THE UNIVERSE

Galileo Galilei 1564 - 1642

SAGR. *You present these recondite matters with such evidence and ease that they seem less appreciated; people lightly esteem knowledge which they acquire with little labor.*

SALV. *If those who demonstrate with brevity and clearness the fallacy of many popular beliefs was treated with contempt instead of gratitude the injury would be quite bearable; but on the other hand, it is very unpleasant and annoying to see men, who claim to be peers of anyone in a certain field of study, take for granted certain conclusions which later are quickly and easily shown by another to be false.*

— Galileo Galilei, Two New Sciences (1638)

THE UNIVERSE

The Foundations, the Variables, and the Structure of the Universe

SAYYAD MASTHAN VALI

Asha Science Press

THE UNIVERSE

The Foundations, the Variables, and the Structure of the Universe

Published by Asha Science Press

Kalidindi - 521344 India

ISBN (Paperback): **978-93-343-9293-7**

First Edition, 2025

— — —

Disclaimer:

This book presents the author's independent scientific interpretations and philosophical reasoning. While every effort has been made to ensure accuracy, the ideas and explanations herein reflect the author's personal research perspective and are not intended as textbook or institutional material. Readers are encouraged to examine the concepts critically and consult additional sources for broader understanding.

DEDICATION

To my father, **Sayyad Ibrahim** *— who showed me the dignity of hard work.*
To my mother, **Sayyad Mastan Be** *— who taught me the value of reason.*
To my wife, **Sayyad Maimunnisa** *— whose perseverance has been my constant example.*

ACKNOWLEDGMENTS

I owe my deep apologies to my wife, Dr. Sayyad Maimunnisa, for long years of absence from my duties and responsibilities during this research and writing.

I express my sincere gratitude to my friends and well-wishers Dr. Mastan vali Shaik, Dr. Ameer Sultana, Dr. Mehaboob Shaik, Dr. Sabirunnisa, Mr. Abdul Mateen, Ms. Jani Begam, Mr. Shaik Jilani, Mr. Nanna Baji, Mr. Bada Baji, Dr. Sardar Basha, Dr. Satyanarayana, Dr. Butchi Krishna Redddy, Mr. Amareswara Rao, and T. V. Narasimha Rao — whose encouragement and honest conversations helped sustain my enthusiasm through the long years of reflection and writing.

Thanks to Mr. Krishna Rao Garu and Mrs. Aruna Kumari Garu and Dharma Rao Garu for their immense support throughout my research period.

Dr. Ali Shaik, Dr. Asha Parveen, Mr. Khaja Bhai, and Mrs. Malin Sister for believing in my ideas and great support to pursue.

I owe a deep debt to my family and all who silently supported this endeavour — especially Mr. Bhure Saida and Mrs. Azeeza, Abdul Bhai, Haseena Bhabi, Subani, Hasan, Karimulla, Rasheed, for their patience and understanding and believing in my ideas to be true and encouraging in times of disbelief.

Thanks to our staff Mr. Santi Vardhan, Ms. Rebecca and Ms. Pushpa for taking care of me.

My grandchildren Armaan Ali and Arhaan Ali for their immense love.

1. Introduction

The Architecture of This Work

This book is built as a single continuous argument about how the universe moves and forms itself.

When I first encountered the ancient philosophers, a single thought stayed with me—perhaps inherited from them, perhaps my own: *"The impossible is absolutely impossible; yet however ridiculous an idea may appear, if it is not impossible, then it remains possible."* That conviction became the seed of this entire research.

I looked toward the asteroid belt and asked: how can small bodies, billions of kilometres from the Sun, circle endlessly around it? How could motion begin without a cause? How could the Sun wait passively for nearby matter to form planets, and yet those planets move at tens of kilometres per second against its own immense pull?

The idea that such motion could begin without an initial impulse seemed—not merely unlikely—but impossible. From that impossibility, this book was born. It is the record of a lifelong attempt to understand motion itself, culminating in the **Massive Mass Ejection Theory**. Whatever reception it may find, I offer it so that future minds will not have to begin again from zero in seeking how the universe truly moves.

It begins with what can be observed, proceeds through the causes that make those observations possible, and culminates in a mechanical model that unites every level of cosmic structure. The organizing idea is simple but profound: **the universe was built by motion, and motion was born from pressure impulse — Massive Mass Ejection — not from rotation or collapse.**

The ideas that follow are not hurried thoughts. They are the result of decades of careful observation, reflection, and doubt. Doubt not only about existing theories, but also about my own limitations, language, and strength. This work has no institutional support, no committee of editors, no external funding. It is the product of a single mind, shaped by life as a doctor, nurtured by long hours of reading, and driven by a lifelong restlessness to understand how the universe truly works.

How This Book Is Structured

The reader is invited to move through the pages as through a sequence of reasoning rather than a set of isolated topics. Each part prepares the ground for the next:

Part I — Foundations: The Principles Beneath All Phenomena

The first part asks what makes science possible. It restores *phenomena* as the starting point of knowledge, not abstract theory. Here the reader learns that every genuine explanation begins with observation, proceeds by reasoning, and returns to nature for confirmation.

These chapters define **the first principles of the universe** — the immutable characteristics of matter and motion that never change — and examine how universals and particulars, principles, conditions, and elements give birth to every event in nature.

Through the guidance of Plato and Aristotle, the book shows that truth is not invented by mathematics but revealed by nature itself. Gravity, impulse, and momentum are not mathematical conveniences but physical realities, each acting according to its own nature.

The Foundations end by uniting philosophy and physics into one discipline: the study of **locomotion as the necessary act of the universe**.

Part II — Variables: The Active Elements of Motion

Once the groundwork is laid, the discussion turns to the six variables that construct all motion — **matter, impulse, momentum, gravity, space, and time.**

Each is examined in both its universal and local behavior. The reader learns that:

- **Impulse** is the only initiator of motion.
- **Momentum** is the continuation of motion once acquired.
- **Gravity** acts only in the normal (vertical) plane, bending but never creating motion.
- **Space and time** are the framework, not the cause, of motion.
- **Matter** is the carrier that receives, stores, and expresses all these actions.

Through pendulum experiments, projectile reasoning, and analogies from Earth to galaxies, these chapters reveal that the same physical grammar governs both terrestrial and cosmic phenomena.

Inertia is replaced by momentum; cause regains its rightful place in mechanics. By the end of this section, the reader possesses a full vocabulary for understanding how motion behaves everywhere.

Part III — Structure: The Architecture of the Universe

Having understood the causes and variables, we arrive at their consequences — the visible structure of the cosmos.

Here the **Massive Mass Ejection Theory** becomes the unifying framework. From stellar outbursts to galactic cores, every formation is traced to pressure-driven expulsions of matter.

Each ejection imparts *dispensable momentum*; gravity later bends that momentum into orbits and systems. Planets, moons, and rings are not residues of a swirling dust cloud but the natural outcomes of repeated acts of ejection and gravitational shaping. Angular momentum ceases to be a mystery and becomes a measurable result of impulse.

The Structure chapters extend this logic outward: galaxies are not collapsing nebulae but long-lived families of ejected systems, each moving with its own acquired momentum. Flat rotation curves, globular clusters, and galactic independence all arise from the same mechanical law that governs a thrown stone or a swinging pendulum. In this view, the universe is not expanding through empty space; it is **moving** — eternally, directionally, and mechanically.

A Journey of Reason

Readers who proceed sequentially will recognize a deliberate rhythm: from **seeing**, to **understanding**, to **knowing**.

The book does not ask for belief but for attention — to the phenomena that surround us and the logic that connects them. Mathematics, philosophy, and experiment appear together, each serving observation. The reward for patience is coherence: one physical principle, expressed at every scale, explaining the unity of matter and motion.

Who This Book Is For

This book is not only for scientists. It is also for students, general readers, and anyone who has ever looked at the stars and wondered: *What truly moves these bodies? Why do they orbit, scatter, collide, and drift across the vastness?*

No mathematical training is required. Where numbers appear, they are used only to illuminate — not to intimidate. The core of this book lies not in formulae but in reasoning, experiment, and nature.

It also speaks to those who may have felt, silently, that many modern theories have become too abstract, too disconnected from physical experience. You are not alone. There is another way to look at the universe — one that begins with observation and ends in coherence.

How to Read This Book

Begin at the beginning. The early chapters may feel philosophical, but they are the scaffolding for all later reasoning. Do not skip them; without them, the later physical sections lose their depth. As the discussion advances, examples from daily life — pendulums, projectiles, rebounds — gradually expand into stellar and galactic events. Each example, however simple, carries the same laws that shape the Milky Way.

By the end, the reader will see that the entire cosmos is a single mechanical system sustained by two forces only: **gravity**, which tames, and **pressure impulse**, which moves.

Purpose and Hope

This book seeks not to oppose science but to return it to its natural foundation: **phenomena, reason, and truth**. Its aim is to restore clarity where abstraction has obscured reality, and to show that the universe can be explained without invoking mystery or mathematical fiction. It is written for the thoughtful reader — scientist or layperson — who believes that simplicity and truth are one and the same

A Word About the Author's Position

I am not a professional physicist. I am a practicing doctor. But I believe that deep scientific insight does not come from titles or laboratories — it comes from honest observation and the courage to ask the right questions. I have spent many years quietly thinking, and many nights unable to sleep because some truth remained just beyond reach.

I offer this work not as a final answer but as a beginning. Some conclusions may prove wrong; others, I believe, will stand the test of time. What matters most is that the method is right: follow nature, not opinion.

A Final Note on Urgency and Legacy

This book is not written in luxury. It is written in urgency. I do not have the decades ahead to wait for perfect words or public approval. What I have, I give. The rest I leave to the minds and hands of those who come after.

If a reader, anywhere in the world, finds even one section that brings clarity where there was confusion, then this effort will have served its purpose.

— *Sayyad Masthan Vali.*

TABLE OF CONTENTS

PART I — FOUNDATIONS

Part I — Foundations

The *Foundations* form the philosophical and observational groundwork of this book. Here, the reader encounters the first truths upon which all later reasoning stands. It is a return to the discipline of seeing — to begin not from speculation but from what nature herself reveals.

The chapters explore the nature of phenomena, the meaning of cause, and the essential distinction between principles, conditions, and elements. They remind us that physics must be built from the behavior of bodies, not from mathematical assumptions. In this part, Aristotle's logic, Galileo's experiments, and Newton's formulations converge into a single realization: **locomotion is the essential act of the universe**, and every event we study must follow from it.

This section provides the reader with the intellectual tools to distinguish between what is imagined and what is observed — the first step toward genuine understanding.

2. Phenomena: Neither Experiments nor Theories Are the Gold Standard of Truth

Why nature must come first in all science—and what happens when we forget that.

In the history of science, perhaps the greatest error has been to believe that theories and mathematical predictions are more fundamental than nature itself. But the true gold standard of physics — more valuable than any theory, more telling than any experiment — is **phenomena**.

A phenomenon is what nature does. It is the undistorted, unmanipulated behavior of physical universe. And it is from here that every theory, model, or measurement must begin. The tendency in modern science to place theory before observation, or to design experiments merely to confirm a theory's predictions, is not only backward — it is deeply unscientific. Theories must emerge from nature, not the other way around.

This inversion of priority has led to a number of conceptual disasters. For example, when photographs appear to confirm light bending near a massive object, or when redshifts are interpreted as evidence of universal expansion, we often mistake the results of a designed experiment for the actual phenomenon. Yet an experiment that fails to reflect nature is as misleading as a failed theory. Just because an experimental result matches a theoretical curve does not mean nature has spoken. It may only mean we have filtered nature through our expectations.

Phenomena are created by nature but are observed by us. Even the most sophisticated detector or satellite cannot improve a phenomenon — it can only measure it with greater precision. And such precision is meaningful only if the device itself is neutral, unforced, and consistent with the broader structure of natural reality.

This foundational approach restores the proper order of scientific reasoning, as understood by Aristotle and later Galileo:

- First, observe phenomena.
- Then, construct logical explanations.
- Only then, test through deliberate experimentation.
- And finally, compare outcomes back to nature — not to the theory alone.

We must insist that no theory, however elegant, and no experiment, however precise, is above the phenomenon it seeks to describe. If nature does not comply, the theory must be abandoned, not nature reinterpreted.

In this book, we begin and end with phenomena. Every law, every principle, and every concept must be traced directly to something observable in nature. Not because we distrust mathematics or experiment, but because we recognize that nature has no obligation to obey our models.

This, then, is the **sine qua non** of physics: phenomena — not equations, not predictions, not simulations — are the final judges of truth.

2.1 Observation of Physical Phenomena

The path to knowledge has only one true entrance: **phenomena.** From the beginning of human thought, observation of natural events — the rising and setting of the Sun, the phases of the Moon, the fall of objects — provided the material for reasoning. Aristotle, Galileo, and Newton all began here. And yet, in modern times, science often treats phenomena as secondary, bending them to fit theories instead of letting them lead.

Why Phenomena Matter

A phenomenon is nature itself speaking. It is not theory, not experiment, not speculation. It is what happens, directly and undeniably. However small or humble it may seem — a pebble rolling down a slope, a pendulum swinging, a droplet scattering into many — it is worth more than the most elaborate speculation that ignores observation.

Phenomena are:

- **Direct:** they occur whether or not we expect them.
- **Neutral:** they are not altered by our opinions.
- **Repeatable:** they can be seen again, by anyone, under the same conditions.

Theories and models may help us think, but they must follow phenomena, not precede them.

How the Ancients Began

The ancients did not have satellites or particle accelerators. They had eyes, ears, and hands. Their science began in what could be observed: The fall of bodies showed gravity acting downward. The arcs of projectiles revealed two motions at once — horizontal and vertical. The swing of a pendulum demonstrated both impulse and regularity. The heavens, with their repeating cycles, hinted at deeper order. Though limited in instruments, they were not limited in wisdom. Their reliance on phenomena gave them truths still valid today.

How Modern Science Drifted

In time, speculation began to overshadow observation. Mathematics became a starting point instead of a tool. Models like curved space or expanding universes were advanced without phenomena to confirm them. Photographs and measurements were often interpreted to fit theories rather than to reveal nature's own behavior.

The danger is clear: when theories replace phenomena, science risks losing contact with reality.

Phenomena as the Standard of Truth

We must restore the proper order:

1. Observe phenomena.
2. Think about causes.
3. Test with experiments.
4. Compare results back to nature.

If the theory fails to match, the theory must go — not the phenomenon. This was Galileo's principle, and it remains the only secure ground.

Examples of Neglected Phenomena

Gravity's one-directional action (normal plane only) has been shown in every projectile and orbit, yet is ignored in favor of abstract models.

The persistence of dispensable momentum in bodies large and small is visible in every ejection and orbit, yet it is often hidden under "initial conditions."

The independence of spin from gravity can be seen in everyday objects and celestial bodies, yet it is not recognized in dominant theories.

Each of these is a phenomenon: small, simple, but decisive. To neglect them is to neglect truth itself.

Conclusion: Returning to Nature

The ancients began with phenomena, and we must return to the same ground. However small the example, however simple the observation, it is more valuable than a grand speculation unsupported by nature. Physics must be built from phenomena upward — not from abstractions downward.

Every law, every equation, every conclusion must answer to what nature does. Nothing else is worthy of the name science.

3. First Principles: The Immutable Characteristics of Primordial Particles

"For we do not think that we know a thing until we are acquainted with its primary conditions or first principles." — Aristotle, Metaphysics.

In every science, the path to true understanding begins with the search for **first principles** — those unchanging, foundational characteristics of primordial particles without which nothing can be explained. Whether in geometry, biology, or physics, first principles form the ground beneath all knowledge. Without them, our explanations are shallow. With them, every phenomenon finds its root.

This is especially true in the science of nature, which is the subject of this book — the universe, its movement and its structure. To understand the cosmos, we must begin with the immutable characteristics of the universe's most fundamental components — what we shall call the **primordial particles** of matter.

What Are First Principles?

First principles are not assumptions. They are not theories, models, or approximations. They are the universal and eternal properties that belong to the most basic constituents of nature – the primordial particles' characteristics and their products.

They are like:

- The fact that a triangle always contains 180 degrees — regardless of how it is drawn.
- The fact that an electron always carries a negative charge — no matter how it moves or where it appears.

Such properties are unchangeable, inherent to the primordial particles, and independent of external conditions. These consistent characteristics of primordial particles create consistent phenomena. They are not created by observation; they are discovered by reason, confirmed by consist observation and experiments, and remain true across all space and time.

Primordial Particles: The Physical Carriers of First Principles

In the material universe, all observable phenomena arise from the behavior of matter — but matter itself is made of more fundamental particles, which we may call primordial particles.

These are:

- Not divisible further into meaningful components
- Not created by current physical processes (they exist as givens)
- Bearers of universal characteristics — mass, structure, polarity, or other properties yet to be fully understood.

These primordial particles are the **alphabet of nature**. From their characteristics, all visible matter, motion, interaction, and structure emerge.

Why First Principles Matter in Physics

The universe is not a collection of random events. It is structured. And structure implies order. Order implies rules. And rules must arise from things that do not change — from first principles. These are the invariable characteristics of Primordial Particles. These characteristics are immutable, so are the First Principles of matter itself.

Only by understanding the immutable characteristics of matter can we understand:

- Why particles attract, repel, or bind
- How forces arise from mass, structure, or imbalance
- How motion is initiated, transferred, or restrained
- How visible forms — from atoms, planets, stars, and galaxies — are formed, shaped and maintained

We must look deeper than equations and patterns. We must ask: **What causes the behavior we see in the first place?**

Examples of First Principles in Natural Phenomena

These are not conditional properties. They are essential characteristics that do not depend on the situation. They are part of what the thing is.

What This Means for Our Study of the Universe

This inquiry begins not with telescopes or equations, but with this realization:

If we understand the first principles of matter and motion, we can understand all natural phenomena: from a falling apple to a spinning galaxy, from a ripple in a pond to the birth of a solar system — all arise from the interplay of unchanging characteristics acting under knowable conditions.

Therefore, before we analyze matter, gravity, impulse, momentum or structure, we must ask: **What do these first principles fundamentally are, and how do they behave by their own nature?**

Conclusion: Foundations Before Phenomena

If we start our understanding of the universe from appearances, we risk getting lost in surface patterns. But if we start from first principles, we have the map to understand all forms, forces, and motions.

In the next section, we will explore how these first principles express themselves in **the universals and particulars of nature** — a view deeply shaped by the philosophies of Plato and Aristotle, to whom the next section is dedicated.

Every phenomenon we see is a consequence of principles we do not see — but can know.

4. Universals and Particulars: A Tribute to Plato and Aristotle

To understand the universe is to understand the relationship between what is universal and unchanging, and what is particular and temporary. Every object we see, every motion we observe, and every structure we study is a particular expression of deeper universal characteristics. This distinction is not merely philosophical; it is foundational for physics. Without it, we confuse single events (particulars) with eternal rules (Universals), and we mistake local observations for complete truths.

In this section, we honor Plato, who sought the truth of all things in unchanging Forms, and Aristotle, who sought it in the structure of reality through classification and logic. Their combined vision gives us the tools to understand how immutable characteristics of variables such as gravity, impulse, and momentum give rise to individual phenomena in specific ways.

What Are Universals?

Universals are the complete and unchanging set of characteristics that belong to the fundamental variables of the universe — matter, gravity, impulse, momentum, time, and space. These characteristics do not depend on a specific situation or event. They define what a variable is. Gravity, for instance, always acts vertically, always attracts mass, and its strength always varies with the inverse square of distance. Impulse force is direction independent, that is, it can act in any direction, instantaneous, and always requires an external cause or confinement to act. Matter always has some arrangement, some mass, some charge, and some structural potential, even if not all of these are expressed in a particular object. Universals are always present, though not always expressed, and together they form the full spectrum of a variable's nature. As shown in Figure 4.1

universals are the forces and characteristics of the phenomena, whereas particulars are that physical events.

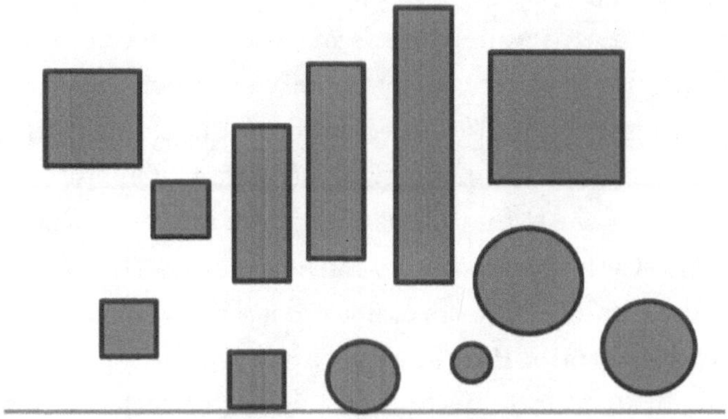

Figure 4.1 Universals and Particulars. Universals express the laws and equations, and forces of nature, while particulars are the figures and locomotion that embody them. Scientific understanding moves both ways: universals explain particulars, and particulars in combination express universal principles.

What Are Particulars?

Particulars are real-world events or objects in which some of the characteristics of one or more universals appear in combination. Each particular incident or event is an expression of some of the characteristics from the whole set of the universal characteristics, a momentary expression of deeper universal truths. A thrown basketball, for example, expresses impulse, gravity, momentum, direction, and time, but not necessarily all aspects of matter. A magnet shows the structural characteristics of matter and its field, but not impulse or locomotion. A human body embodies a vast arrangement of matter and structure, but only some expressions of motion at any given time. Each of these is a particular expression of universals, shaped by specific conditions and contexts.

How Do Universals Express Themselves in Particulars?

Universals become visible through selection and combination. A particular phenomenon expresses some characteristics of a variable, while others remain dormant, inactive, or irrelevant in that case.

The form, function, and behavior of the particular event are determined by which characteristics are expressed and how they interact in that particular condition. A falling apple, for example, expresses gravity's downward pull, matter's mass and structure, and the passage of time, but not necessarily impulse or directional force. A projectile expresses impulse, momentum, direction, and gravity's correction, but not the polarity or structure of matter. No single phenomenon reveals the full nature of the universal characteristics every time. Only by studying many particulars and tracing them back to their universal roots can we grasp the whole.

Plato and Aristotle: Parallel Pursuits of Truth

Plato taught us to look beyond the visible, to seek the unchanging Forms — what we here, call universals. These Forms are not located in space and time, but they explain what is common and essential to all things. Aristotle, by contrast, grounded philosophy in observation and logical classification, insisting that knowledge must arise from particular things, but always in relation to their underlying principles.

In this work, we follow both masters: from Plato, the idea that unchanging truths lie behind every phenomenon, and from Aristotle, the method of discovering them through careful observation, reasoning, and analysis. Every particular is a temporary expression of one or more universals, and to understand any phenomenon, we must trace it back to the unchanging characteristics behind it.

Why This Distinction Matters for Science

Physics cannot advance unless we learn to distinguish between what is permanent and what is transient. When we study gravity in a single experiment, we see only a partial expression, not the whole characteristics of gravity. When we observe an individual motion or object, we are witnessing a particular, not the complete account of its variables. Modern theories often mistake such temporary observations, or the mathematical curves derived from them, for universal truths. But only by separating the enduring from the passing can we build a coherent science of the universe.

Conclusion: Particular Events, Universal Causes or Forces

Every fall, every throw, every orbit, and every collision is a particular event. Yet each one arises from the universal characteristics of variables acting in definite ways under definite conditions.

In the next section, we will explore how universals participate in the formation of particular events through principles, conditions, and elements — the inner grammar of physical phenomena. The universe is not made of accidents. It is made of structured particulars, shaped by universal laws.

4.1 Principles, Conditions, and Elements: How Phenomena Are Formed

If universals are the complete, unchanging characteristics of each physical variable, and particulars are their specific, visible expressions in the world, the next question is: how do universals become active in particular events? Why do some characteristics appear, while others remain hidden?

To answer this, we must look at the inner grammar of phenomena — the structure that determines how physical events come into being. Every phenomenon, whether simple or complex, is shaped by three essential components: **principles, conditions, and elements.**

Principles: The Laws Built into Each Variable

Principles are the intrinsic behavioral laws of each variable. They describe how a variable acts by its very nature, either always and everywhere or only when a certain cause is present. Gravity, for example, always pulls inward, always acts on mass, and always diminishes with the square of distance. By contrast, impulse force appears only when pressure builds and is released, as in the throw of a stone, the contraction of a muscle, or the eruption of a volcano. Principles define the nature of a variable across all cases; they are not determined by the event, but by the variable itself.

Conditions: The Circumstances That Shape Appearance

Conditions are the **contextual circumstances** that determine which characteristics of a variable are expressed and to what extent. They include mass, direction, temperature, position, or the medium through which motion occurs. Conditions do not change the principle itself, but they govern how much of it is revealed in a particular case. A heavier body does not alter the law of gravity, but its motion will differ because of its mass. The direction of a throw does not change the nature of impulse, but it alters the trajectory of the projectile. Temperature may activate or suppress physical reactions without altering their underlying laws. Conditions are the reasons why the same principle produces different appearances under different circumstances.

Elements: The Participants in the Phenomenon

Elements are the actual participants, component parts, in a physical event — the material bodies and the physical variables involved. They include both the tangible materials such as iron, gold, water, or air, and the universal variables such as matter, impulse, gravity, and momentum. Each phenomenon is composed of some combination of these elements, acting together within the setting of conditions. A falling stone, for instance, involves the body of matter itself, the principle of gravity, the condition of mass and distance, and the variables of time and space that frame its descent.

Illustration: Throwing a Stone

Consider the simple act of throwing a stone upward. The principles involved are gravity, which always pulls downward, and impulse, which acts in the direction of the throw. The conditions are the mass of the stone, the angle of release, and the resistance of air. The elements are the stone itself, the gravitational pull of the Earth, and the impulse delivered by the thrower's hand. Although the principles never change, the outcome will vary depending on the mass of the stone, the force and angle of the throw, and whether the event occurs in air, water, or vacuum.

Why This Framework Matters

This layered understanding of phenomena prevents confusion by showing us what governs an event, what shapes its appearance, and what it is composed of. Principles are the governing rules, conditions are the shaping circumstances, and elements are the participants. By keeping these distinctions clear, we can analyze phenomena with greater precision and avoid the misinterpretations that arise when causes and contexts are confused.

Conclusion: The Architecture of Phenomena

Every phenomenon is not a mystery but a structured event, formed by the universals of nature expressed under definite conditions through identifiable elements. Once this architecture is understood, phenomena can be read like sentences in the language of nature.

In the next section, we will reflect on how such knowledge is reached, not only through observation but also through reasoning and demonstration — a method that Aristotle first gave form to, and which remains as necessary for science today as it was in his time.

5. Syllogistic Reasoning and Demonstration: The Method of Knowing

Every science begins with observation. But observation alone is not enough. We may watch a body fall, a pendulum swing, or a stone arc through the air, yet remain spectators rather than thinkers. To transform observation into knowledge, we must apply reasoning — and not loose speculation, but disciplined reasoning that moves from universal principles to particular events and back again.

This is the role of **syllogistic reasoning**. When applied correctly, syllogism allows us to uncover universal truths, to demonstrate why phenomena behave as they do, and to ensure that our conclusions are as reliable as any experiment. Aristotle called this **"demonstrative syllogism,"** and it remains a powerful tool for science today.

What Is Syllogistic Reasoning?

A syllogism is a structured chain of propositions that leads to a necessary conclusion. It requires a major premise (a universal principle), a minor premise (a particular case), and a conclusion that follows with certainty. For example:

- Major premise: All bodies under gravity accelerate vertically toward a center. (without initial sideways force)
- Minor premise: A stone is a particular body accelerating under gravity. (without initial sideways force)
- Conclusion: Therefore, the stone accelerates vertically toward the Earth's center. (without initial sideways force)

This is more than logic. When each premise arises from observed phenomena or first principles, the conclusion becomes a demonstrated truth. Unlike speculation, it cannot be dismissed; unlike experiment alone, it explains why the event must happen that way.

Demonstration Through Gravity's Normal Plane

Consider the fundamental fact that gravity acts only in the normal (vertical) plane. This can be expressed syllogistically:

Major premise: Gravity causes acceleration only in the vertical direction; it never alters horizontal velocity.

Minor premise: A projectile moves horizontally by impulse, while simultaneously being pulled downward by gravity.

Conclusion: Therefore, the projectile's horizontal motion is unaffected, (speed does not change in horizontal plane) by gravity, while its vertical component of motion is fully governed by it.

This syllogism does not merely describe what happens; it demonstrates the nature of gravity itself. It shows that gravity cannot create or change horizontal motion, and that all such motion must originate from another cause, such as impulse.

Why Syllogism Matters for Science

Syllogism matters because it forces us to separate the universal from the particular. It prevents us from mistaking a temporary curve on a graph for a universal law. It keeps us honest when experiments appear to confirm our expectations. And it gives us a method that scientists must apply throughout their lives and careers: always reasoning back to first principles, always testing conclusions against phenomena, always demonstrating, never merely assuming.

Experiments may confirm, but syllogism explains. Observations may reveal, but syllogism secures. Without it, science risks becoming a catalogue of appearances; with it, science becomes a search for causes.

Conclusion: Reason as the Bridge

The bridge between observation and knowledge is not mathematics alone, nor experiment alone, but reasoning. Syllogism gives structure to our thought and certainty to our conclusions. In this book, we will use syllogistic reasoning not once, but repeatedly, as the method by which we move from phenomena to principles and from principles back to the universe at large.

In the next section, we will see how locomotion is necessary for the origin of the universe and how this method leads naturally to the recognition that all matter and all locomotion are one system, governed by the same variables everywhere in the cosmos.

6. Locomotion Is Necessary for the Origin and Formation of the Universe

"Living in the world without insight into the hidden laws of nature is like not knowing the language of the country in which one was born."
*— **Hazrat Inayat Khan (1882–1927)**, Sufi spiritual guide, musician, and writer*[1]

The movement of the Sun and other stars around the Milky Way's core, or the motion of stars in other galaxies around their respective cores, would be absolutely impossible without the process of **locomotion**. The formation of the Solar System, the continual motion of the planets and smaller bodies around the Sun, and even the arrangement of galaxies across space, are all consequences of locomotion. To understand the universe, therefore, one must first understand **motion itself**.

Locomotion is as old as the universe. The very first activity of existence was motion—the first stir within the primordial state. Without locomotion, matter could never have aggregated to form stars or galaxies; no solar system could have taken shape, and no body could have begun its journey through space. Thus, **the study of locomotion is the first step toward understanding the universe**.

Questions That Lead Toward Insight

How does a pendulum work? Why does its period remain the same for pendulums made of cork, wood, lead, or gold—bodies of vastly different mass—yet change when the length of the pendulum is

---

[1] Schneider, Michael S. A Beginner's Guide to Constructing the Universe: The Mathematical Archetypes of Nature, Art, and Science (p. 21). HarperCollins. Kindle Edition

altered? What is the relation between pendulum oscillations, freely falling bodies, and projectiles?

Why do oceans have tides and waves while still water remains calm? Why does a mere breeze raise ripples on the surface of a pond?

Every planet exhibits more than one kind of motion: it spins on its axis while revolving around the Sun. What is the relationship between these two motions—spin and orbit? Why are the spins of different planets inclined at varying angles? Why do most planets move in the same general direction while a few show retrograde motion?

Why are the heavy, rocky terrestrial planets found near the Sun, while the massive gaseous planets are far away? Where did the comets, asteroids, Kuiper Belt, and Oort Cloud bodies originate? Why are cometary orbits so elongated? What causes all these differences, and can we truly know how the Solar System formed?

Is there a relation between one star and another—for instance, between our Sun and its nearest neighbor, Alpha Centauri? Are all stars in motion, or are some immobile as once believed? Is there a correlation between a star's mass and its orbital speed within the galaxy? Why do galaxies vary so widely in size and brightness? What determines the extent of a galaxy? And above all, **are there definite causes** behind these patterns, or are they merely coincidental?

Until we can answer these questions, we cannot claim to understand our galaxy—or the universe itself.

The Common Thread

Though these questions seem different, they are all bound by one common factor: locomotion. Motion underlies every formation, every arrangement, every observed regularity in the heavens.

Why do planets move at their characteristic velocities around the Sun? Why does the Sun move within the Milky Way at its specific speed? Why does every star in every galaxy trace a defined path around its galactic core? What is the true nature of space and time, if both only reveal themselves through motion?

Locomotion is not merely an effect—it is the **essential condition** for all phenomena. It is the pulse of existence itself. Understanding locomotion, and the variables that generate and regulate it, is the only way to understand how the universe was formed and how it continues to evolve.

Looking Forward

In the chapters that follow, we will examine locomotion not as an abstract idea but as a necessary reality—a phenomenon inseparable from matter and the first act of the universe. We will trace its causes from the immutable characteristics of primordial particles, explore its measurable variables, and see how these variables give rise to the physical structures we observe—from the swing of a pendulum to the motion of galaxies.

Thus, before we discuss *the possibility of locomotion*, we must first acknowledge **its necessity**—for without motion, there could have been no universe at all.

6.1 All Matter and Locomotion Is One: Why Local Physics Applies to the Whole Universe

> *"Philosophy is written in this grand book, the universe, which stands continually open to our gaze. But the book cannot be understood unless one first learns to comprehend the language and read the letters in which it is composed."*[1]
>
> *Galileo Galilei 1564 – 1642.*

To understand the universe as a whole, we must first ask two simple questions: is the matter in distant galaxies the same as the matter here on Earth? And do the principles that govern motion in a laboratory apply equally to stars and planets? The answer is yes — not merely as a philosophical belief, but as a demonstrable truth.

The Same Matter, Everywhere

Whether we study the tip of a leaf or the spiral arms of a galaxy, the material involved behaves according to the same laws of nature.

---

[1] Dialogues Concerning Two New Sciences; Galileo, Henry 1914

Electrons do not carry different charges in distant stars than they do in our instruments. Gravity does not change its form from one region of space to another; it always acts inward, always attracts, and always follows the same relationship with distance. The universe is not divided into regions with separate physics. What is observed here applies everywhere, because the ingredients of nature do not vary from place to place.

The Same Motion, Under the Same Principles

It is not only matter that is one; locomotion, too, is governed by a single system. Whether a pebble falls in a well, a pendulum swings in a cathedral, or a planet orbits a star, the same variables are at work: impulse initiates the motion, momentum carries it, gravity regulates it, and matter provides the body through which it occurs. Time and space frame the event, but do not alter the principles. The scale may change, but the causes remain the same.

Experimental Confirmation: Pendulum and Free Fall

Two classical observations demonstrate this unity.

The **pendulum** shows that oscillation period depends only on string length, not on the material or mass of the bob. A pendulum made from wood, iron, or gold swings with the same rhythm if the length is equal, revealing that gravity acts uniformly regardless of the matter involved.

Free fall shows the same truth. When two objects of very different mass are dropped together, they fall with the same acceleration and strike the ground at the same time, provided air resistance is removed. This proves that gravity acts equally on all matter, and that acceleration under gravity is independent of the body's weight or composition.

These simple observations confirm a profound fact: the same laws govern matter and motion everywhere.

Beyond the Experiments: Bouncing and Impulse

Yet these observations also reveal that not all forces are the same. When bodies strike the ground, the heavier one bounces less and the lighter one bounces more. The difference is not due to gravity, which acts equally, but to pressure impulse, which is mass-sensitive. Thus, even the differences confirm the rule: the same principles apply universally, but their effects depend on the variables involved. Gravity is uniform; impulse is variable. Together they explain both the sameness and the diversity of motion.

The Implication for Science

No matter where we look — Earth, Sun, or galaxy — motion begins with impulse, is carried by momentum, and is regulated by gravity. All bodies, from the smallest particle to the largest star, share this common system. To understand the universe, it is enough to study it here, because the laws of motion do not change with distance.

Conclusion: A Universe Built on Unity

Matter is one. Locomotion is one. And the laws that govern them are universal. This is not poetry but science: it is the foundation upon which we may read the cosmos as a whole.

In the next section, we will explore the logical consequences of this unity by looking at the nature of motion itself — its types, causes, and classifications.

Summary and Transition: What the Reader Has Gained from the Foundations

At this point in the journey, the reader has passed through the true entry gates of universal understanding — not by way of abstraction, but through clarity, structure, and reason. The Foundations have not been a collection of loose reflections, but a deliberate sequence leading from observation to principle, from principle to universality, and from universality back to particular events.

We began with **phenomena**, the undistorted behavior of nature itself, and recognized that no theory or experiment can rise above what phenomena reveal. We then turned to **first principles**, the immutable characteristics of primordial particles, which anchor all scientific reasoning. Next, through the distinction of **universals and particulars**, we saw how enduring truths manifest in individual cases, and why no single event ever tells the whole story. We traced this further into **principles, conditions, and elements**, the inner grammar by which events are shaped. And with **syllogistic reasoning**, we restored the discipline of logic as the bridge between phenomena and knowledge. Finally, we affirmed the **unity of matter and locomotion**, showing that the same causes govern both the smallest experiment and the grandest galactic motion.

Taken together, these ideas give the reader not just definitions, but a complete framework for thinking about the universe. The foundations teach us that every motion must be traced to an impulse, every persistence of motion must be carried by momentum, and every restraint must be explained by gravity acting in the normal plane. They also show us that physics is not a fragmented set of local rules, but one coherent system of causes that applies equally to Earth, stars, and galaxies.

From here, the journey moves into a new phase. Having secured the ground, we now turn to the **variables of locomotion themselves** — matter, gravity, impulse, momentum, time, and distance. Each will be studied not in isolation, but in relation to the others, for it is only through their interplay that the universe builds its structures.

The Foundations have given us the compass. The Variables will provide the map. With both in hand, we will be ready to read the structure of the universe itself.

7. Definitions and First Concepts: A Common Language for Nature

Before we examine the variables of locomotion in detail, we must agree on a common language. Words that appear familiar in daily life — mass, motion, force, gravity — often carry imprecise meanings that blur scientific thought. To move forward with clarity, we must define these terms not as jargon, but in their natural sense, as they appear in the physical world.

A **phenomenon** is any event in nature that can be observed directly, without requiring interpretation or theory. The fall of a stone, the swing of a pendulum, the freezing of water, or the orbit of a moon are all phenomena. They are the raw evidence upon which science must be built.

A **theory** is a human attempt to explain one or more phenomena through reasoning, sometimes aided by mathematics. A theory is useful only when it can be tested against observation. It is never final, and it must be abandoned or corrected when phenomena contradict it.

A **force** is not a substance but an interaction that causes a change in motion. Gravity is a force that attracts matter inward toward a center. Pressure impulse is a force that pushes matter outward from a point of impact or confinement. Forces are actions, not things; they can be measured only through their effects on bodies.

Gravity is the natural inward (Normal or Vertical Plane) pull that all matter exerts on other matter. It acts only in the normal (vertical) plane, always toward the center of mass. Gravity cannot push, cannot rotate, and cannot initiate horizontal motion. It acts by attraction, to regulate and restrain, not to propel.

A **pressure impulse** is a sudden delivery of force over a short duration. It sets bodies into motion by imparting velocity. Unlike gravity, which is continuous, impulse is momentary and directional. It is the true origin of locomotion in the universe.

Momentum is the continuation of motion once a body has been set in motion by pressure impulse force or gravity. It is not inherent in matter; it must be acquired through impulse or gravity. A body at rest has no momentum. Once in motion, its momentum carries it forward until it is consumed by resistance, collision, or gravity's inward pull. Momentum is the inseparable product of mass and acquired velocity, measurable through its effects and conserved through interaction.

Indispensable Momentum: The inherent quantity of matter itself — the potential for motion contained within mass, independent of any external impulse.

Dispensable Momentum: The externally acquired momentum imparted to a body by impulse or collision; it is consumed during motion and governs trajectories.

Mass is the quantity of matter in a body. It determines how strongly the body responds to impulse, how much gravity it exerts, and how much momentum it can carry. Mass does not change with location; it is an essential characteristic of matter itself.

Velocity is the speed of a body in a given direction. It is the measurable outcome of impulse or force. Momentum depends on both mass and velocity together. Velocity is the measurable expression of dispensable momentum; describes rate and direction of acquired motion.

Acceleration is the rate of change of velocity. It is never spontaneous, but always requires a cause, such as gravity pulling a falling body.

An **orbit** is the curved path a body takes under the influence of a central gravitational force. Orbits are not caused by gravity alone, but by the balance between an acquired horizontal momentum and gravity's vertical restraint.

An **impulse** is the bridge between force and momentum. Defined as the product of force and the time for which it acts, impulse explains how motion begins. A rocket launch, a hammer strike, or a supernova explosion are all expressions of impulse. A sudden, directional release of energy or pressure that gives a body its initial motion; the creative force of locomotion.

Pressure Impulse Force: The instantaneous, high-magnitude force responsible for segregation of matter and initiation of motion at all scales.

A **primordial particle** is the smallest unit of matter that cannot be divided further while still retaining physical identity. These particles are the bearers of the universe's first principles: mass, attraction, and response to force.

Attraction is the natural pull of matter inward toward a center. It is not a suction or a mystical field, but a measurable tendency of mass. **Repulsion** is not the opposite of attraction but the result of built-up pressure or impact, arising from collisions, compressions, or high-energy release.

Aggregation: The natural inward action of gravity that collects matter toward the denser center of a system.

Effective Gravitational Extent (EGE): The boundary radius where the gravitational acceleration of a core falls to a minimum effective value a; beyond this, binding ceases.

Massive Mass Ejection Theory: The framework proposing that stellar and galactic structures arise from enormous pressure-driven expulsions of matter from dense cores, each event imparting momentum to create orbits and systems.

Segregation of Matter: The dispersive counterpart to gravitational aggregation; the outward distribution of material due to impulse or expansion.

Finally, **locomotion** is the continued movement of matter from one place to another. It is not an inbuilt property but an acquired state, caused by impulse and regulated by gravity.

Locomotion persists until its momentum is exhausted or counteracted. This is universal act of movement of matter through space; the synthesis of impulse, momentum, and gravitational moderation.

These definitions are not abstractions but the vocabulary of reality. They form the language in which this book will speak. With them established, we can now examine each variable in turn, beginning with matter — the carrier of all physical characteristics and the stage upon which every force and motion acts.

8. Physical World vs Mathematical World: A Foundational Inquiry

> *"If you do not rest upon the good foundation of nature, you will labor with little honor and less profit. Those who take for their standard any one but nature—the mistress of all masters—weary themselves in vain."*
> *— Leonardo da Vinci (1452–1519)*[1]

The First Foundation: Nature Is Primary

Every true understanding of the universe begins with nature itself. It is not the equations, not the diagrams, not even the models — but the observable, sensible phenomena that confront us daily. As Leonardo da Vinci rightly said, nature is the mistress of all masters. Any science that does not rest on her foundation is a castle built in air.

The journey of natural philosophy begins by looking at what is, before we ask what can be calculated. Without this grounding, all efforts, however intelligent, risk being neither true to nature nor useful to humankind.

The Role of Mathematics: A Necessary Tool, Not the Origin

> *"No investigation can strictly be called scientific unless it admits of mathematical demonstration."*
> *— Leonardo da Vinci*[2]

At first, this might appear to elevate mathematics above all else. Yet in context, da Vinci was not reversing his earlier wisdom. He was

---

[1] (Schneider, Michael S. A Beginner's Guide to Constructing the Universe: The Mathematical Archetypes of Nature, Art, and Science (p. 35). HarperCollins. Kindle Edition.)

[2] (Schneider, Michael S. A Beginner's Guide to Constructing the Universe: The Mathematical Archetypes of Nature, Art, and Science (p. 272). HarperCollins. Kindle Edition.)

affirming that once nature is observed, mathematics becomes the essential tool for clarity, precision, and demonstration.

Mathematics does not generate the truth of nature; it expresses it, tests it, and extends it. The scientist must first grasp what is physically happening, and only then express it in mathematical form.

When the Roles Are Reversed: The Root of Modern Misconception

> *"All the effects of Nature are only the mathematical consequences of a small number of immutable laws."*
> *— Pierre-Simon de Laplace (1749–1827)*[1]

This statement, while profound, has often been misused. Many have read it as if nature were a by-product of mathematics, or as if equations came first and nature followed them. That is not how the laws of nature were discovered.

The laws are born from physical observation: consistent behaviors, compared across conditions, tested repeatedly, and only then formulated mathematically. Newton's Third Law — "For every action there is an equal and opposite reaction" — was not invented at a desk. It was witnessed in every collision, push, and fall. Similarly, the Law of Universal Gravitation emerged only after the attraction between bodies was observed and measured, from falling apples to orbiting moons.

Without the experience of weight, or the sight of a moon in orbit, no equation could ever have been written. Mathematics can refine truth but cannot invent it.

The Overshadowing of Nature by Mathematics

> *"Mathematics takes us still further from what is human into the region of absolute necessity, to which not only the actual*

[1] (Schneider, Michael S. A Beginner's Guide to Constructing the Universe: The Mathematical Archetypes of Nature, Art, and Science (p. 32). HarperCollins. Kindle Edition.)

world, but every possible world, must conform."
— Bertrand Russell (1872–1970)[1]

Here, Russell captures the majesty of mathematics — its reach into all possible worlds. But in this very reach lies the risk. If we begin to treat mathematics not as a servant of nature but as its master, we displace reality. We start to see equations as truths before evidence, models as more real than phenomena, and experiments adjusted to fit theories rather than the other way around.

This quiet reversal is the true danger. When nature becomes the stage on which mathematics performs, we lose touch with the very soil of science.

Rediscovering Unity in Nature's Complexity

"This world is a vast unbroken totality; a deep solidarity joins its contrary powers."
— Sri Aurobindo Ghose[2]

Reality is not a machine that follows only simple equations. It is a living totality of interactions, balances, and tensions. Mathematics helps us simplify, but oversimplification fragments the whole. We must find simplicity within nature's harmony, not impose it from outside.

"These phenomena in water and air may, we think, be regarded as the letters of a script which it is necessary to use like the alphabet of nature. Those who wish to remain at the stage of pure phenomenology relinquish the ability to read this writing and thus the ability to understand its meaning. They see the letters, but not words or sentences."
— Theodor Schwenk[3]

---

[1] (Schneider, Michael S. A Beginner's Guide to Constructing the Universe: The Mathematical Archetypes of Nature, Art, and Science (p. 510). HarperCollins. Kindle Edition.)

[2] (Schneider, Michael S. A Beginner's Guide to Constructing the Universe: The Mathematical Archetypes of Nature, Art, and Science (p. 133). HarperCollins. Kindle Edition.)

[3] (Schneider, Michael S. A Beginner's Guide to Constructing the Universe: The Mathematical Archetypes of Nature, Art, and Science (p. 326). HarperCollins. Kindle Edition.)

Phenomena are the letters. Natural laws are the words. Mathematics is the grammar we use to write them. But the script begins with the letters of nature itself.

> *"Without looking out of the window, one may see the way of heaven."*
> *— Lao Tzu (c. 604–531 B.C.)*[1]

Insight does not come from abstraction alone, but from a faithful sequence: observe phenomena, trace consistencies, test through experiment, formulate laws, and only then translate them into equations. To reverse this order is to risk building castles of elegance with no foundation in the real.

Conclusion: Returning to the True Order

Mathematics is a region of necessity; nature is a region of truth. Mathematics serves; nature commands. When kept in their rightful order, they work together: phenomena as the seed and soil, mathematics as the instrument of cultivation. If we reverse them, we may gain elegance — but lose the world itself.

---

[1] (Schneider, Michael S. A Beginner's Guide to Constructing the Universe: The Mathematical Archetypes of Nature, Art, and Science (p. 351). HarperCollins. Kindle Edition.)

9. Observation and Sequence of Scientific Understanding

"Phenomena are the direct clues to the secrets of the Universe."

Science begins not in theory but in the encounter with phenomena — the real, observable events of the natural world. The falling of an apple, the oscillation of a pendulum, the rising of tides, the orbit of a planet, the scattering of light, the flicker of a flame — all are phenomena. They are nature speaking in her own language, long before mathematics translates or theories attempt to explain.

What Are Physical Phenomena?

A phenomenon is not an invention, not a model, and not a theory. It is what nature does, without our interference. A phenomenon may be simple, such as the free fall of a stone, or complex, such as the drift of galaxies. What unites them is that they are real, finite in time and place, and governed by underlying variables.

Phenomena must not be confused with experiments. An experiment is a test designed by us; a phenomenon is what occurs regardless of us. Experiments may reveal phenomena, but only if they are faithful to nature. When designed to prove a theory, they risk filtering nature through expectation. Phenomena stand higher than both theories and experiments, because they cannot be falsified by opinion.

Why Do We Observe Physical Phenomena?

We observe phenomena not for their spectacle but to uncover their causes. Each phenomenon points beyond itself to the variables and principles that produce it. The swing of a pendulum reveals the uniform action of gravity. The path of a projectile reveals the independence of horizontal momentum from vertical acceleration. The orbits of planets reveal the balance of impulse and gravitational restraint.

Observation has three purposes: to identify causes, to recognize variables, and to classify events. A single phenomenon may show part of a law, but no single event shows all of it. Truth arises only by connecting many phenomena into a pattern.

Reasoning and Demonstration

Observation alone does not secure knowledge. The mind must connect observations through reasoning. Aristotle's syllogism remains as valid in physics as in philosophy: premises drawn from phenomena, when combined correctly, yield necessary conclusions. A falling body is not just an image of gravity but a demonstration of gravity's nature, once reason traces the cause.

Thus, observation and reasoning work together: observation supplies the evidence, and reasoning reveals the order. Without observation, reasoning floats ungrounded; without reasoning, observation remains mute.

The Rightful Sequence of Scientific Understanding

True science respects the following order:

1. Observe phenomena as they appear in nature.
2. Analyze consistencies and differences.
3. Design experiments to test these consistencies.
4. Formulate principles and laws from repeated verification.
5. Translate them into mathematical form for clarity and communication.
6. Return again to phenomena to test and confirm.

To reverse this order — to let mathematics or models dictate what phenomena *must* be — is to risk replacing reality with illusion.

Conclusion: The Gateway to the Universe

Every great discovery has begun with an observation of phenomena: Galileo with the pendulum, Newton with falling bodies, Kepler with planetary motions. These were not theories first, but realities first. They remain the gateway to all understanding of the universe.

To observe with patience, to reason with discipline, and to test with humility — this is the path. In the next section, we turn from phenomena themselves to the deeper question: how do universal principles and conditions shape every particular event we see?

9.1 Observation of Particular Events to Understand Causes

Every physical event we observe is a particular — a momentary expression of universal forces acting under definite conditions. The universals do not change. Gravity always attracts, impulse always pushes outward from a point of cause, momentum always carries motion forward, and time always advances uniformly. Yet the way these universals appear in any given event depends on the circumstances of that event — its mass, position, direction, resistance, and environment.

Universals as the Same Everywhere

The laws of nature are constant. The fall of a leaf, the swing of a pendulum, the orbit of a planet, and the drift of a galaxy are all governed by the same universal variables: gravity, impulse, momentum, matter, timc, and distance. There is no separate gravity for Earth, Sun, or stars; there is no different kind of momentum in galaxies compared with projectiles. The universals are one, consistent across the entire cosmos.

Particulars as Conditional Expressions

What varies from event to event are the particulars. A falling feather and a falling stone are both governed by the same gravitational pull, but the conditions — the feather's surface, the resistance of air, and the distribution of mass — alter the appearance of their motion. A ball thrown upward and a comet flung into orbit both move by impulse and gravity, but their trajectories differ because of differences in speed, distance, and environment.

Particulars, then, are not new laws but temporary expressions of universal forces. They are the shapes and pathways through which the unchanging variables reveal themselves under specific conditions.

The Relationship Between Cause and Expression

When a universal force acts, it is shaped by the medium in which it operates. Gravity acts uniformly on all masses, but the rebound of a heavy ball differs from that of a light one because impulse is mass-sensitive. Impulse itself does not change, but its expression in the particular case depends on the body receiving it. Thus, the same cause leads to different expressions, not because the law varies, but because the conditions modify the outcome.

Why This Distinction Matters

Modern science often mistakes a particular curve, measurement, or experimental result for a universal truth. But no single event contains the whole of gravity, momentum, or impulse. Only by tracing the universal behind the particular can we avoid confusion. The proper task of physics is to separate what belongs to the variable itself from what belongs to the conditions of its expression.

Conclusion: Unity Behind Diversity

All particular events — from the simplest fall to the grandest orbit — are fragments of a deeper whole. They differ in appearance, but not in cause. The universals remain constant; the particulars change according to situation, condition, and quantity.

10. The Nature of Locomotion in the Universe

We have distinguished three types of motion. We can now turn to the one that forms the foundation of physics itself: **physical, uncontrolled motion**. Unlike artificial motion, which depends on machines, or controlled natural motion, which depends on biology, physical motion is free of continuous intervention. It begins with an impulse, carries forward through momentum, and is restrained only by gravity or resistance. This is the motion that governs projectiles, pendulums, orbits, and the vast drift of galaxies.

Physics is not primarily about what exists; it is about what moves. And everything in the observable universe is in motion. From the fall of a stone to the orbit of planets, from the swing of a pendulum to the rotation of galaxies, reality is always dynamic. Yet motion is not inbuilt. It is not a natural property of matter. It must always be caused, acquired, or induced.

Motion as a Consequence, Not a Property

No object in the universe possesses motion as its default state. Motion does not arise spontaneously in the body itself. It must begin with a cause — a push, a release, an impact, an ejection. This may seem obvious, yet many modern accounts of planetary, stellar, and galactic dynamics assume that motion is inherited, as if bodies were born moving. But such an assumption avoids the essential question: *where did the motion come from in the first place?*

If we are to understand the universe, we must ask how motion begins, how it is maintained, and how it ends. This inquiry must include not only the motions familiar on Earth but also cosmic locomotion — stars orbiting galactic cores, galaxies dispersing, and systems rotating through space.

The Origin of Cosmic Motion: Pressure Impulse

When we look to the heavens, we do not find engines or decisions behind celestial trajectories. We find paths that must have been set in motion. Their origin lies in events of great force: mass ejections, collisions, or bursts of pressure. These deliver a **pressure impulse** — a concentrated force acting for a short duration, imparting velocity and momentum to matter.

Pressure impulse explains why comets begin their journeys, why supernova remnants scatter, and possibly even how solar systems are born. It is the true first cause of all celestial locomotion. Gravity cannot initiate this motion. It acts only as a centripetal force, restraining bodies inward. Pressure impulse disperses them outward. Together they shape the universe: impulse drives, gravity tames.

A Universe in Motion: Acquired, Not Inborn

Every orbit is a balance between an acquired horizontal momentum and a central gravitational pull. Without an initial horizontal impulse, a planet would fall into its star. Without gravity, it would fly away into space. Motion itself is not a property of matter, but the result of past events.

The same truth applies to galaxies. Their stars do not move because space itself expands or spins, but because entire systems carry accumulated momentum — built up through repeated mass ejections, collisions, and interactions in galactic cores.

Motion, therefore, is not a defining feature of matter. It is something given to matter, and something that may be taken away by resistance, collision, or opposing force.

Conclusion: The Cornerstone of Inquiry

This understanding of locomotion — its types, causes, and implications — forms the backbone of all later study in this book. Planetary orbits, galactic structures, and cosmological drift all rest upon this foundation. And at its root lies a simple and unshakable truth:

Momentum is not an inbuilt characteristic of matter. It is acquired. This cornerstone will guide our inquiry into every phenomenon of the universe.

11. Gravity Acts Only in the Normal Plane: The Forgotten Constraint of Nature

Most people imagine gravity as a force that "pulls everything down" in all directions at once. This picture is not only vague but physically incorrect. Gravity does not act everywhere equally. It acts only in the **normal plane** — that is, vertically, toward the center of mass.

This truth is not speculative. It is confirmed by direct and repeatable experiments, especially those of Galileo, the father of modern science.

Galileo's Experimental Proofs

In his inclined plane experiments, Galileo showed that a body accelerates as it rolls downward not because of friction or any hidden property of momentum, but because of the vertical component of gravity along the slope.

He also demonstrated that in the absence of vertical influence, horizontal motion remains unaffected. In projectile motion, a ball launched horizontally from a table continues moving forward at a constant speed, while simultaneously accelerating downward due to gravity.

From this we learn two decisive facts: vertical acceleration proves gravity is acting, and the absence of horizontal acceleration proves gravity does not act sideways. This is not theory but observable reality. Horizontal motion does not require gravity, and gravity does not alter horizontal velocity. See the figure gravitation acts only in the normal plane. Figure 11.1.

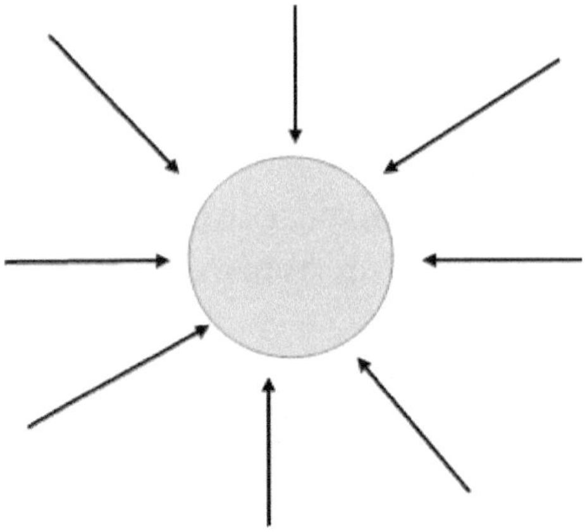

Figure 11.1 Gravity acts only in the normal plane. Gravity does not repel or act outward in the geodesic plane. It only exerts force in the vertical (normal) direction, curving motion downward while leaving horizontal motion unaffected.

Negative Premise as Evidence

Aristotle reminded us that a negative premise, when consistently confirmed across all cases, can become positive proof. Gravity never produces horizontal acceleration — not in projectiles, not in free fall, not in orbits. Its effect is always normal, always vertical, always directed to the center.

The total absence of horizontal gravitational acceleration across all observations is itself positive evidence of a universal truth: gravity is constrained to one plane. This is one of the rarest and most certain kinds of scientific conclusions — a truth demonstrated by the silence of phenomena.

11.1 Gravity Acts Only in the Normal Plane

The most decisive proof that gravity acts exclusively in the normal (vertical) plane comes from the simplest and most universal experiments: the free fall and the projectile.

If we separate each type of motion and observe them frame by frame, one striking feature emerges—**gravity never creates or modifies horizontal motion**. See Figure 11.2.

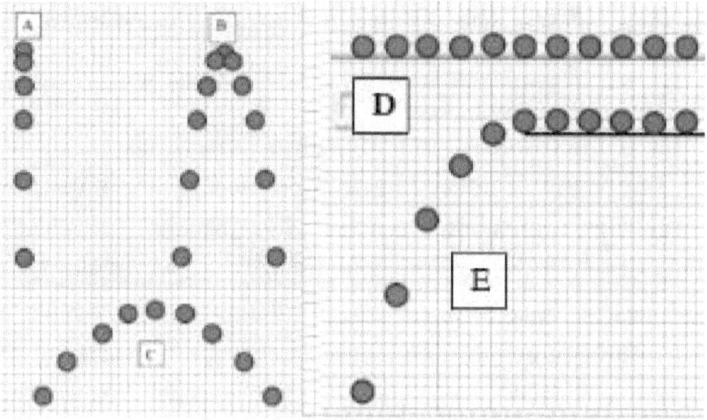

Figure 11.2 Free Fall, Projectile, and Impulse: Gravity Acts Only in the Normal Plane.

Illustrations A through E show that whenever motion begins without an impulse, there is no horizontal displacement; when motion begins with an impulse, gravity alters only the vertical component while the horizontal remains constant. In every case—free fall, oblong or circular projectile, or horizontal release with fall—gravity acts strictly in the normal plane. Tangential or orbital motion arises solely from initial pressure impulse, proving that gravity bends paths but does not drive them.

In **A**, the body released from rest falls straight downward with increasing vertical spacing between successive positions. The widening distance marks vertical acceleration, yet the body remains fixed horizontally.

In **B**, when the initial impulse is stronger or weaker, the curvature changes accordingly—oblong or semi-parabolic—but still the horizontal spacing does not vary during flight.

In **C**, the projectile launched with an initial horizontal component follows a circular or parabolic arc. The horizontal spacing between equal-time positions remains constant even while vertical distances widen. This shows that gravity changes the vertical component alone, leaving the horizontal untouched.

In **D** and **E**, representing extended mechanical analogues of the same phenomenon, the same pattern persists: gravity draws matter inward along the normal, while the tangential path continues unaltered.

At every instant the motion divides into two distinct components:

- **The horizontal component**, set solely by the impulse at launch and remaining constant in magnitude.
- **The vertical component**, governed by gravitational acceleration, increasing uniformly downward.

This simple observation, available to any eye, proves that gravity produces no side-ways or tangential acceleration. Its entire domain of influence lies in the normal direction—toward the primary body's centre of mass.

All horizontal or orbital motion throughout the universe must therefore arise from **pressure impulse**, never from gravity itself.

The Illusion of Artificial Experiments

Modern physics often confuses engineered systems with nature. Elevators accelerating downward, rockets simulating weightlessness, or spaceships moving at relativistic speeds are not natural expressions of gravity. They are machine-driven analogies, not reality.

Galileo saw the difference clearly. He based his reasoning not on artificial contrivances but on the behavior of bodies in the Earth's field — a cannonball fired (no more interference after the act), a stone dropped, a ball rolling. His conclusions belong to nature, not to theory alone.

The Reality of Natural Motion

Return to the cannonball. It curves not because gravity pulls it sideways, but because gravity accelerates it downward while its horizontal momentum continues unchanged.

This explains the parabolic path of projectiles, the continuous free-fall of satellites, and the balance that allows the Moon to orbit Earth without either escaping or collapsing. In every case, horizontal motion is untouched by gravity, while vertical motion is fully governed by it.

Why Horizontal Motion Must Have a Cause

If gravity cannot initiate or sustain horizontal motion, then there must be another cause. Every horizontal trajectory begins with an impulse: a physical push on Earth, or a supernova-like ejection in the cosmos. This pressure impulse imparts momentum, while gravity only restrains, curves, or limits it inward.

This distinction is not minor. It is central to understanding orbital dynamics, galactic rotation, satellite motion, and the origin of planetary systems.

Final Insight: The One-Direction Constraint

The greatest misunderstanding of gravity in modern physics is to treat it as omnidirectional, bending or shaping motion in all planes. In reality, gravity is one-directional. It acts only in the normal plane, toward the center.

This unidirectional constraint is precisely what allows horizontal motion to persist without interference. And it is why ideas such as gravitational lensing or spacetime curvature, which imagine gravity bending light or warping space in every direction, fail the test of physical experiment.

Gravity curves motion only in one way. It accelerates bodies toward a center, never sideways, never outward. This forgotten constraint is the cornerstone for understanding both terrestrial and cosmic locomotion.

Every law of nature has both a power and a limitation. Gravity's power is universal attraction — it pulls every mass toward a center. Its limitation is equally absolute: **it acts only in one direction, the normal plane.**

This one-directional constraint is not a weakness of gravity but its defining truth. It explains why horizontal motion persists undisturbed, why planets continue in orbits without being slowed sideways, and why galaxies maintain their drift despite immense gravitational fields. Gravity does not and cannot reach sideways to alter a body's velocity. It acts downward, inward, normal to the surface of attraction — always toward the center, never across.

This insight resolves one of the oldest puzzles of motion. The horizontal trajectory of a projectile does not fade because gravity "pulls it back." It continues because gravity has no power in that plane. The orbit of a planet is not created by gravity dragging it sideways, but by gravity constantly pulling inward while momentum carries it forward. Even the Moon, suspended in eternal free fall, moves unaltered in its horizontal path because gravity is powerless there.

The one-direction constraint is a rare kind of certainty. It is demonstrated not by a single dramatic experiment, but by the total absence of exceptions across all phenomena. Every projectile, every orbit, every fall testifies to it. In science, absence can be proof when absence is universal.

This truth must also correct many modern misconceptions. Theories that imagine gravity bending space in all directions, pulling light into curves, or stretching the universe itself, ignore this foundational constraint. Gravity curves motion only in one way: toward a center, in the normal plane. It never disperses, never twists, never accelerates sideways.

By recovering this forgotten truth, we restore gravity to its proper place. It is the restraining force, not the creator of motion. It is the regulator of trajectories, not the initiator. Its one-directional action is precisely what allows momentum — once given by impulse — to remain untouched in the horizontal plane.

This is the final insight: **gravity is unidirectional. Its universality lies not in acting everywhere, but in acting always the same way.**

12. The Primacy of Impulse: How Motion Begins and Why It Matters

If gravity restrains and momentum sustains, what begins motion in the first place? The answer is impulse — the short, concentrated force that sets matter into locomotion. Without impulse, the universe would be static. With it, everything moves, from a tossed pebble to the drift of galaxies.

What Is Impulse?

Impulse is force delivered over a finite interval of time. It is the push of a hand on a stone, the strike of a hammer, the explosion of a supernova, or the eruption of a galactic core. In every case, the essential feature is that force acts briefly but powerfully, imparting momentum and velocity to matter.

Once the force ends, the body carries forward with the momentum it has acquired. This is why impulse is the true beginning of all locomotion.

Why Gravity Cannot Begin Motion

It is important to distinguish impulse from gravity. Gravity pulls continuously but always inward, always normal. It cannot create horizontal velocity. A ball left in the air without a throw will not move sideways; a planet without an initial ejection would not orbit; a galaxy without violent beginnings would not rotate.

Gravity regulates, limits, and curves trajectories, but it never initiates them. The starting point of motion is always impulse.

The Universality of Impulse

Impulse is direction-independent. It can push upward, downward, sideways, or radially outward. It is the fountain jet that rises in defiance of gravity, the cannon blast that launches a projectile, the volcanic eruption that hurls ash into the sky, the stellar explosion that scatters matter into nebulae. Wherever sudden force acts, impulse gives matter its initial motion.

This universality explains why impulse is present in phenomena both small and vast. It governs the beginning of a child's thrown ball as surely as the scattering of supernova remnants or the mass ejections from galactic cores.

Why Impulse Matters

Recognizing the primacy of impulse corrects a long-standing confusion in physics. Too often, motion is explained as if it were an inherent property of matter, requiring no cause. But this assumption leaves unanswered the most fundamental question: *how did the motion begin?*

By placing impulse at the foundation, we restore causality to physics. Every trajectory, every orbit, every drift can be traced back to an originating impulse. Without it, matter remains still. With it, matter acquires momentum, which gravity can then curve or restrain.

Conclusion: The First Cause of Locomotion

In the chain of motion, impulse comes first, momentum second, and gravity third. Impulse begins, momentum carries, gravity restrains. This order cannot be reversed, nor can it be ignored.

To understand locomotion, we must therefore begin not with gravity or inertia, but with impulse — the universal initiator. It is the spark that sets matter in motion, the origin of every trajectory, and the first principle of dynamics in the universe.

13. Distinguish Motion: What We See, What We Don't, and What to Study

We now turn to the kinds of *motion* that things display. For not every motion is equally visible or equally understood. Some are directly before our senses, others are hidden but can be inferred, and some remain uncertain. To advance science, we must know which motions can be studied directly, which must be traced indirectly, and which are best left outside physics until evidence appears.

Motions We See Directly

These are motions that present themselves to our eyes without need of inference. A stone falling, a pendulum swinging, a bird flying, or a ball rolling on an inclined plane — all are motions we can observe and measure with ease. They form the first laboratory of science. It was by watching such motions that Galileo discovered acceleration and uniformity, and that Newton framed laws of dynamics.

Motions We Do Not See, but Know by Effects

Some motions are invisible in themselves, yet undeniable in their consequences. We cannot see the Earth rotate, but we see the alternation of day and night. We cannot watch the Moon's orbit in one glance, but we trace it across the sky and confirm it. Similarly, the circulation of stars around galactic centers cannot be witnessed directly, but long-term observation of their positions and velocities confirms it.

These motions require reasoning and accumulation of data. They are not less real because they are unseen; they are more demanding because they must be pieced together.

Motions We Imagine but Cannot Yet Confirm

Beyond these lie motions that are proposed but not verified. The expansion of space, the rotation of the universe as a whole, or speculative "inflation" epochs belong here. They are not motions we can observe, nor are they motions we can confirm by effects with certainty. They may serve as hypotheses, but they cannot yet be science.

What Physics Must Study

Physics must confine itself to motions that are either seen directly or known by their consistent effects. These include projectiles, pendulums, collisions, orbits, tides, planetary revolutions, stellar and galactic rotations. Each of these motions reveals the action of impulse, momentum, and gravity in ways that can be studied, measured, and tested.

Motions that belong only to imagination must remain outside physics until phenomena bring them within reach. To confuse speculation with observation is to build castles in air. The discipline of science is not to deny imagination, but to keep imagination subordinate to reality.

Conclusion: The Path Forward

By distinguishing motions into what we see, what we infer, and what we only imagine, we give science its true direction. The task of physics is to study phenomena that are either visible or demonstrable by consistent effects. These are enough to uncover the laws of locomotion, without resorting to speculation.

In the next section, we will examine more deeply the two realities that govern all these motions — matter and locomotion — and see how their union explains the universe at every scale.

13.1 Matter and Locomotion: Two Realities, One Universe

The universe is built on two inseparable realities: matter and locomotion. Matter provides the substance, the carrier of characteristics. Locomotion provides the activity, the expression of those characteristics in time and space. To understand either one apart from the other is impossible; to confuse them is to lose clarity.

Matter: The Substantial Carrier

Matter is the enduring stage upon which all physical events take place. It possesses intrinsic properties — mass, volume, arrangement, polarity — whether in motion or at rest. A stone lying still in the hand retains its weight and composition. A star suspended in space carries within itself mass, density, and chemical structure even before it moves. Matter does not need motion to be what it is. It is the substantial carrier of potential.

Locomotion: The Acquired Expression

Locomotion, by contrast, is never intrinsic. It does not exist until matter is acted upon. A stone does not move until it is thrown; a planet does not orbit until a great impulse has set it on its path; a galaxy does not rotate until its core has ejected matter with sufficient force. Locomotion is always acquired. It arises from impulse, continues through momentum, and is tamed by gravity. It lasts only so long as momentum is sustained, and it ends when opposing forces consume it.

Their Indivisible Unity

Though distinct, matter and locomotion cannot exist apart in the physical world we study. There is no locomotion without matter to move, and there is no matter entirely free from the possibility of locomotion. Matter without motion would be a dead abstraction; motion without matter would be meaningless. Together, they form the duality that makes the universe intelligible.

Why This Distinction Matters

Confusion in physics has often come from blurring this line. By treating motion as if it were built into matter, science has imagined planets "born moving," or galaxies "spinning because space spins." Such explanations abandon cause. On the other side, to treat matter as passive, ignoring its mass, polarity, or resistance, is to overlook why motion appears as it does. Only by recognizing both realities — the carrier and the expression — do we arrive at truth.

Conclusion: One Universe, Two Realities

The cosmos is not a collection of objects alone, nor a mere field of motions. It is the union of both. Matter endures; locomotion flows.

Matter provides the characteristics; locomotion reveals them. Together they form one universe — stable, yet dynamic, enduring, yet in motion.

In the next section, we will explore how this framework helps us distinguish between things that can be studied directly and things that remain hidden, setting the stage for the study of both sensible and insensible realities.

14. Sensible and Insensible: How to Study the Unseen Universe

In the earliest philosophies of nature, things were divided into two groups: the *sensible*, which could be grasped directly by the senses, and the *insensible*, which could only be known indirectly. This division still carries great value for physics, because not all realities can be touched, weighed, or seen, yet many are no less real.

Sensible: The Realm of Direct Experience

Sensible things are those that present themselves immediately to human perception. A tree can be seen, water can be touched, fire can be felt, iron can be weighed. These things require no inference and no instruments. They are the most secure starting point of knowledge, because they stand before us without mediation.

Insensible: The Realm Beyond Direct Senses

Other realities do not reveal themselves so directly. We cannot touch gravity, yet we see its effects everywhere. We cannot see momentum, yet its presence is undeniable in the continuation of motion. Time and distance cannot be grasped in the hand, yet all events unfold within them.

These insensible realities are known through phenomena — by consistent effects that point back to causes. Gravity is confirmed by the fall of bodies, momentum by the rebound of collisions, impulse by the flight of projectiles. The reality of the insensible lies not in imagination, but in repeated observation of effects.

The Method of Studying the Insensible

To study the insensible requires discipline. First, one must collect phenomena faithfully, without forcing them to fit expectations. Second, one must reason from effects to causes, following the chain of logic. Third, one must test conclusions repeatedly, ensuring that the unseen principle holds across many cases.

In this way, we can study what we cannot touch. The unseen becomes visible through its consequences.

Why This Division Matters

Much confusion in science arises from treating imagined constructs as though they were insensible realities. A true insensible variable is confirmed by effects, whereas a hypothetical entity has no such confirmation. Gravity is insensible but real. Curved space is hypothetical until phenomena confirm it. To keep these categories clear is to protect physics from drifting into speculation.

Conclusion: Seeing the Unseen

The sensible gives us certainty; the insensible gives us depth. Together they form the whole field of physics. By observing what can be seen and reasoning about what cannot, we arrive at truths that span from the falling of a stone to the rotation of galaxies.

The division between sensible and insensible things gives us the first tool for inquiry, but by itself it is not enough. To move forward, we must refine our distinctions. Not everything unseen is the same. Some are real but known only by effects; some are imagined but unverified; some are disproven entirely.

This is why a broader classification is necessary. By placing all "things" into a clear fivefold framework, we protect science from confusion, and we ensure that our study of locomotion rests only on what belongs to nature. In the next section, we will develop this classification, so that we may know not only how to study, but what to study.

14.1 What Kind of "Things" Exist? A Fivefold Classification for Understanding the Universe

To study the universe, we must first be precise about what kinds of "things" it contains. Not every "thing" is equally real, equally observable, or equally useful for physics. Without clear categories, science risks mixing what is observable with what is imagined. Observe the comparison table below Table 14.1.

Category 1: Sensible Things

These are directly available to human senses. A stone, a flame, water, or a tree can be seen or touched without inference. They form the most secure starting point for knowledge.

Table 14.1 Five Categories of Things

CATEGORY	PHYSICAL?	OBSERVABLE?	EXAMPLES
1. Sensible Things	Yes	Directly, by the senses	Rock, tree, fire, water
2. Instantaneous Observable Physical Things	Yes	Known through a single effect	Photon (photoelectric effect), electromagnetic wave, magnetism
3. Multifactorial Observable Physical Things	Yes	Known only through many effects and reasoning	Gravity, momentum, pressure impulse
4. Non-Substantial Hypotheticals	No	No — imagined only	Curved space, multiverse, ether, mythical beings
5. Non-Existents (Nowheres)	No	No — disproven or forever outside inquiry	Ghosts, disproven physical concepts, purely fictional entities

Category 2: Instantaneous Observable Physical Things

These are not directly sensed but are known through one immediate effect. A photon is invisible, but its strike on a plate, releases electrons. Electromagnetic waves are unseen, but their presence is confirmed through signal detection.

Category 3: Multifactorial Observable Physical Things

These cannot be confirmed in a single event. They are established only by connecting many observations. Gravity is not seen directly, but falling bodies, tides, and orbits confirm it. Momentum is not visible, but rebounds, collisions, and trajectories prove its presence. These are the most important realities for physics, and they require careful reasoning.

Category 4: Non-Substantial Hypotheticals

These are constructs of thought. They may be useful models or speculations, but they are not confirmed by phenomena. "Curved space as a fabric," the "multiverse," or the old idea of ether belong here. They remain abstractions until grounded in observation.

Category 5: Non-Existents — Nowheres

These are things that do not exist. Some have been disproven (ether, perpetual motion machines); others belong to belief or fiction (ghosts, mythical beings). They lie outside the scope of physics.

Why This Matters

This fivefold classification gives science a framework for separating what must be studied from what must be set aside. It shows that the true variables of locomotion — gravity, impulse, and momentum — belong to the multifactorial category. They are real, but must be traced through many consistent effects.

No other classification in physics is drawn in this way. Without it, science risks elevating hypotheses to the status of realities, or overlooking variables that cannot be sensed directly but are essential to motion. By applying this structure, we keep our inquiry disciplined, guided by observation, and focused on nature rather than imagination.

15. Cause, Effect, and the Chain of Reasoning: How We Build Scientific Truth

The universe does not speak in words. It speaks in events — in causes and effects. A falling apple, the arc of a comet, the vibration of a string — these are not accidents but consequences. To understand nature, we must ask the right question: *What caused this to happen?* And to answer it, we must learn to think in chains, linking what we observe with the forces behind it.

Every Phenomenon Demands a Cause

It is not enough to say "a thing moved." We must ask: what initiated the motion, what sustains or resists it, and what variables control its speed, direction, and duration. This is the heartbeat of scientific reasoning. No physical event happens without a physical cause. And the link between cause and effect is never mystical; it is logical, traceable, and discoverable.

The Role of Observation and Analysis

Galileo's greatness lay not in inventing instruments but in seeing the world as a system of causes. He observed falling bodies, rolling balls, inclined planes — and saw consistent patterns. He asked what caused them, and tested repeatedly to confirm his answers.

Newton did the same when he considered the Moon. He did not assume it orbited for no reason. He deduced that two causes were at work: a pulling force (gravity) and a continuing motion (momentum). From this reasoning, the law of universal gravitation was formed. He was not guessing; he was building a chain of logic that tied observations to causes.

The Syllogistic Method: Thinking in Steps

As Aristotle taught, truth emerges from proper sequencing of known propositions: if A is true, and B follows from A, then C must be true. This is not abstract philosophy but the foundation of science.

Such reasoning is testable. It can be confirmed or contradicted by phenomena. That is what makes it scientific.

Isolated Facts Are Not Science

Science is not a collection of facts. It is the reasoned understanding of how one fact leads to another. We cannot stop at an observation; we must trace its cause.

For example: we observe a body falling. We measure its acceleration. We confirm the same rate across many bodies. We infer the presence of a universal force. We verify that the force acts toward Earth's center. We call it gravity. This is not imagination, but discovery built from effects.

Effects Reveal the Invisible

Most of the universe's causes are invisible, but their effects are plain. We do not see gravity itself, but we see its pull. We do not see momentum, but we see motion carried forward. We do not see impulse, but we see the launch it produces.

Causes are like roots beneath a tree — unseen, but revealed in the structure above. By studying the branches and leaves, we reconstruct the roots with certainty.

A Warning on Theoretical Shortcuts

Modern science sometimes begins with equations, then looks for causes to fit. This reverses the proper order. It produces mathematical models that match data but lack grounding in physical reality.

The **correct chain of knowledge** is simple:

Observe the effect > Propose a cause > Test the cause > Accept it only when repeated results confirm it.

This is the chain of reasoning on which science must depend.

Science as Reconstruction of the Invisible

Science is detective work. We begin with visible clues — falling apples, orbiting moons, spinning galaxies — and work backward to uncover the forces, pressures, velocities, and origins that caused them. Each variable is a suspect; each experiment is an interrogation; each conclusion is a verdict, always subject to retrial if new evidence arises.

This is not simply a method. It is the very meaning of scientific truth.

16. Classification of Motion: The Three Types of Locomotion

The following table summarizes the three essential kinds of motion: Table 16.1.

Table 16.1Three Kinds of Motion

TYPE OF MOTION	DEFINITION	EXAMPLES	CAUSE
Artificial	Motion created or maintained by human or mechanical means	Car, rocket, drone, machine	Needs continuous external power or control
Controlled Natural	Motion arising within living organisms, biologically regulated	Bird flight, fish swimming, walking	Initiated and sustained by internal mechanisms
Physical (Impulse generated))	Motion begun by impulse and continuing without control by artificial means	Projectile, pendulum, orbit, galactic drift	Starts with impulse, carried by momentum, restrained by gravity or resistance

Science must begin by recognizing that not all motion is the same. To confuse fundamentally different kinds of motion is to confuse their causes. A rocket launch is not the same as a falling stone, and a bird in flight is not the same as a drifting galaxy. To build a sound physics of locomotion, we must classify motion according to its origin and manner of continuation.

Why This Classification Matters

Artificial motion belongs to the realm of engineering. Controlled natural motion belongs to biology. But the third type — physical motion — is the domain of physics proper. This is the motion of the universe, the motion of planets, stars, galaxies, and projectiles. It is here that the fundamental variables of matter, gravity, impulse, and momentum must be studied.

Physics must therefore build itself not on artificial or biological examples, but on the pure cases of physical motion where no hidden intervention exists. Only then can we reach the first principles of locomotion.

Uncontrolled Physical Motion is the most fundamental and widespread. It includes projectiles, planetary orbits, galactic drift, and cosmic structures in motion. Here, motion begins with a physical impulse and continues without intervention, carried by momentum and restrained only by forces such as gravity or resistance.

16.1 Impulse-Generated Motion: The True Origin of Physical Locomotion

Every physical motion in the universe — whether the orbit of a planet, the fall of a stone, or the drift of a galaxy — begins with a single cause: **impulse.** An impulse is not a continuous force but a sudden, short-lived burst of energy that transfers motion into matter. Once it occurs, the body acquires momentum, which carries it onward into further motion.

Regular and Cosmic Examples

Stone Thrown by Hand. The moment the hand releases the stone, the force ends. Yet the stone continues forward with momentum until slowed by resistance or pulled downward by gravity.

Water Jet from a Burst Pipe. A rupture creates a pressure impulse. The water surges outward until resisted by air or gravity.

Gunshot or Cannonball. The explosion in the barrel is a violent impulse. The projectile moves not because of continuous force, but because momentum was imparted in that instant.

Volcanic Eruption. Pressure impulse propels magma and rock upward; gravity then restrains and redirects the fragments.

Solar or Stellar Ejection Events. Coronal mass ejections, solar flares, or supernovae hurl matter into space. The expelled material acquires enormous (momentum) velocity and becomes the seed of future bodies.

Collisions Between Celestial Bodies. When two objects collide, each receives an impulse in proportion to mass and velocity. These collisions create new motions without further intervention.

Contrast with Artificial Motion

Artificial motion — trains, engines, rockets under continuous thrust — is not pure impulse. It depends on an ongoing power source. When the energy supply stops, the motion halts, unlike physical motion which continues naturally until momentum is consumed.

The difference is decisive:

- **Impulse-generated motion** continues by itself once the initiating force ends.
- **Artificial motion** ends the moment external intervention stops.

This is why artificial systems, though useful in engineering, cannot serve as true analogies for cosmic locomotion. They are sustained by design, not by nature.

Why Study Physical (Impulse-Generated) Motion?

The structure and motion of the universe — galaxies, stars, planets — did not come from machines or living organisms. They are products of:

- Primordial impulse events (such as galactic core ejections),
- Naturally preserved momentum (dispersive, later tamed), and
- Passive governing forces (gravity and resistance).

Only physical, impulse-generated motion reveals the true transfer, preservation, and consumption of momentum. It shows us how galaxies evolve, how stars orbit, how matter clumps and disperses. Studying manipulated systems teaches engineering, but studying impulse-generated motion teaches physics.

Summary

Impulse-generated motion is the essence of physical motion. It arises without human or biological input, continues without artificial intervention, and reveals the causal chain of locomotion in its purest form. It is here — not in artificial systems or voluntary motions — that the laws of the universe must be sought.

- **Natural motion = voluntary, living organisms.**
- **Artificial motion = engineered, machine-driven.**
- **Physical motion = impulse-generated, universal.**

17. One Impulse, Many Motions: Momentum Transfer Across Bodies

One of the most profound truths of nature is this: a single impulse can give rise to countless motions at once. Motion is not confined to a single object; it spreads, fragments, reflects, and reciprocates across all affected masses. This principle is the true engine of cosmic locomotion.

Every Impulse Distributes Motion

When a tumbler of water is struck upward, the water does not rise as a block. It separates into hundreds of droplets, each acquiring its own momentum depending on mass and angle. The impulse is singular, but its effects are many.

The same occurs in explosions. An atomic or chemical blast shatters a solid structure into countless fragments. Each fragment carries away part of the energy as independent velocity. At the same time, the source itself recoils. This is not confined to mechanics; it governs stars and galaxies as well.

Gunfire: A Mirror of Symmetry

The firing of a gun illustrates the principle with perfect clarity. The bullet is propelled forward by a pressure impulse; the gun recoils backward. Newton's Third Law — every action has an equal and opposite reaction — is not an abstraction. It is the mechanism of momentum transfer.

On a cosmic scale, the same law governs supernovae. The explosion propels stellar matter outward, while the core itself receives an opposite momentum. The recoil may be subtle due to the core's immense mass, but repeated events accumulate measurable motion.

The Supernova as a Cosmic Gunshot

A supernova or galactic core ejection is not a one-way push. When pressure is released violently, vast masses are hurled outward as secondary bodies — fragments that may become planets, moons, or dispersed matter drifting for millennia.

At the same time, the origin (core) also gains momentum. The heavier the source, the smaller its recoil, but it is never zero. Over many such events, even a galactic core can acquire dispensable momentum, carried silently across billions of years.

This principle explains why galaxies drift, why cores precess, and why solar systems can emerge from a single ejection event. A solar system need not form from mysterious coalescence; it can be born from a controlled blast that produces many orbiting bodies and imparts subtle recoil to the source.

Simultaneous Birth of Many Trajectories

A single impulse can scatter thousands of bodies at once:

- **Sprinkled water:** one flick creates many droplets, each with its own path.
- **Glass shattering:** one impact produces thousands of shards.
- **Bomb fragmentation:** one detonation disperses fragments in all directions.
- **Supernova ejection:** billions of tons of matter become new trajectories.

Momentum is not always one-to-one. It can be one-to-many, with each fragment carrying a share of the initial energy, while the source itself retains an opposite motion.

Newton's Third Law on a Galactic Scale.

Usually taught as a classroom rule, Newton's Third Law is in fact the governing law of cosmic motion. In every explosion, collision, or impulse:

- If a small body is thrown far, the larger body shifts slightly the other way.
- If many bodies are ejected, the source gains the vector sum of their motions as its own recoil.

Over time, even massive galactic cores accumulate motion through this process. This explains the drift of galaxies and the coherent directions of their stars and systems.

Conclusion: Impulse Is the Source, Momentum the Carrier

Cosmic structure is not built from silence or equilibrium. It is built from impulse events — explosions, collisions, and ejections — each transferring measurable motion to all involved bodies.

A single impulse does not just create one motion; it creates a system. The resulting distribution of momentum sets the stage for orbits, drifts, and structures at every scale.

17.1 Origins of Impulse: Pressure, Temperature, and Energy Release in Nature

If all motion begins with impulse, we must ask: where does impulse itself come from? It is not arbitrary. In every domain of nature — from volcanoes to stellar cores, from gunpowder to muscle contraction — impulse arises from **pressure buildup**. And pressure depends on the relationships between energy, temperature, volume, and containment.

Impulse is not mysterious. It is the natural consequence of physics, especially the mechanics of gases, heat, and constrained matter.

The Preconditions of Impulse

For impulse to occur, three conditions must be present:

1. **Energy buildup** — thermal, chemical, or nuclear.
2. **Containment or restriction** — preventing free expansion.
3. **A release point** — rupture, fracture, or valve, through which energy escapes.

Without all three, no directional impulse is possible. Heat alone is not enough. Even great energy cannot impart motion unless confined.

Why Containment Matters

Classical gas laws show why:

- If temperature rises in a fixed volume, pressure increases.

- If volume expands freely, pressure does not accumulate.
- If volume is restricted, even a small thermal increase creates immense pressure.

This principle explains how engines work, why volcanoes erupt, why stellar fusion occurs only in compressed cores. In every case: no pressure, no impulse.

How Impulse Forms in Nature

1. **Thermal Expansion in Confined Volume.**

When gas is heated in a sealed chamber, pressure builds as particles move faster. Once the container gives way, matter escapes with velocity. Example: a pressure cooker whistles only because the sealed chamber converts heat into pressure and then into motion at the vent.

2. **Chemical Explosions.**

Gunpowder or nitroglycerin stores chemical energy. When triggered, bonds break, producing sudden heat and expanding gases. In a closed barrel, the bullet acquires momentum in an instant. The force does not continue; only the momentum remains.

3. **Geological Impulse Events.**

Magma, gas, and superheated fluids are confined beneath the Earth's crust. When pressure exceeds structural limits, eruption occurs. Rocks, ash, and lava are ejected by impulse, their paths later shaped by gravity.

4. **Stellar and Nuclear Reactions.**

Stars compress hydrogen under extreme gravity. Fusion begins only when pressure and temperature pass critical thresholds. In supernovae, the collapsing core produces such pressure that entire outer layers are blasted outward in one colossal impulse, seeding massive mass ejections outwards which form new planets comets and small orbiting bodies.

5. **Biological Impulse.**

Muscles store chemical energy in ATP. When activated, ionic gradients and calcium flows release this energy into contraction.

The result is a directional impulse, whether in a step, a punch, or a flick. Even here, pressure and release govern motion.

Impulse as the Bridge

Impulse may be summarized as:

Impulse = Confined Energy + Pressure + Sudden Release

It is not created by energy alone, but by energy that is restrained, built into pressure, and suddenly liberated. When the structure yields — a volcano, a cannon, a star — matter becomes the carrier of momentum.

Impulse is therefore the bridge between stored energy and locomotion. It is the precise point where energy becomes motion, where the still becomes moving.

Conclusion: Containment Creates Direction

Without restriction, energy disperses. With resistance, pressure builds. With rupture or gaping, motion is born. From stars to stones, from machines to muscles, the same law applies: **locomotion begins when stored energy, confined and then released, becomes impulse.**

18. Momentum, Not Inertia: Replacing a Placeholder with Physical Reality

For centuries, inertia has been treated as a cornerstone of physics — the idea that a body at rest stays at rest, and a body in motion continues in motion unless disturbed. Yet closer examination shows that inertia is not a cause, not a force, not a measurable variable. It explains nothing, predicts nothing, and cannot be applied to real systems. It is a placeholder — an illusion of explanation.

By contrast, momentum is real. It is created by impulse, carried by matter, and shaped by gravity. It is quantifiable, transferable, and exhaustible. Momentum gives us the true mechanics of locomotion.

Why Inertia Fails

Inertia assumes motion persists without cause, but in nature:

- No body is ever free of forces; all are under gravitational control.
- No motion begins spontaneously; every trajectory starts with an impulse.
- No persistence is indefinite; momentum is always consumed by resistance, friction, or gravitational interaction.

Inertia is not a physical property of matter. It is only a statement of tendency — without mechanism, unit, or transferability.

Momentum as the Real Quantity of Motion

Every motion begins with an impulse — a sudden, directional application of force. That impulse is stored in the body as **momentum**:

- **Quantifiable:** momentum = mass × velocity.
- **Transferable:** collisions, rebounds, and ejections share momentum between bodies.
- **Exhaustible:** momentum is spent through resistance, drag, or gravitational work.

This framework explains real systems. A planet orbits because its acquired momentum is balanced by centripetal gravity. A pendulum swings because momentum from the initial impulse is gradually dissipated by resistance. A projectile curves because its horizontal momentum persists while gravity accelerates it vertically. In every case, momentum — not inertia — explains the outcome.

Gravity Exposes the Weakness of Inertia

Inertia imagines endless continuation. But nature reveals otherwise:

- A falling object accelerates not by inertia, but by gravity acting downward.
- A satellite stays in orbit not from inertia, but from a balance of horizontal momentum and gravity's centripetal pull.
- A projectile arcs and falls not from inertia, but because momentum is tamed by vertical acceleration.

Inertia cannot account for gravity's universal role. Momentum, however, incorporates it seamlessly: impulse creates momentum, and gravity reshapes it.

Respect for History, but a Break from Illusion

Inertia was a useful stage in the history of thought, correcting Aristotle's belief that motion required continuous pushing. But like humors in medicine or crystalline spheres in astronomy, its time has passed. Science must now move forward, explaining motion by causes, not placeholders.

This is not a rejection of Galileo, Descartes, or Newton, but a continuation of their method: to follow what is observable, causal, and necessary.

The Four Essential Variables of Motion

To explain any motion — from a falling apple to a rotating galaxy — we must consider four real variables:

- **Matter**: the carrier of mass and structure.
- **Impulse**: the origin of motion.
- **Momentum**: the continuation of motion.
- **Gravity**: the regulator and tamer of motion.

These together, not inertia, form the foundation of true mechanics.

Conclusion: Motion Belongs to Reality, Not Notion

Inertia is a notion without power. Momentum is a reality with presence, cause, and consequence. With due respect to the past, we must replace abstraction with physical truth.

Motion is created by impulse, carried by momentum, and restrained by gravity. That is the foundation on which physics must rest.

18.1 Momentum — Indispensable and Dispensable

In classical mechanics, momentum is defined as the product of mass and velocity, $p = m \cdot v$. While this equation remains numerically correct, it does not reveal what momentum truly is. For a complete understanding of cosmic motion, we must separate two distinct realities that the single word momentum conceals.

1. Indispensable Momentum — The Capacity for Motion

Indispensable momentum is the **inherent potential for motion** possessed by every body of matter.

It is not motion itself but the **capacity to receive and carry motion**.

It is inseparable from the body, as natural to it as mass or volume.

A body at rest has no velocity, but it never loses its indispensable momentum, for that quality is identical with its very existence as matter.

It neither begins motion nor ends it; it is the *substrate* on which all forces act and into which motion can be placed.

In this view, **mass itself is indispensable momentum**—the silent reservoir that makes locomotion possible when an impulse arrives.

2. Dispensable Momentum — The Acquired Motion

Dispensable momentum is the **real, directional motion** a body acquires when acted upon by an external impulse.

It is *event-borne*: created by pressure impulse, collision, or ejection. It possesses direction, magnitude, and duration; it can be transferred, shared, or gradually altered, but never generated from within the body itself.

When resistance is negligible—as in cosmic space—dispensable momentum endures for immense timescales, changing only under the gravitational influence of other bodies.

In nature, dispensable momentum is the **cause of motion** in every sense. It is the reason a projectile travels, a planet orbits, a star drifts through its galaxy, and a galaxy itself moves across the cosmic field.

3. Gravity as the Divider

The action of gravity defines how dispensable momentum behaves. Gravity acts **only in the normal plane**—the plane directed toward the attracting body's center. It has no effect in the horizontal or geodesic direction. This one-plane action is the hidden order behind all observed motion.

When a projectile is launched, its dispensable momentum has two components:

a **vertical (normal)** component, acted upon by gravity, and

a **horizontal (tangential)** component, untouched by gravity.

The constant interplay between these two components produces the familiar **curved path**—the trajectory that joins straight-line impulse with downward acceleration. Were gravity to act equally on both, the projectile would slow and collapse directly into its source; no orbit, arc, or structure could ever form. Because gravity pulls only in the normal plane, the tangential component of dispensable momentum persists unchanged, and stable orbits become possible. This same principle governs the heavens. Every orbital path—planetary, stellar, or galactic—is the large-scale continuation of the projectile pathway first observed on Earth.

4. Primary and Secondary Bodies

When two bodies are related gravitationally, the **primary body's gravity** can curve or modulate the **secondary body's**

dispensable momentum, redistributing speed between the inward and outward portions of its path. However, no body can consume or neutralize its **own** dispensable momentum by means of its own gravity. A body's self-gravity shapes its structure but does not erase its motion.

- The **Sun's** galactic motion is modulated by the Milky Way's core gravity; the Sun is a secondary in that relationship.
- The **galactic core**, as the primary, carries its own dispensable momentum accumulated from countless ejections and encounters. Its motion cannot be consumed by its own gravity; only external gravities can alter its drift.

This distinction explains why motion, once created, **persists**. Self-gravity holds matter together; it does not act as a brake upon the motion that matter already possesses.

5. Why Motion Persists — From Projectiles to Galaxies

Because a body cannot consume its own dispensable momentum, every impulse-driven motion endures until influenced from outside. A projectile continues its flight until resistance or another body intervenes. A planet retains its orbit until acted upon by external perturbations. A galactic core retains its trajectory through space long after the ejections that first propelled it.

At cosmic scale, this principle explains the drift of galaxies and the observed recession of distant systems. Each galactic core carries unspent dispensable momentum from ancient mass-ejection events. Their continuous outward traversal is not an expansion of space but the straightforward persistence of motion once imparted.

Thus, there is **no need for an external "dark energy"** to push galaxies apart; their motion is self-consistent with the classical law that momentum endures until acted upon by another force.

6. The Unequal Responses of Matter

The same impulse distributes dispensable momentum unequally among bodies of different mass. Lighter bodies acquire greater velocity; heavier ones shift more subtly. Yet the governing principle remains universal:

- *Matter* (indispensable momentum) is the carrier and capacity.
- *Impulse* is the origin of motion.
- *Dispensable momentum* is the acquired, directional motion that builds structure.
- *Gravity* is the regulator that modulates the motions of other bodies, never a body's own.

7. **The Consequence for Cosmology**

We therefore need no self-canceling accounts of bodies "using up" their motion through their own gravity. Motion ceases only through **external resistance**, **collision**, or **external gravity**.

The enduring drifts of stars and galaxies are legacies of dispensable momentum imparted long ago and gently guided by surrounding fields. This framework unites the microcosm and the macrocosm: the curve of a stone in flight, the oscillation of a pendulum, the orbit of a planet, and the galactic paths across the cosmos all obey the same law.

Indispensable momentum is the ever-present capacity for motion; **dispensable momentum** is the acquired motion that the universe has been carrying since its first impulse. The concept can be fully understood by observing the table of comparison and contrasting features Table 18.1.

Through this understanding, the persistence of cosmic motion—and the seeming acceleration of galaxies—need no mysterious dark energy: they are the natural and continuing consequence of locomotion itself.

Orphan Bodies and the Legacy of Dispensable Momentum

Not all bodies remain bound within the systems that gave them birth. Some stars, planets, and smaller objects are expelled from their parent systems through powerful impulses or gravitational encounters. These **orphan bodies**—also called rogue stars, wandering planets, or intergalactic masses—move freely through space, far from any dominant gravitational control.

Their motion is not mysterious. Each carries within it the **dispensable momentum** inherited from its origin. The galaxy or stellar core that once acted as its primary body imparted an outward pressure impulse and set it in motion. When that body later drifted beyond the gravitational extent of its source, no further external regulation remained, and it continued along its own straight-line or gently curved path.

The persistence of these wanderers is direct evidence that **dispensable momentum endures**. Once a body escapes a gravitational domain, its acquired momentum is no longer modulated by the parent field; it travels indefinitely until encountering another mass or field strong enough to curve or capture it. Each orphan body is therefore a fragment of history in motion—a solitary witness to ancient ejections and collisions that built the structure of the universe.

Their existence removes the need to imagine extra forces propelling galaxies apart. The same principle that keeps a thrown stone in flight also carries entire stars across interstellar space. The universe is filled with such silent travelers, each continuing its journey on the strength of dispensable momentum long ago bestowed.

Table 18.1 Indispensable vs. Dispensable Momentum

FEATURE	INDISPENSABLE MOMENTUM	DISPENSABLE MOMENTUM
Definition	Inherent capacity for motion; the *mass itself* of a body — permanent, inseparable, and ever-present.	Acquired, event-borne motion imparted by an external impulse (pressure burst, ejection, or collision).
Physical Meaning	The *potential* to receive and carry motion.	The *actual* directional motion that a body possesses after impulse.
Origin	Exists by the mere existence of matter; not	Produced by specific physical events —

FEATURE	INDISPENSABLE MOMENTUM	DISPENSABLE MOMENTUM
	created or destroyed by events.	pressure impulse, impact, or recoil.
Relation to Mass	Identical with mass; proportional to matter's quantity.	Depends on both mass and acquired velocity (p = mv).
Measurability	Not measured separately; implicit in the measure of mass.	Quantitatively measurable through velocity or observable motion.
Direction	None; omnipresent and undirected.	Always directional, determined by the impulse that created it.
Duration / Persistence	Permanent while the body exists.	Persists until acted upon by external gravity, resistance, or collision.
Consumption or Loss	Cannot be consumed or reduced; it is the body's existence itself.	Can be transferred, redistributed, or exhausted through external interaction.
Gravity's Action	Own gravity maintains structural cohesion.	External gravity acts only on the *normal-plane* (vertical) component; the tangential component continues unaltered.
Physical Consequence	Provides the substrate upon which impulses act.	Responsible for all motion and trajectories — free fall, projectile arcs, orbits, and drifts.

FEATURE	**INDISPENSABLE MOMENTUM**	**DISPENSABLE MOMENTUM**
Example (Local)	The still pendulum bob before release; mass waiting for impulse.	The pendulum in motion; the projectile in flight; the planet in orbit.
Example (Cosmic)	The quiescent matter within a galactic core before ejection.	The expelled stellar or galactic mass continuing its path through space.
Role in Projectile Motion	The body's mass that receives the push.	The imparted horizontal and vertical motion forming the curved trajectory; gravity acts only on the vertical part.
Role in Primary vs Secondary Bodies	Self-gravity shapes the body's structure.	The body's own dispensable momentum cannot be consumed by its self-gravity; only external gravity modulates it.
Cosmic Persistence	Enduring presence of mass.	Source of galactic drift and cosmic motion; explains recession without invoking "dark energy."
Philosophical Expression	"What a body *is*."	"What a body *has*."
Summary Statement	Indispensable momentum is the permanent potential for motion — the being of matter.	Dispensable momentum is the acquired, directional motion — the doing of matter.

Summary:

All motion in the universe arises from the interaction between indispensable and dispensable momentum. Indispensable momentum is the permanent capacity for motion—mass itself—while dispensable momentum is the real, directional motion imparted by pressure impulse. Gravity acts only on the normal-plane (vertical) part of dispensable momentum, allowing the horizontal component to persist and form curved trajectories, orbits, and galactic motion. Because no body can consume its own dispensable momentum, the motion of stars, galaxies, and galactic cores continues indefinitely, producing the observed cosmic drift without any need to invoke dark energy. In this framework, every phenomenon—from a falling stone to a moving galaxy—follows the same universal principle of locomotion.

19. Spin: A Pure Act of Pressure Impulse

Spin Origin: Not a Gift of Gravity

Spin — whether in a cricket ball, a planet, or a star — never arises from gravity. Gravity acts only in the normal (vertical) plane and governs linear motion; it has no power to generate rotation. Spin begins only when a **pressure impulse** is applied, either as a torque, a shearing force, or an asymmetric push on a body's mass distribution.

Once spin is imparted, it persists. In the absence of friction or opposing torque, the rate of spin remains unchanged, no matter how strong the gravitational field may be.

Example: A cricket bowler can throw a ball straight, or add a twist that makes it spin. The spin is entirely the result of the bowler's impulse. Gravity pulls the ball downward but does nothing to alter the spin.

Gravity and Spin: Independent Domains

In free space, a spinning asteroid or satellite continues to rotate indefinitely. Gravity may bend its linear trajectory toward a larger mass, but it cannot alter the body's spin rate or axis. This independence is evident across the solar system: planets, moons, and asteroids retain their spin despite being under constant gravitational attraction from the Sun or larger bodies.

Apparent Spin Variations: The Coin-Toss Illusion

Sometimes spin seems to change, but this is an illusion created by changing radial motion. A tossed coin appears to spin faster at its highest point and slower near the ground, but the spin is constant. The illusion comes from gravity altering the translational velocity, not the rotation.

The same effect applies to Earth's orbit. At perihelion (closest to the Sun), Earth's linear speed is greater; at aphelion, it is slower.

Yet Earth's spin rate remains constant. Apparent changes are observational, not physical.

The Moon: No Spin at All

The Moon demonstrates the distinction between true spin and orbital appearance. Conventional astronomy says the Moon spins once per orbit (tidal locking). But in reality, the Moon shows the same face to Earth continuously. If it truly rotated on its axis, we would eventually see all sides.

The better analogy is a toy train around a circular track without spinning: its inner side always faces the center. The Moon's orientation is maintained by curved linear motion under Earth's gravity, not by rotation.

True Spin vs. Apparent Spin

True Spin: Seen in bodies like Earth or Jupiter, where internal dynamics or external impacts have imparted real rotation.

Apparent Spin: Seen in the Moon, where, constant orientation results from orbital curvature, not axial rotation.

Conclusion: The Moon's True Nature

The Moon is not a spinning body. It is a secondary body moving in orbit, with its orientation fixed by translational motion, not by rotation. Its apparent spin is an illusion created by orbital curvature.

This recognition not only corrects a long-standing misinterpretation, but also reinforces the principle: spin exists only where impulse has created it. Gravity does not produce spin.

Impulse as the Universal Cause of Spin

The diversity of spin across the solar system proves that spin cannot be inherited from a uniform rotating gas cloud (nebular hypothesis).

- Mercury: almost no spin.
- Venus: retrograde spin, opposite to most planets.
- Uranus: tilted sideways, rolling on its axis.

These anomalies make sense only if spin originates from **specific impulse events** — impacts, ejections, or asymmetric forces.

Why Cosmic Bodies Keep Spinning

Once a body acquires spin from an impulse, it is no longer modulated by the gravity of its primary body. The Sun spins because of impulse events in its history; planets spin from their own collisions and ejections; galactic cores spin from accumulated impulses over billions of years. None of these spins can be consumed by their own gravity.

Spin continues as long as dispensable rotational momentum lasts — which, in space, can mean eternity.

Conclusion: Spin as Independent Locomotion

Spin is not a gravitational phenomenon. It is born from impulse, persists independently, and is unaffected by a body's own or its primary's gravity. The variety of planetary and stellar spins across the cosmos confirms this principle.

Spin is the purest form of impulse-born motion: once given, it endures.

Conclusion: The Moon's True Nature

The Moon is not a spinning body. It is a secondary body moving in orbit, with its orientation fixed by translational motion, not by rotation. Its apparent spin is an illusion created by orbital curvature.

This recognition not only corrects a long-standing misinterpretation, but also reinforces the principle: **spin exists only where impulse has created it. Gravity does not produce spin.**

20. Locomotion as the Central Problem of Physics

Physics, at its root, is not about what exists, but about what moves. All the universe's phenomena — from the fall of a stone to the drift of galaxies — are forms of locomotion. To study physics is to study motion, and to misunderstand locomotion is to misunderstand the universe itself.

Why Locomotion Is Central

Matter, by itself, is passive. Energy, by itself, is potential. Neither has meaning in physics until expressed as motion. Locomotion reveals the action of all variables — impulse, momentum, gravity, resistance. It is the single thread that runs through every natural event.

- Without locomotion, mass is indivisible lump.
- Without locomotion, energy or momentum cannot be measured.
- Without locomotion, impulse has no role.

Locomotion is where matter and force meet in reality.

Locomotion: overlapping variables

For centuries, locomotion was obscured by overlapping variables: inertia confused with momentum, gravity treated as both cause and effect, spin mistaken for orbital motion. These misinterpretations prevented a clear framework for how motion begins, continues, and ends.

By separating variables and focusing on locomotion itself, we recover clarity.

Three Planes of Inquiry

To understand locomotion, we must examine it in three contexts:

Artificial Motion — created and sustained by human or intelligent intervention.

Natural Motion — initiated and guided by living organisms through internal impulses.

Physical Motion — arising from impulse events, governed only by gravity and momentum, without intervention.

It is this last category — **physical motion** — that forms the subject of physics and of this book.

Why This Matters for the Universe

Every cosmic structure is the result of locomotion:

- Planets orbit because of acquired momentum balanced by gravity.
- Galaxies drift because of dispensable momentum accumulated through ejections.
- Stars spin because of specific impulse events in their past.

The persistence, variation, and limits of locomotion are what shape the universe we observe.

Conclusion: The Focus of Physics

Physics must be the science of locomotion. It must ask:

- Where does motion come from?
- How is it carried?
- How is it restrained?
- How does it end?

Only by answering these can we understand both the smallest experiment and the largest galactic motion.

Locomotion is not a side-topic of physics. **It is physics itself.**

20.1 Foundations Recap: What We Have Learned

The purpose of this first part was to clear the ground for a science of the universe that rests not on speculation, but on **phenomena, reason, and first principles.**

We began by affirming that **phenomena are the gold standard of truth.** Neither theories nor experiments have value unless they answer to what nature actually does. The smallest observable event — a falling stone, a projectile's arc, a pendulum's swing — is more decisive than the most elaborate speculation if that speculation ignores reality.

From there, we returned to the **first principles of matter and motion.** All knowledge must be grounded in what does not change. Universals and particulars, principles and conditions, and the five-fold classification of "things" gave us a clear framework: some realities are directly sensible, others only indirectly, while purely imagined constructs must never be confused with nature itself.

We saw that **reasoning, properly ordered, is the method of science.** From Aristotle's syllogism to Galileo's observations and Newton's deductions, the path of truth is always: observe, infer, test, and return to nature.

Having cleared these preliminaries, we came to the heart of physics: **locomotion.** Matter by itself is passive. Energy by itself is potential. Only in motion do they find meaning. Every phenomenon in the universe is an expression of locomotion, and to misunderstand motion is to misunderstand the universe.

We then turned to the **causes of motion.** Not inertia — which explains nothing — but **impulse.**

- Impulse is the sudden application of force, born of pressure and containment, that transforms rest into motion.
- Momentum is the real continuation of motion, measurable, transferable, and exhaustible.
- Gravity is the regulator, acting always in the normal plane, shaping but never originating motion.
- Mass is the carrier — the indispensable momentum, the capacity to hold motion when it is imparted.

We saw that **one impulse can give rise to countless motions** — droplets from water, shards from glass, fragments from a supernova. We saw that **spin is always an act of impulse, never of gravity**, and that the Moon itself reveals the difference between true spin and mere orbital orientation.

Finally, we corrected the deepest error of modern physics: **inertia is not the foundation of motion.** Motion is created by impulse and carried by momentum. And momentum exists in two forms:

- **Indispensable momentum** (mass itself, the potential to carry motion).
- **Dispensable momentum** (acquired motion from impulse, which persists until altered by another body).

This distinction explains why cosmic motion never dies out by itself: a body's own gravity cannot consume its own dispensable momentum. Galactic cores, stars, and planets continue in motion until acted upon by external forces, not because of inertia, but because of real momentum acquired in real events.

PART II — VARIABLES

Part II — Variables

Having established the foundation, we now enter the realm of **Variables** — the living agents of motion. This part examines how matter, gravity, pressure impulse, and momentum interact to produce every visible motion in the universe.

Here, inertia gives way to momentum; cause returns to the center of mechanics. The pendulum, the projectile, and the rebound become universal symbols of motion, demonstrating that the same mechanical principles operate from the smallest stone to the largest star.

Each variable is studied in its purest role: gravity as the taming force, impulse as the creative force, and momentum as the messenger that carries motion through time and space. Together they form the dynamic grammar of nature — the vocabulary through which the universe writes its own story.

21. Why Locomotion Has Been Misunderstood: The Problem of Overlapping Variables

1.1.1 Phenomena and Variables

A single physical phenomenon is a combination of many variables. Variables are also called as parts or elements of a concept. For example, observe an act of locomotion. Locomotion is defined as displacement of body from one place to another. Locomotion can be observed as a multifactorial phenomenon; many variables are at work at the same time

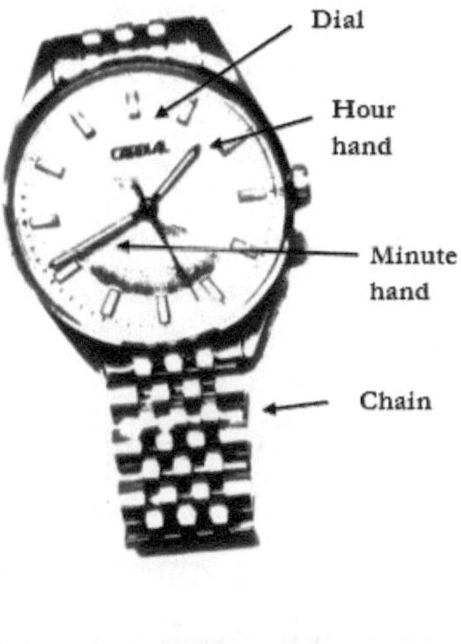

Figure 21.1 Variables are parts of a Concept or Phenomenon.

A "Variable" is a measurable or definable factor that can change or influence an action. For example, in a watch, the dial, minute hand, and chain of the watch are variable – each one affecting the reading of time. See the variables at work Figure 21.1.

21.1.1 Time is a variable, but not a cause

When a body is immobile (not moving) or moving from one place to other (or in locomotion) – Time is passing continuously. Time is not a cause of locomotion. When the material body is in motion – still the time is passing. When the body is immobile – still the time is passing. Not only locomotion, whether we do anything, or not do anything – the time is the same. It is passing irrespective of any incident, or cause, or effect. In other words, time is not a cause or effect of any incident or phenomenon or activity. Time is not a substance of anything. It is the unavoidable and inseparable part of the existence of universe itself. Time is measured as duration. But it is not in the clock, not in the matter. It is not a 'substance' at all. Its presence is nowhere, but it is unimaginable without the existence of time.

21.1.2 Duration: as a measure of time

Time is not a human invention, but measurement of time is a human invention. We measure time in association with motion. So, it is necessary to understand time and duration. With the help of time, duration is measured which makes the understanding of phenomena meaningful and measurable. Duration is also not a cause, or effect, or substance.

21.1.3 Matter – Two Forces: Gravity, Pressure Impulse

Throughout the history of physics, the concept of motion—locomotion—has been measured, theorized, and mathematized to astonishing levels of complexity. Yet despite this effort, its true nature remains poorly understood. This is not because of lack of intelligence or tools, but because the core variables involved in motion have never been clearly separated. Forces have been confused with impulses, momentum has been treated as inertia, gravity has been mistaken for the cause of motion rather than its regulator, and mass has been blurred with weight. These conceptual overlaps have clouded our understanding of how bodies actually move in nature.

Another error is to equate **momentum with velocity.** Velocity is only a rate of motion; momentum is the product of mass and velocity together. Two objects may move at the same speed, yet their momentum differs drastically depending on their mass. By reducing momentum to mere speed, the indispensable role of mass is lost, and the real mechanics of motion are overlooked.

Equally misleading is the tradition of treating **inertia as if it were a cause of motion.** Inertia explains nothing: it has no mechanism, no measure, and no role in real interactions. Motion is caused by impulse, carried by momentum, and shaped by gravity or resistance. By giving inertia too much weight, physics obscured the real structure of locomotion and left students with the impression that motion continues "on its own."

Confusion also arises in the way **gravity is described as the origin of motion.** Gravity does not create motion; it regulates existing motion. It can tame, curve, or restrain, but every orbiting body already moves because of a prior impulse. Misplacing gravity as the cause leads to contradictions: Why does Earth not fall into the Sun? Why do satellites curve instead of spiraling? Why does a projectile maintain horizontal speed? These puzzles vanish when we see gravity as regulator, not initiator.

Another overlooked factor is the role of **containment and structure.** Impulse only forms when pressure is restricted. Heat or energy without volume limitation dissipates harmlessly; but when confined and suddenly released, impulse is born. From the pressure cooker's whistle to volcanic eruptions to stellar flares, motion begins only when containment yields. To neglect this is to leave the true cause of motion unexplained.

Modern physics has gone further still, sometimes assigning **motion to abstractions such as space or spacetime.** Yet space is not matter; it has no mass, no resistance, no capacity to carry momentum. Motion belongs only to matter, caused by impulse acting on mass. When geometry is mistaken for cause, motion is removed from reality and placed in mathematical fiction.

Compounding this, **multiple variables are often combined into single expressions.** Terms like "dynamic mass" or "relativistic momentum" merge force, energy, and matter into abstractions without clarifying which component is actually acting. Such terms obscure the distinct roles of impulse, momentum, gravity, and mass.

At the root, the greatest misunderstanding has been the failure to see that **motion arises from four interacting variables together:**

- Matter (mass, the carrier)
- Impulse (the initiator)
- Momentum (the continuation)
- Gravity (the regulator)

When these are confused, physics becomes a patchwork of partial theories and incomplete explanations.

Conclusion: Clarity Through Separation

Understanding motion does not demand more complex equations but clearer thinking. We must separate the variables, define their roles, and trace their interaction in real phenomena. Only then can we overcome centuries of confusion about locomotion.

With this clarity, we can now proceed to examine each variable in turn, establishing its true nature and function. In this way, the framework of motion will be rebuilt—not from abstractions, but from the realities of matter, impulse, momentum, and gravity.

21.2 The Core Variables of Motion: Matter, Impulse, Momentum, Gravity, Distance, and Time

To understand how the universe moves—how it builds structure, follows paths, and evolves over time—we must begin by identifying the fundamental variables involved in all locomotion. These are not abstract conveniences or mathematical fictions. They are real, physical principles, observable in nature, and inseparable from every phenomenon.

Four of these variables are active. They generate, sustain, and regulate motion. Alongside them, two additional variables form the background stage—space and time—not as causes of motion but as conditions that shape how motion unfolds.

The Four Active Variables

All motion begins with **matter**, for without a body there is nothing to move. Matter provides both the mass that resists displacement and the base that receives impulse and carries momentum. Motion is never a property of space, fields, or time—it is always a change in the position of something material.

The second variable is **impulse**, the initiator of motion. Impulse is a sudden, directional transfer of energy that sets a body in motion. It can be generated by pressure imbalance, confined explosions, chemical release, or ejection. No body begins to move without an initiating impulse. Motion is not spontaneous—it is always caused.

Once set in motion, a body continues because of **momentum**, the real quantity of acquired motion it possesses. Momentum is proportional to mass and velocity, transferable in collisions, and gradually consumed by resistance or tamed by gravity. It exists in two forms: indispensable momentum, which is simply the mass itself, and dispensable momentum, the motion a body acquires through impulse. Motion persists only as long as dispensable momentum remains.

The fourth active variable is **gravity**, which does not create motion but regulates it. Gravity acts as a tamer, guide, or limiter of momentum. It operates only in the normal (vertical) plane, alters trajectory but never horizontal speed, and sustains orbits by balancing centrifugal momentum. Every orbit, fall, or curve arises from the interplay between acquired momentum and gravity's regulatory force.

The Two Background Variables

In addition to these active factors, two background variables are present in every act of motion: space and time.

Distance and direction—what we loosely call **space**—do not themselves move or exert force, yet they shape all trajectories. They define how far a body travels, give orientation to its path, and determine how gravitational influence weakens with distance squared. Space is not an actor, but its relational framework becomes visible through the behavior of masses in motion.

Time as duration, likewise, is not a force or a substance, but the inevitable witness to change. Motion or rest alike occur within it. We age even while sitting still; processes of decay, growth, or accumulation unfold whether or not we move. Time does not push, pull, or resist, but it records every change and marks the order in which events occur. We can observe the specific characteristics of each variable in a table below. Table 21.1

Conclusion: Motion as a Relationship

What we call "motion" is not a single force or tendency. It is the relationship between six variables—four active and two background. To understand how a body moves, we must know:

- what it is (matter),
- how it was pushed (impulse),
- how far it continues (momentum),
- how its motion is shaped (gravity),
- where it moves (space), and
- how long it takes (time).

In the sections that follow, each variable will be examined individually, beginning with matter—the foundation of all motion. Only by understanding these six variables, and the harmony and tension between them, can we hope to understand how the universe constructs itself. We summarize the important features of all the variables of locomotion in a table below.

Table 21.1 The Six Variables of Locomotion

VARIABLE	ROLE IN MOTION
Matter	The carrier of motion; provides mass that resists displacement and serves as the base to receive impulse and carry momentum.
Impulse	The initiator of motion; sudden transfer of energy (pressure imbalance, explosion, release) that sets a body into motion.
Momentum	The continuation of acquired motion; proportional to mass × velocity; transferable, consumable, and exists in indispensable (mass) and dispensable (acquired) forms.
Gravity	The regulator of motion; acts only in the normal plane, curves or tames motion, sustains orbits by balancing centrifugal momentum.
Space (Distance & Direction)	The relational stage; defines orientation, distance, and how gravitational influence weakens with distance squared. Not a cause, but the framework of motion.
Time (Duration)	The witness of all change; not a force, but records duration, sequence, and inevitability of processes.

22. Characteristics of Matter

To understand the structure and behavior of the universe, we must begin with its most fundamental component: matter. Yet matter is not a single, uniform entity. It expresses a wide range of characteristics that differ across scale and circumstance—mass, sensitivity to gravity, chemical behavior, response to pressure impulse, cohesion, elasticity, thermal behavior, and more. These characteristics never appear alone in nature; they co-exist in every physical phenomenon we observe. The challenge, therefore, is to study each variable in intellectual isolation even though, in reality, they are always intertwined.

This task becomes clearer when we recognize two major stages in the history of matter. The first is the stage of **primordial particles**—the foundational building blocks from which all higher matter originates. These particles accumulate in galactic cores and stellar furnaces and exhibit essential traits such as mass and structure. From them arise the quantum-scale phenomena we observe: particles and quanta with characteristic velocities, largely indifferent to gravity. The second stage is the formation of **material bodies**, where those same primordial particles aggregate into **elements**, stars, planets, and solid objects. It is in these secondary bodies that the variable characteristics of matter become most visible and measurable.

In this section, we study these characteristics not as isolated physical substances but as **conceptual variables** that clarify the structure and motion of material bodies. We will analyze each variable—mass, volume, density, temperature, elasticity, cohesion, and others—as if it could be separated from the rest. This is not to distort nature, but to understand it better.

Each example or phenomenon is chosen because it allows one variable to dominate in expression. A falling object highlights gravitational response. A tightly wound spring reveals elasticity. A heated metal rod displays thermal expansion. Through such cases, we can begin to distinguish the independent contributions of each variable and see how they combine to shape the behavior of matter.

It must be emphasized: there is **one kind of matter** in the universe, and its many behaviors arise from the inherent characteristics of its earliest particles. The variety we observe—from solid to liquid to gas, from reflective to absorptive, from sluggish to highly responsive—results from different combinations and expressions of these foundational variables.

Mass: The Fundamental Quantity of Matter

Mass is the most basic and indispensable characteristic of matter. Every object in the universe, from the smallest dust particle to the largest galaxy, possesses mass. It is through mass that matter exists, endures, and exerts influence. Mass is not an incidental property; it is the defining attribute of material being.

Mass gives matter its presence. It is the reason a thing can be touched, weighed, measured, and resisted. In this sense, mass is not simply a numerical entry in equations—it is the very being of matter in the universe. Without mass, there is no material reality.

Classical mechanics often treats mass as a passive quantity, useful for calculating force, momentum, or energy. Yet mass is active in its own right. It is the root of gravitational attraction and the very cause of aggregation. Whenever bodies come together—stones falling to the ground, planets orbiting stars—it is mass that makes such interactions possible.

Importantly, mass is not the same as weight. Weight is the force a body experiences due to gravity acting on its mass. In the absence of gravity, a body may be weightless, but it never becomes massless. Thus, mass is more fundamental and permanent than weight.

Mass is also indispensable for all other variables to appear. A body cannot have volume, density, temperature, elasticity, or momentum unless it has mass first. Even motion requires mass: without it, no momentum can be carried, no impulse received, no force transmitted.

We may think of mass as the carrier of all characteristics. A rock at rest still has mass. A planet in motion still has mass. A collapsed star still has mass. Though every other property may change—shape, color, state of matter—mass persists as the unchanging foundation beneath all physical change.

At the quantum level, some phenomena appear massless—such as photons. Yet even these are byproducts of mass-bearing events. As matter develops in stages, primordial particles give rise to interactions and transformations that emit energy as electromagnetic radiation. Such byproducts do not exert gravity because they lack mass, but everything that shapes cosmic structure—atoms, stars, planets, galaxies—has mass at its core.

Thus, in studying matter, mass must come first. It is not only the first variable we examine; it is the foundation upon which the universe of matter rests.

Volume: The Incompressible Presence of Matter

Every mass-bearing object must occupy space. That occupied space is what we call volume—the three-dimensional extent of matter. From the smallest primordial particle to the largest galaxy, no material body exists without volume.

In traditional physics, volume is treated as a geometrical measure: the space an object fills. But volume is more than a measurement. It is the natural boundary of matter—the irreducible presence that resists compression into nothingness. Mass and volume are inseparable. If something has mass, it must also have volume, however minute and beyond our observation.

This has profound consequences. No matter how great the pressure or how advanced the technology, no particle can be compressed beyond its natural minimum volume. Matter may be rearranged, fragmented, or recombined, but its volume cannot be erased. Even in neutron stars or the theoretical conditions of black holes, the idea of infinite compression must be treated cautiously as a mathematical fiction rather than a physical reality.

Volume is also the stage for interaction. Without it, matter would have no boundary to resist, no interface to transmit pressure, no surface to reflect or absorb waves. Volume makes matter capable of collision, containment, and relation.

Furthermore, volume makes density possible. Without volume, we cannot determine how much mass exists in a given region of space. And because density influences buoyancy, collapse, and gravitational stability, volume is central to every material process in the universe.

In short, volume is not abstract or optional—it is inherent to primordial particles and conserved through every transformation of matter. In the universe there may be regions without matter, but there is never matter without volume.

Temperature: The Internal Activity of Matter

Temperature is often thought of as an external condition, something measured on a scale. Yet in reality, temperature is not a thing in itself. It is the expression of internal activity—the agitation, vibration, and interaction of the particles that compose every material body.

At its root, temperature arises from accumulated motion. When particles collide, compress, or fuse, they generate internal kinetic activity. Nuclear fusion, chemical reactions, and phase changes all involve such transformations. What we perceive outwardly as heat or cold is the gross effect of this hidden activity.

In the early universe, temperature emerged in the dense clustering of primordial particles, where interactions reached thresholds that triggered fusion. We see the same today in stars and galactic cores, where nuclear reactions release immense energy in the form of heat.

In the laboratory, chemical reactions illustrate the same principle. Combustion releases heat as bonds break and reform. Endothermic reactions absorb heat from their surroundings. In both cases, temperature is a consequence of rearrangement, not a cause.

Temperature cannot exist apart from matter. A solitary proton drifting in space has no meaningful temperature. Only when particles interact, vibrate, or are subjected to pressure or radiation does temperature acquire meaning.

Temperature is dynamic: it fluctuates with energy flow, yet within limits. Absolute zero marks the cessation of molecular motion—not the absence of energy in the universe, but the lower bound of what matter can express. Extreme heat, likewise, can only exist while matter remains bound; beyond certain thresholds, it disintegrates into plasma or radiation.

Temperature does not create mass or compress volume. It cannot generate density on its own. Yet it transforms phase, enables chemical change, and distributes energy. It is the invisible breath of motion within matter, shaping how it behaves without altering what it fundamentally is.

When we study temperature, we are really studying the inner life of matter—its agitation, its restlessness, its transitions. Temperature is not superficial; it is a window into the hidden activity that animates the material world.

Density: The Measure of Aggregation

Density is the relationship between mass and volume. It tells us how much matter occupies a given region of space. At the most familiar level, we recognize it when one object sinks in water and another floats. At the cosmic level, density determines whether a cloud of gas collapses into a star or disperses into space.

Yet density must always be understood as **derivative, not fundamental.** It depends entirely on two more primary variables: mass and volume. Matter must first exist with mass and occupy volume; only then can we speak of its density.

This leads to a crucial realization: density cannot exceed the irreducible characteristics of matter itself. Every primordial particle possesses a minimum volume. However small, it cannot be compressed into nothingness. Therefore, no material body can ever achieve a density greater than that set by the intrinsic properties of its constituent particles. The idea of "infinite density," so often imagined in theories of singularities, is a mathematical abstraction, not a physical reality.

In practice, density varies by how particles aggregate. Closely packed atoms form solids; loosely arranged molecules form gases. Liquids fall between these extremes. Even in astrophysical objects, the principle is the same. A white dwarf is denser than ordinary matter because atoms are squeezed into near contact; a neutron star is denser still because particles are pressed to their nuclear boundaries. Yet in each case, the limit is set not by imagination but by the volume of the particles themselves.

Density is therefore not an independent property but a consequence of how matter arranges itself. It shapes buoyancy, resistance, collapse, and structure, but it is never greater than the combined minimum volumes of the particles involved.

Thus, when we study density, we are not discovering a new characteristic of matter but observing how matter, already endowed with mass and volume, arranges itself in different conditions. Density reveals the pattern of aggregation, but its limits remind us that nature never abandons the foundation of primordial particles.

Pressure Impulse: The Motion-Generating Force of the Universe

In modern cosmology and astrophysics, pressure is often mentioned but rarely understood in its full physical and structural implications. It is usually treated as a background quantity—a balancing factor inside stars or interstellar gases. Yet this view overlooks its primary role in generating motion, especially on cosmic scales. We assert here, based on both observation and reason, that **pressure impulse is the true origin of motion in the universe—not gravity.**

To see this clearly, we must begin with what pressure is. Pressure is not a substance, nor is it hidden inside a quantum particle. It is a consequence of three conditions: temperature, which increases particle energy; volume, which defines the space available for motion; and structural constraint, which temporarily prevents expansion.

When heat accumulates within a confined volume, the internal activity of matter increases and pressure builds up. As long as the boundary holds, this pressure remains latent. But once the structural limit is exceeded—once the boundary yields—a sudden release occurs. That release is not a slow diffusion but an impulse: a burst of motion, a directional force that carries mass away from its source. This is the **pressure impulse.**

We observe this principle clearly in laboratory experiments: in heated gas chambers, in explosive chemical reactions, in combustion engines, and in phase transitions where matter erupts from one state to another. Yet strangely, this same principle is rarely applied to the cosmos, even though the universe itself is full of pressure systems.

Stars are pressure systems by definition—thermal bodies with immense internal temperature, contained by their own gravitational cohesion. When fusion rates change, or outer shells collapse or accumulate, pressure builds beneath the surface. A supernova is not primarily a gravitational phenomenon—it is a pressure impulse event. The core collapse contributes, but it is the accumulated pressure under confinement that drives the explosion.

At larger scales, galactic cores exhibit the same principle. These ancient, massive regions accumulate not only mass, but heat, friction, and rotational effects. Over time they may reach a threshold where internal pressure exceeds containment. The result is not a slow gravitational drift but a sudden, directional ejection of matter, momentum, and motion. Planets, comets, stars, and even globular clusters may all have originated from such core pressure ejections. This is not speculation but the only physically grounded mechanism we know that can create large-scale motion without assuming pre-existing momentum.

Gravity does not generate motion. It only regulates, restrains, and balances it. Pressure impulse, by contrast, **initiates motion.** It is the first cause of displacement, direction, and velocity. Once a pressure impulse occurs, the expelled body acquires dispensable momentum. Gravity may then tame it into orbit, or leave it to drift indefinitely, if the dispensable momentum is beyond gravitation of the primary body. But the original cause—the spark of locomotion—is always pressure under confinement, suddenly released.

This perspective explains why stars spin, why planets orbit, why galaxies rotate, and why cosmic structures show directional expansion and drift. It also explains why gravity cannot account for the origin of motion: gravity pulls inward, while motion begins outward. Only pressure impulse explains this asymmetry.

In short, pressure impulse is not a secondary balancing factor but one of the most foundational forces in the cosmos. It is not merely part of an equation—it is the true motion-generating act, the unidirectional event that begins every system of locomotion.

22.1 Characteristics of Matter in Relation to Locomotion

By its very nature, matter is motionless. It neither moves on its own nor seeks movement. It occupies space, carries weight, resists force (apparent – if the impulse is not enough to displace the mass), and endures through time—but left alone, it remains still. Motion is never a built-in property of matter. It is always the result of an external cause.

This simple truth is often neglected in modern theories that attribute inertia or intrinsic momentum to matter. But if we return to clear reasoning and direct observation, we see that motion must always have a beginning—a cause that sets matter into movement. That cause does not come from matter itself, but from forces acting upon it.

To understand locomotion, we must first understand how matter receives, stores, and expresses force. This requires a study of matter's characteristics, not as abstract variables, but as conditions that allow or resist motion.

Mass is the essential carrier of motion. A body must have mass in order to be moved and to continue in motion with momentum. Volume defines the space the mass occupies, shaping how it can interact with other bodies and forces. Density influences how matter accelerates, resists, or responds under different force conditions. Temperature stirs internal agitation, preparing matter for transformation but not giving it direction. Pressure, created by heat and structural constraint, builds potential energy, awaiting release. And finally, pressure impulse—the sudden, unidirectional discharge of accumulated pressure—is the decisive event that initiates motion in nature.

Thus, every characteristic of matter plays a role in enabling, resisting, or expressing motion. Without these characteristics, motion would not only be impossible—it would be meaningless.

We often observe motion without acknowledging its roots. A falling object, a spinning planet, a drifting star—each seems natural, even eternal. Yet all motion must be caused, and all causes must act upon something. That something is matter. And the way matter responds is determined by its characteristics.

In this section we have seen matter not as a passive backdrop but as the necessary medium through which all motion is expressed. The study of its characteristics gives us the limits and capacities within which forces must act. Only by first understanding matter itself can we then understand the causes that overcome its stillness—most notably, gravity and pressure impulse, the two universal forces that set matter into motion.

22.2 Matter Is Motionless

In the earliest days of human thought, the universe was imagined as alive, a self-moving and self-unfolding being. Nature seemed to work toward goals, to fulfill inner purposes. Aristotle, inheriting this tradition, argued that living beings possess an inner source of motion. Plants grow, animals move, humans act. Yet he also saw what is still true: this motive power is not present in matter itself. A stone does not move unless pushed. A body at rest remains at rest. Matter, in truth, is motionless.

Unlike living beings, physical bodies do not move themselves. They require an external force—gravity, impact, explosion, or impulse—to displace them. The entire science of locomotion begins with this recognition.

This distinction is not only physical but cosmic. The universe is full of matter—stars, planets, galaxies—yet almost all of it is lifeless and still, awaiting external forces to act upon it. Life is rare and complex, but even life is governed by the same forces. Gravity and pressure impulse act upon the living just as they act upon the lifeless.

One principle follows: matter is the subject of forces, but never the source of its own motion. Motion is always caused.

22.3 A Material Body Cannot Stop on Its Own

Once a body is set in motion, it cannot stop itself. There is no internal mechanism by which matter reduces or cancels its own momentum. Motion continues as long as momentum remains, and ceases only when momentum is consumed by friction, resistance, or gravitational pull.

This does not imply mystical perpetual motion. It means simply that in the absence of opposing forces, matter continues in motion indefinitely. Matter has no choice to slow down or stop; it obeys only external conditions.

This is a vital correction to traditional mechanics. Much has been said about inertia, velocity, and acceleration, yet rarely has it been made explicit that a body in motion cannot regulate its own momentum. This recognition is crucial for a clear understanding of motion and its causes.

22.4 Material Body Moves in the Direction of the Acting Force

Matter never moves of its own accord—it moves only in response to forces. Two universal forces generate motion in the universe: gravity and pressure impulse.

Gravity is a constant attractive force, acting in proportion to mass and inversely with the square of distance. Its action is always toward the center of the primary body, and therefore always in the vertical or normal plane to that body. Gravity accelerates bodies downward but never creates horizontal motion. Every observed horizontal displacement originates elsewhere.

Pressure impulse is episodic and directional. It arises under confinement, when temperature and structure build pressure until release. The result is a sudden push outward, imparting motion to matter. Unlike gravity, which pulls continuously, pressure impulse acts once, then vanishes. The expelled body continues only by the momentum acquired in that moment, later shaped by gravity.

In this way, matter always moves in the direction of the acting force—downward when gravity dominates, outward when pressure impulse initiates.

22.4.1 Studying Motion in the Horizontal Plane

The clearest way to isolate these effects is to observe motion on a horizontal plane. Here, gravity acts only vertically and does not influence horizontal speed. If no impulse is applied, the body rests. If a single impulse is applied, the body moves forward at constant velocity, unable to increase or decrease its own momentum without another force. Gravity creates acceleration only in the normal plane without any effect on horizontal plane. See the Figure 22.1

On inclined planes the situation changes: downward slopes add acceleration by gravity, upward slopes subtract it. But on the perfect horizontal plane, impulse alone causes motion. This demonstrates again that matter:

- does not move unless acted upon, and
- does not change speed unless acted upon again.

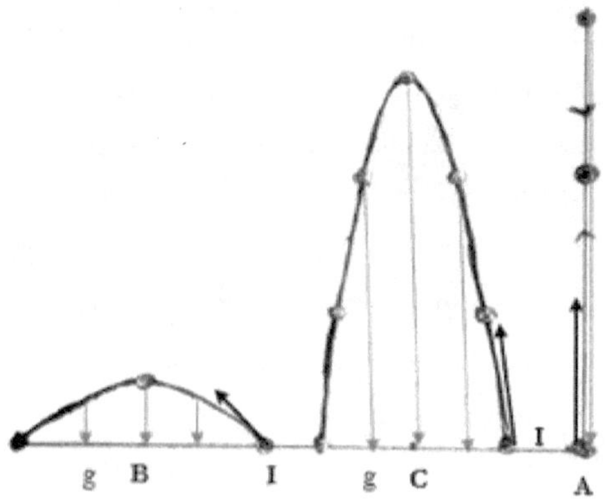

Figure 22.1 Pathways of a thrown object under gravity. The three trajectories—vertical (A), near-circular (B), and oblong (C)—represent bodies launched with different initial impulses under the same gravitational field. The arrows marked g show gravity acting only in the normal (vertical) plane, while the arrows marked, I represent the initial pressure impulse acting tangentially. Throughout motion, gravity alters only the vertical component of momentum; the horizontal component remains unchanged. Thus, gravity neither increases nor decreases velocity in the horizontal plane, proving that the horizontal speed of a projectile is preserved except where opposed by other resistances.

22.4.2 Gravity and Pressure Impulse Are Not Beyond Matter

Matter is the medium of motion. There is no gravity without mass to attract, no impulse without mass to be expelled. Motion is never a thing apart from matter—it is always matter itself in displacement.

Here we confine our attention to the locomotion of material bodies, not to light or quantum fields, which will be treated later. By first understanding matter's stillness and its response to forces, we establish the groundwork for a true science of locomotion.

22.5 Matter Is the Source of Gravity and Pressure Impulse

All motion in the universe arises through forces—but where do these forces themselves come from? The answer, both simple and profound, is this: they come from matter.

Through pendulum experiments and free-fall observations, we know that all material bodies—regardless of their size, shape, or composition—respond the same way in a gravitational field. A stone, a feather, or a drop of mercury all accelerate identically when freed from resistance. This demonstrates that gravity is not dependent on surface characteristics or chemical constitution but on mass alone.

From this emerges a deeper realization: while matter appears passive and motionless, it is also the source of the two great motion-causing forces in the universe:

- **Gravity**, which attracts and gathers bodies together.
- **Pressure impulse**, which pushes and disperses bodies apart.

Motion in Different Systems

- **Living organisms** initiate motion internally. Through metabolism and muscular activity, they generate pressure impulse between their body and the surface, producing locomotion.
- **Artificial systems**—engines, motors, vehicles—create motion through combustion, chemical release, or electrical conversion. These, too, produce pressure impulse, often in controlled, incremental ways.
- **Most matter in the universe**—planets, stars, gas clouds, dust—possesses no internal source of motion. It is motionless, and yet paradoxically, it is the source of both gravity and pressure impulse, the very agents that cause all motion. Planets, stars, gas clouds, dust, and galaxy cores are moved by the same forces acted upon by them.

22.6 Echoes from Ancient Thought

This puzzle was glimpsed long ago by Empedocles, who proposed that the cosmos was governed by two opposing forces: *Love* (which unites and attracts) and *Strife* (which separates and disperses). Today, we might rename these forces *Gravity* and *Pressure Impulse*. Aristotle rightly observed that "the characteristics of the forces are more important than their lisping names."

The universe indeed contains these two opposing agents:

- Gravity, the force that aggregates matter.
- Pressure impulse, the force that segregates matter.

These are not metaphors but physical realities, confirmed by observation and experiment.

22.7 Two Opposite Expressions of Matter

When an object is placed on Earth, gravity draws it downward until it comes to rest. The falling body's momentum is consumed by Earth's attraction. This is the taming action of gravity.

When a pressure impulse acts on a body, it imparts momentum and sends it outward. This is the trigger of motion, the dispersing agent that separates matter, launches fragments into orbits, and ejects mass across galactic distances.

Thus, gravity and pressure impulse are the twin expressions of matter's interaction with itself:

- One gathers and holds.
- One releases and scatters.

Closing Reflection: Matter as the Moving Body

Matter is the subject of all motion, yet it is not the origin of that motion. It does not move itself, nor can it change speed or direction without the action of external forces. Matter is motionless by nature—it is the receiver, not the initiator.

All observed movement arises because matter has been acted upon—by gravity, by pressure impulse, or by the forces derived from them. A body moves only in the direction of the force applied. It cannot start itself, and it cannot stop itself either.

And yet once motion begins, it is carried within the body as momentum—a subject we will study in detail later. Momentum gives continuity to motion, but it is not intrinsic to matter. It must be acquired. It must be given.

23. Gravity: The Taming Force of the Universe

We have already established that matter is the source of the two great motion-causing forces in the universe: gravity and pressure impulse. These are not metaphors but real, physical principles observable in nature. Gravity is the force that gathers, attracts, and tames, while pressure impulse is the force that pushes, releases, and scatters.

Having explored matter's role as the subject of motion, we now turn to the first of these two forces: gravity—the silent, ever-present influence that holds planets in orbit, draws bodies to the ground, and gently or powerfully brings all motion to rest. Gravity is not merely a pulling force. It is a structural and balancing presence that does not initiate motion but regulates and terminates it. It is the great taming force of the universe, shaping all trajectories and guiding all mass-bearing bodies toward equilibrium.

In the following sections we will examine the fundamental characteristics of gravity: how it acts, where it acts, its unique directionality, and its role in consuming motion and returning bodies to rest. Our approach begins not with mathematical formulations but with a careful study of how gravity behaves in the physical world, through phenomena as simple as a falling stone or as profound as the curved paths of planets.

23.1 Characteristics of Gravity in Relation to Locomotion

We do not yet know how gravity truly works. We do not know what "thing" exists between two material bodies that pulls them together. But just because its essence remains hidden, we need not surrender the search. The unknown should never block us from investigating the knowable.

What we do know is this: gravity is a mysterious attractive force between all material bodies. Though its mechanism is not fully understood, its effects are consistently and constantly observable. Its presence is universal and its behavior is reliable. Because of this, gravity offers us a field of knowledge grounded in physical phenomena, even if the invisible nature of its cause remains elusive.

As with many truths in nature, we begin not with explanation but with observation. Through diligent study of how gravity behaves—how it acts on bodies, how it controls motion, how it consumes momentum—we can uncover real characteristics that help us understand locomotion more accurately. Too often science has tried to leap to theory before it has fully grasped the phenomena. Here we take the opposite approach: to examine gravity as it behaves, especially in relation to the movement of bodies, and from that build our understanding of its true role.

We begin not with assumptions but with careful attention to what gravity does—not what it is.

23.2 Gravity Is an Inbuilt Characteristic of Matter

Gravity is not something added to matter from the outside. It is not an extra feature. It is an inbuilt characteristic of matter itself, a property without which matter would not behave as it does, nor form into the structures we observe in the universe.

If we treat matter as the subject, then gravity is its necessary predicate. Every force we assign to gravity—every attraction, every pull, every tendency to gather—is in fact a characteristic of matter itself. There is no gravity without matter, and wherever matter exists, gravity is already present.

This is not a poetic expression but a logical principle. A material particle without gravity could never aggregate. It could not come to aggregate with other particles to form larger bodies.

Therefore, every piece of matter involved in constructing the universe must inherently possess gravity. It is not optional. It is essential.

This is why gravity qualifies as one of the "first principles" of the universe: not just because it plays a foundational role, but because it is necessarily tied to the very definition of matter.

Importantly, gravity does not depend on the shape of a body—it depends solely on the quantity of matter it contains. A ten-kilogram cube and a ten-kilogram sphere are equally attracted to Earth. Gravity does not "see" the outer form; it acts according to mass, not geometry.

Shape, however, does affect how that body behaves when in contact with other surfaces. A cube resting on a flat base appears snug and stable. A sphere of equal mass balances on a point and rolls more easily. Its gravitational attachment appears less stable, not because gravity is weaker, but because the surface resistance to motion is less. Yet if either body is lifted, the force required to overcome gravity is identical, because gravity responds only to mass, not to shape.

In this way gravity reveals itself as intrinsic to matter, universal in presence, and indifferent to the surface appearance of the body. It is always there, acting quietly, forming, holding, attracting—simply because matter exists.

23.3 Gravity Is the Matter-Aggregating Force

Every primitive particle in the universe must have the characteristic of gravity. This is not speculation—it is a necessary condition for the universe to exist in any coherent structure. Whether matter originated at a single point and was dispersed by a pressure impulse, or whether it arose in multiple scattered regions, one truth remains: without gravity, aggregation is impossible.

If matter began from a single point and spread outward, how could it return or form clusters without a force drawing it back? If matter originated scattered across infinite space, how could it come together to form stars and galaxies without an innate tendency to attract? In every model, gravity must be present as a built-in characteristic of the particle itself.

Regardless of charge, temperature, or chemical nature, each particle must be capable of exerting and receiving gravitational force. This makes gravity the sine qua non—the indispensable characteristic—of all material particles. Without it, there is no explanation for why particles form bodies, why orbits exist, or why dispersal ever gives way to structure.

Gravity is not a form of charge, spin, or polarity. It is not magnetism. It is simply the pure aggregating quality of mass. Other properties—electrical, thermal, mechanical—are additional characteristics layered on top. Matter may carry many features, but gravity is always one of them. It cannot be absent.

And gravity has only one role. It pulls material bodies together. It does not create motion. It does not segregate. It does not repel. It gathers and holds.

This becomes clear when contrasted with pressure impulse, the great segregating force. If pressure impulse separates, scatters, and moves, then gravity is the counteracting agent that returns, slows, or binds.

Only by understanding both forces thoroughly—and their consequences—can we explain how matter begins to move, how it forms orbits, and how the universe transitions from dispersal to structure. We are not explaining with metaphor. We are identifying physical characteristics revealed through observation and reason. And gravity, in its simplest form, is the one force that makes structure possible by pulling matter back together.

23.4 Gravity Is a Universal Force

Wherever there is matter, there is gravity. This is what we mean when we say gravity is a universal force. It is not confined to one region, one type of body, or one part of the universe. From the smallest particle to the largest galaxy, whenever matter exists, gravity is present.

The force of gravity is the same whether you stand in India, China, the United States, or at the poles of the Earth. It does not change between north and south, east and west. Its nature is constant and consistent. The gravitational pull experienced on Earth is not different in kind from that on the Moon, the Sun, or any star. Gravity is universal in scope and identical in form.

Wherever material bodies are found in aggregation—whether in solar systems, galaxies, or clusters—gravity is present. Without it, there would be no orbits, no stable systems, and no structures in the universe at all. Gravity is the very cause of cosmic architecture.

But here we must make an important clarification: gravity is ubiquitous with matter, not ubiquitous in space. Gravity exists only where matter exists. It is not a free-floating property filling the void apart from matter; it is a predicate of matter itself. If there is no matter, there is no gravity.

The strength of gravitational attraction between two bodies depends on the mass of each and on the distance between their centers. This makes gravity both quantitative, measurable in magnitude, and qualitative, consistent in behavior. It is always an attractive force between two bodies of matter, nothing more. It does not possess thermal, electrical, or magnetic qualities.

At present we may not be able to give a final definition of gravity, because a true definition must include all its essential characteristics. But we can understand it piece by piece—through observation, experiment, and reflection. That is the method we follow: not speculation, but the gradual uncovering of truth, beginning with the simple and moving toward the complex.

23.5 Gravity as the Centripetal Force

Gravity is the centripetal force—the force that always pulls a body toward the center of another, more massive body. It is not tangential; it does not create sideways motion. It is always directed inward, toward the gravitational center of the system.

In our terminology, we call the larger body the Primary Body and the smaller body influenced by it the Secondary Body. When the secondary body is released, gravity causes it to accelerate toward the center of the primary. This is the essence of centripetal force.

In a gravitational field, all bodies accelerate uniformly regardless of their mass, shape, or composition. A feather and a rock fall at the same rate when freed from resistance. This consistent acceleration is not due to the properties of the body itself but to the invariable action of gravity on mass.

Through this acceleration, gravity imparts momentum to the body. In this way, gravity resembles pressure impulse, for both can create motion by producing momentum. Yet gravity is impartial to the origin of momentum. Once a body possesses momentum—whether given by an impulse or by free-fall acceleration—gravity treats it the same. It bends, curves, or stabilizes the motion already present.

Thus, gravity is more a modulator than an originator. It may initiate motion in the special case of free fall, but in most planetary and cosmic contexts its role is to tame, bend, and sustain the motion that pressure impulses or other causes have begun. Without this centripetal action, bodies would move in straight lines forever. Gravity curves their paths, shapes orbits, and disciplines the initial energy given by pressure events.

23.6 Gravity Is Always Present with Matter

Gravity is not episodic. It is not temporary or conditional. It is always present with matter, whether the body is at rest or in motion. This distinguishes it sharply from pressure impulse, which is episodic, appearing only when special conditions—heat, chemical reaction, or rupture—create it.

In everyday life we see this constancy clearly. When you lift a stone from the ground, you are not suddenly bringing it under gravity. Gravity was already acting on it before you touched it, during the lift, and after you release it. Gravity does not switch on and off; it is continuous.

The strength of gravitational pull varies with mass and distance, but its presence never vanishes. As long as matter exists, gravity exists with it. Unless the mass of the primary body changes, or the radial distance shifts significantly, the gravitational force remains stable. It is not a sporadic event but a permanent attribute of matter.

This constancy is one of the most important differences between gravity and pressure impulse. One is a continuous background presence; the other a sudden, directional event. Together they explain how matter can both disperse and gather, how the universe sustains motion while at the same time producing structure.

23.7 Gravity Does Not Depend on Atomic or Nuclear Reactions

Finally, we must emphasize that gravity is an inbuilt characteristic of matter itself. It does not depend on atomic structure, chemical composition, or nuclear activity. Bodies without nuclear fusion or chemical reactions—planets, moons, or asteroids—still possess gravity, simply because they are made of matter.

In contrast, nuclear and atomic reactions produce pressure, heat, and explosive motion. These can create pressure impulses that move matter outward, but they are not the source of gravity. Even the smallest dust particles in interstellar space exert gravitational attraction, though they are chemically inactive.

Recognizing this prevents us from falling into serious misconceptions. Some models of stellar evolution suggest that when nuclear fusion ceases, gravity alone compresses the star into an infinitely dense singularity. But this is an error. Yes, when internal reactions end, pressure production ceases, and gravity dominates. But gravity cannot compress matter beyond the natural minimum volume of its particles. Each primordial particle has an indivisible size. Gravity can gather, but it cannot crush matter into nothingness.

What results when reactions end is not infinite compression but compaction toward structural stability, limited by the essential size of matter itself.

By separating gravity from temperature and nuclear reactions, we gain a clearer view: gravity is always present with matter, pressure impulse is episodic, and matter can be aggregated but never annihilated into a point. This perspective restores physical clarity where speculation once prevailed.

23.8 Gravity Is Different from Magnetism and Electricity

Gravity is a purely attractive force between material bodies. It acts universally and consistently, without polarity and without exception. There is no repulsive aspect to gravity. Its nature is always to draw bodies together, never to push them apart.

Magnetism, by contrast, is a selective force that includes both attraction and repulsion. Magnetic materials possess two poles—north and south—and the behavior of these poles is directional: like poles repel, while opposite poles attract. This bipolarity has no parallel in gravity. Gravity has no poles. It does not behave differently in different orientations. It acts uniformly on mass and always pulls.

Magnetism is also a restricted property. It is found only in certain materials with specific atomic or molecular structures. Not all matter is magnetic, but all matter is gravitational. Gravity is universal; magnetism is selective.

Although both forces are invisible, their behavioral difference is absolute. Gravity is always attractive, while magnetism can be both attractive and repellent. This makes them entirely distinct, each governed by different principles and different causes. One cannot be reduced to the other.

The same distinction applies when comparing gravity with pressure impulse. Pressure impulse is a dispersing force, pushing matter outward in bursts. Gravity is a gathering force, acting constantly. To conflate them, or to fold them into a single "unified" picture, obscures their real and opposite natures. As Aristotle reminded us, it is the characteristics of forces that matter, not the names we give them.

Electric force is also distinct. It arises from the motion of electrons—the small, negatively charged particles of matter. Their movement produces electricity, which can be stored, transmitted, and directed. Gravity cannot be stored or turned off. It does not travel along wires or circuits. It acts silently and continuously wherever matter exists.

Even though electricity and magnetism are often grouped together because moving charges generate magnetic fields, both still remain separate in origin from gravity. Magnetic behavior arises from the alignment of electrons and protons within matter. Gravitational behavior arises from mass itself.

The modern tendency to merge electricity, magnetism, and gravity into a single "grand unified" framework may appear mathematically elegant, but elegance is not evidence. Each of these forces must be studied on its own terms, through its own characteristics and effects.

Gravity is not electromagnetism. Magnetism is not gravity. Electricity is not magnetism. And pressure impulse is not any of these. Each is real, physical, and unique in its action.

23.9 Gravity Is Present Even in Rest

Gravity does not require visible motion to be active. It is present even when bodies are at rest. Its influence is not limited to falling objects or orbiting planets; it acts silently and continuously, shaping stillness as much as motion.

We can observe this through simple experiments. If we throw a cube and a sphere of equal mass onto a surface, the cube comes to rest more quickly, while the sphere continues to roll or bounce. This is not because gravity is weaker for the sphere, but because of its shape. The cube, with a broad base, offers more stable contact with the ground, allowing gravity to consume its momentum quickly. The sphere, touching only at a point, remains less stable and allows momentum to persist.

This is why wheels roll: their shape resists full gravitational stability, and their momentum lasts longer. In vehicles, when the frame stops suddenly, attached parts stop at once, but loose objects continue rolling forward because gravity requires time and surface engagement to consume their momentum.

The same principle applies in projectile motion. As a body rises, gravity slows its vertical momentum until its momentum quantity comes to equalize with gravity at its peak. As it descends, gravity restores momentum, accelerating it downward again. In both cases, gravity is actively regulating the motion, not merely pulling.

Thus, gravity acts both in motion, as the cause of acceleration or retardation, and at rest, as the stabilizing force holding bodies in place. It is never episodic. It is always present, visible in change and invisible in stability, the quiet background that governs the continuity of motion.

23.10 Acceleration: Aristotle of Stagira, Strato of Lampsacus, Galileo Galilei, and Sir Isaac Newton

The understanding of how bodies fall—how they move under the influence of gravity—has evolved through centuries of observation, correction, and refinement. Some of the most influential contributions came from Aristotle, Strato, Galileo, and Newton.

Aristotle, reasoning from appearances rather than experiments, concluded that heavier bodies fall faster than lighter ones, and that all bodies fall at constant speed rather than accelerating. Though his authority endured for nearly two millennia, his conclusions were flawed.

Strato of Lampsacus, a successor in Aristotle's school, corrected this error through careful observation. Watching drops of water fall, he noticed that they spread apart as they descended: close together at the top, farther apart near the ground. This could only mean acceleration. Strato also observed that stones dropped from greater heights created deeper impact craters. Though he did not yet articulate the role of momentum, he recognized that acceleration itself was real. We now understand that the deeper impact comes from greater momentum acquired during a longer fall: more time under gravity produces more acceleration, more velocity, and thus greater momentum.

Galileo Galilei carried this inquiry further and decisively overturned Aristotle's doctrine that heavier bodies fall faster. From the Leaning Tower of Pisa, he dropped two lead balls— one nearly a hundred times heavier than the other— and showed that both struck the ground simultaneously. Galileo demonstrated that all bodies, regardless of mass or composition, fall with the same acceleration under gravity. He proved the universality of gravitational acceleration, and that it is independent of a body's own weight.

Galileo extended his experiments with pendulums. He discovered that pendulums of different weights but equal string lengths have the same period of oscillation. Again, he showed that weight itself is irrelevant to gravitational acceleration.

Newton then gave these insights a mathematical form. He recognized that acceleration is the process by which a force generates momentum in a body. Whether a stone falls from a tower or a rocket is propelled into space, the motion arises from momentum acquired through a force.

The unified insight is this: acceleration is not a tendency, nor an effect of weight—it is the measurable process of gaining momentum. And momentum is always caused by a force, either gravity or pressure impulse. Once momentum is acquired, gravity no longer distinguishes its origin; it merely bends it, modulates it, or consumes it.

Thus, the impact craters Strato observed were not the effect of weight alone, but of momentum—the true physical quantity governing locomotion. By tracing how forces create momentum and how momentum governs motion, we move from speculation to coherence, from partial theories to a universal and testable framework for understanding motion throughout the universe.

23.11 Free Fall and the Galileo Odd Number Rule

One of the most important breakthroughs in the history of physics was Galileo Galilei's demonstration that falling bodies do not move at constant speed, nor do heavier ones fall faster than lighter ones. Instead, all bodies in free fall accelerate uniformly. This insight, grounded in careful observation and measurement rather than speculation, laid the foundation for modern mechanics.

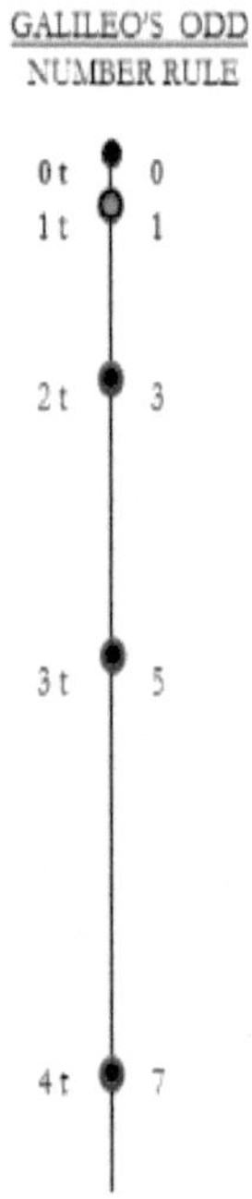

Figure 23.1Free Fall Odd Number Rule. In equal time intervals (t, 2t, 3t, 4t ...), the distances covered increase in the sequence 1, 3, 5, 7... This illustrates Galileo's rule for a uniformly accelerated motion.

When a body is released near the Earth's surface, free of resistance, it undergoes constant acceleration due to gravity. This acceleration, denoted as g, is about 9.8 meters per second squared. Thus, after one second the body falls at 9.8 m/s, after two seconds at 19.6 m/s, after three seconds at 29.4 m/s, and so on. Each second adds an equal increment of velocity, confirming what Galileo called *uniform acceleration*: equal increases of speed in equal intervals of time.

Galileo also observed a striking pattern in the distances covered during each second of fall. In the first second, the body covers a certain distance; in the second, about three times that; in the third, five times that, and so forth. The sequence follows the simple progression of odd numbers: 1, 3, 5, 7, 9... This elegant rule, known as the *Odd Number Rule*, shows that while velocity increases linearly with time, the distance traveled increases quadratically. The acceleration can be observed in a Free Fall body Figure 23.1.

The cause of this acceleration is momentum. Gravity is the agent that supplies momentum to the falling body, adding it in equal amounts during each equal unit of time. This explains why velocity grows steadily and why the impact of a falling object increases with height. The longer a body falls, the more momentum it acquires, and the greater its eventual effect.

What Galileo revealed, therefore, was more than a law of falling bodies. His experiments uncovered the deeper principle that gravity acts as a continuous force, steadily imparting momentum. Whether in the fall of a stone, the motion of a pendulum, or the arc of a projectile, the law of uniform acceleration shows that motion is always a consequence of force transferred into momentum.

23.12 Unidirectional Normal (Vertical) Plane Force

Among all the characteristics of gravity, one stands above the rest—so foundational that if it were proven false, the entire framework of this inquiry would collapse. Gravity acts only in the normal (perpendicular) plane. It does not act in the horizontal or geodesic plane.

This realization, simple in expression yet profound in consequence, marks a turning point in understanding the structure and motion of the universe. All known motion—of rivers, projectiles, pendulums, or falling apples—is shaped by this one distinction: gravity causes acceleration only in the vertical plane.

Acceleration in the Normal Plane Only

From Aristotle to Galileo, the behavior of falling bodies was a central puzzle. Aristotle believed heavier bodies fall faster, and that falling occurs at constant speed. Strato of Lampsacus corrected him, observing that water drops spread apart as they fell, showing that bodies accelerate. Galileo confirmed this with experiments and gave precise form to acceleration, proving that all bodies, regardless of mass, fall with equal acceleration. His *Odd Number Rule* demonstrated that falling bodies traverse distances in the ratio 1, 3, 5, 7... for equal intervals of time.

But all of these accelerations occur only in the vertical plane. Every demonstration—from drops of water to projectiles—confirms that gravity produces acceleration perpendicularly to the surface, not along it.

No Acceleration in the Horizontal Plane

In the horizontal plane there is no gravitational acceleration. Galileo's inclined plane experiments reveal that the final speed of a rolling body depends solely on the vertical height descended, not on the length or slope of the incline. The horizontal component contributes nothing to the body's acceleration.

Thus, a horizontal plane supports uniform motion, unaffected by gravity. Gravity cannot accelerate motion along a flat or parallel surface.

Projectiles and the Curved Path

Projectile motion is the union of two distinct motions: uniform motion in the horizontal plane and accelerated motion in the vertical plane. The horizontal component of momentum remains constant. Gravity neither reduces nor increases it. The vertical component, however, first decreases as the projectile rises, then increases as it falls—always under gravitational acceleration.

This is the gold standard of gravitational understanding: gravity acts vertically, never horizontally.

The Consequences of This Realization

If gravity does not act horizontally, then what causes horizontal motion? The answer lies in pressure impulse and momentum. Gravity regulates and curves motion but does not create it. Horizontal locomotion in nature must always originate in an impulse, then persist as momentum until another force intervenes.

Everyday Demonstrations

This principle is not abstract. It is visible everywhere.

- Stir a cup of coffee: the swirl arises from the stirrer's impulse; gravity only pulls the surface back to level.
- Throw a ball: it moves forward because of the initial push, then falls because gravity acts vertically.
- Observe a rolling sphere: its forward motion is due to impulse and momentum; gravity only pulls it downward.

The horizontal plane belongs to momentum and impulse. The vertical plane belongs to gravity and aggregation.

A Personal Turning Point

The day I fully understood that gravity has no effect in the horizontal plane was the most beautiful insight I had ever experienced. It was a moment of stillness and clarity: six hours of astonishment at the realization that such a simple fact could unlock the mystery of universal motion.

And it is this insight—simple, observable, and testable—that reveals the true role of gravity and why it cannot be the source of all motion in the cosmos.

23.13 Gravity Is a Quantitative Force

Gravity is not only a universal and unidirectional force—it is also quantitative. Its strength is directly proportional to the amount of matter in a body.

A 10-kilogram mass experiences gravitational pull proportionate to 10 kilograms. A 100-kilogram mass is pulled with a force proportionate to 100 kilograms. A million-kilogram mass has gravity of a million-fold magnitude.

This may sound obvious to the modern reader, but it is one of the most fundamental laws of physics: gravity increases in direct proportion to the quantity of mass. Without mass, there is no gravity. With more mass, the gravitational pull is greater. If the mass remains constant, then the gravitational force does not change—regardless of the shape, composition, or outer form of the body.

This quantitative nature of gravity underlies all later gravitational equations, from Newton's law of universal gravitation to Einstein's field formulations (though we will later examine the flaws in assuming curved space). At the root, the law is simple and observable: matter attracts in proportion to its quantity.

23.13.1 Historical Blindness to Force

Although clear today, this realization was not always known. For much of human history, gravity remained invisible in thought, even while its effects shaped every action.

The ancient Egyptians, for example, built the pyramids—marvels of architectural ingenuity—by lifting and moving blocks weighing several tons. They resisted gravity, but without fully grasping its nature as a proportional force. Their methods relied on brute strength, ramps, and balance. Wheels existed in their time, but they were not used in construction, not because of technical absence, but because the deeper idea of leveraging force through shape and mechanics was not yet realized.

It took centuries of observation and refinement before humanity discovered the underlying principle: that every body has a measurable gravitational pull proportional to its mass, and that this pull governs both earthly motion and the structure of the cosmos.

Once this truth was recognized, it opened the door to new ways of working with, rather than merely against, gravity. Machines, pulleys, levers, inclined planes, and wheels became tools not just for survival, but for mastery—harnessing proportional force rather than relying only on human or animal strength.

Gravity as a quantitative force thus stands as one of the simplest, yet most profound, insights in the history of science: it links the smallest stone to the largest galaxy in one law of attraction.

23.14 Gravity Depends on Two Variables: Mass and Radial Distance

The force of gravity, though constant in its presence, is not uniform in magnitude. It depends on two variables: the mass of the bodies involved and the radial distance between them. These two factors alone determine the strength of gravitational attraction throughout the universe. The greater the mass, the greater the gravitational pull; the greater the distance, the weaker the pull, decreasing with the square of separation.

This principle is often expressed as:

Gravitational Force (F) $\propto$ (Mass$_1$ × Mass$_2$) / Distance^2

This law describes not only the attraction between two bodies but also the nature of acceleration under gravity. The force always acts in the normal, radial direction—pulling the secondary body toward the center of the primary body. When free to move, the secondary acquires momentum in that direction, gaining speed as a direct result of gravitational acceleration.

23.14.1 Newton's Distinctions Reconsidered

Isaac Newton, in his great synthesis, distinguished between absolute, accelerative, and motive quantities of gravity. While these distinctions were mathematically useful in his time, they obscure the essential physical simplicity of gravity. In reality, gravity is a single, universal phenomenon: an attractive force that acts between masses, dependent only on their size and distance, and always expressed as acceleration in the radial direction. It is not layered or multifaceted—it is one measurable reality.

23.14.2 Gravity Creates Mass-Proportionate Acceleration and Momentum

One of the most elegant and counterintuitive aspects of gravity is its uniform acceleration across all masses. Galileo's experiments made this clear: a heavy sphere and a light one, when dropped together, fall with equal acceleration. This is because the force of gravity increases in proportion to mass. A body twice as heavy receives twice the pull, but it is proportionate to its mass, the acceleration remains the same.

This uniform acceleration is what allows a feather and a stone to fall together in a vacuum. It is also what makes gravity unique among forces. Pressure impulse, by contrast, is not mass-proportionate in this way. A fixed impulse sends a small body flying with high velocity while barely shifting a larger one. Gravity, however, acts impartially, producing equal acceleration for all masses, though the resulting momentum (mass × velocity) is naturally greater in the heavier body.

Thus, gravity generates mass-proportionate momentum. As velocity under free fall is the same for all bodies, the greater the mass, the greater the momentum acquired. In this way, momentum under gravity increases directly with mass, unlike in impulse-driven events where lighter and heavier bodies diverge sharply in their response.

23.14.3 Gravity Is Radial-Distance Dependent

Alongside mass, the other governing factor is radial distance. The farther the secondary body is from the primary, the weaker the gravitational force. This weakening follows the inverse-square law: double the distance, and the force is reduced to one quarter.

This law explains why planets farther from the Sun move more slowly in their orbits, why satellites must be carefully placed to maintain their paths, and why the influence of a body eventually diminishes beyond measurable limits. Yet the direction of gravity remains constant: always radial, always normal to the surface of the primary body.

23.14.4 No Acceleration in the Geodesic Plane

Here lies the crucial point: gravity never acts in the geodesic, or horizontal, plane. All acceleration belongs to the normal plane. When we see horizontal motion, whether of a projectile, a planet, or a galaxy, it is not gravity that creates it. Such motion originates from impulse and momentum. Gravity only modifies it, curving trajectories inward without ever supplying velocity in the horizontal direction.

Thus, gravity is both simple and profound: proportional to mass, dependent on distance, and restricted to the normal plane. It is not the cause of all motion, but the regulator of motion already acquired. The horizontal belongs to momentum; the vertical belongs to gravity.

23.15 Newton's Law of Universal Gravitation

The force of gravity, though ever-present, was not mathematically expressed until the work of Sir Isaac Newton, who distilled the behavior of gravitational attraction into a precise and universal law.

The law states:

"The attractive force between two bodies is directly proportional to the product of their masses, and inversely proportional to the square of the distance between them."

In mathematical form:

$$\boldsymbol{F = \frac{GMm}{r^2}}$$

Where:

- $\boldsymbol{F}$ = gravitational force between the two bodies
- $\boldsymbol{M}$ = mass of the primary body
- $\boldsymbol{m}$ = mass of the secondary body
- $\boldsymbol{r}$ = radial distance between the centers of the two bodies
- $\boldsymbol{G}$ = universal gravitational constant

The constant of proportionality, G, was not calculated by Newton himself but by Henry Cavendish in the late 18th century, using his famous torsion balance experiment. Its measured value is:

$$G = 6.6743 \times 10^{-11}\ \mathrm{N{\cdot}m^2/kg^2}$$

This equation remains one of the most profound and elegant relationships in all of physics. It allows us to calculate the gravitational force between any two objects—from pebbles to planets—with astonishing precision.

The Equation's Deep Simplicity

Despite its power, Newton's law reveals a beautifully mass-independent effect on secondary bodies. Gravity exerts a proportionate force on all bodies based on their mass. But when calculating acceleration due to gravity on a secondary body, that body's own mass cancels out of the equation.

This explains Galileo's famous insight: all bodies fall with the same acceleration under gravity, regardless of weight. The acceleration depends only on two factors:

- The mass of the primary body
- The radial distance from the primary body's center

Thus, to calculate how Earth influences a falling apple, you need only Earth's mass and the distance from its center. To calculate how the Moon influences Earth, you need the Moon's mass and its distance. The universality of this principle makes Newton's law a cornerstone of mechanics and astronomy.

23.15.1 Locomotion and the Law of Gravity

Our broader inquiry is not about gravity alone, but about locomotion—the universal process by which bodies move. In this framework:

- Gravity provides acceleration and momentum in the normal (vertical) plane.
- Pressure impulse provides motion in the horizontal plane or in any direction.

- Momentum carries that motion forward once it has been initiated.

Newton's Law of Universal Gravitation serves as the bridge linking these realities. It shows that the same force governs the fall of an apple, the orbit of the Moon, and the structure of galaxies.

At the same time, we must avoid overextending Newton's own distinctions between absolute, accelerative, and motive quantities. These divisions, while useful historically, obscure the physical essence. Gravity is not many things—it is one:

Gravity is a mass-based, radial, attractive force that creates acceleration and momentum in material bodies.

It is not episodic. It is not repulsive. It is not magnetic. It does not act in the horizontal plane. It is unidirectional, vertical, proportional, and universal—an inseparable predicate of matter itself.

23.16 What Can We Understand Further from the Law of Universal Gravitation?

If we look closely at Newton's Law of Universal Gravitation:

$$F = \frac{GMm}{r^2}$$

we find that among all the terms in the equation, only one value is truly universal and constant:

***G*— the Universal Gravitational Constant.**

This constant is currently accepted as:

$$G = 6.6743 \times 10^{-11}\ \mathrm{N{\cdot}m^2/kg^2}$$

First measured by Henry Cavendish in the 18th century, its decimal precision has been refined by modern experiments, yet it remains one of the most stable constants in all of physics.

Constancy Amidst Vast Variation

In the equation:

- G is constant.
- M **and** m the masses of the interacting bodies, are constant in most natural systems (except during collisions, supernovae, or galactic disruptions).

- r, the radial distance between the centers of mass, is the most commonly varying factor, changing over time due to orbital motion or displacement.

Despite this variability—from fractions of a meter to trillions of kilometers—the law remains robust. Calculations made with Newton's law perfectly match experimental results across all scales:

- From pendulum experiments on Earth,
- To the orbital paths of planets and satellites,
- To the structure of galaxies.

This universal applicability reveals something profound: the law is not only theoretical—it is a working principle of the universe.

Constancy in Form, Variability in Magnitude

The law shows that:

- Gravity's **form** remains constant — it is always attractive, always radial.
- Gravity's **intensity** depends on the context — proportional to mass, inversely proportional to distance squared.

This duality makes each gravitational interaction uniquely measurable, yet universally explainable.

Thus, Newton's law is not merely a mathematical relationship. It is a **practical guide** to understanding locomotion and structure across the cosmos. And it reinforces the guiding principle of this book:

To understand the particular, we must first grasp the universal.

23.17 Summary: Characteristics of Gravity

Gravity is one of the two great forces responsible for locomotion in the universe. Unlike pressure impulse, which acts episodically and disperses matter, gravity is a constant, aggregating force—a quiet but persistent architect of structure and order.

Here is a summary of gravity's essential characteristics:

1. **Gravity is an Inbuilt Characteristic of Matter**

Gravity is not imposed upon matter—it is a predicate of it. Every material particle in the universe, however small, possesses gravitational character. If there is no matter, there is no gravity. Wherever matter exists, gravity is inherently present.

2. Gravity is a Universal Force

Gravity operates throughout the universe. Its effects are consistent on Earth, in the solar system, and across galaxies. It acts between all bodies that have mass, and its behavior does not change with location, shape, or chemical composition. However, gravity is only present where matter exists—it is not ubiquitous in empty space.

3. Gravity is an Aggregating Force

Gravity attracts and binds. It draws matter inward, causes bodies to coalesce, and brings moving bodies to rest. It plays no role in repulsion or dispersion. All orbits, clusters, and planetary systems are made possible by this aggregating action.

4. Gravity is Always Present and Not Episodic

Gravity acts continuously and uniformly. Unlike pressure impulse, which arises from specific events (explosions, reactions, or actions), gravity is always on—a constant presence accompanying matter. Its quantity remains unchanged unless the mass or radial position of the interacting bodies changes.

5. Gravity is Directional: It Acts Only in the Normal (Vertical) Plane

This is gravity's most crucial feature. Gravity causes acceleration only in the perpendicular (normal) direction, not in the horizontal or geodesic plane. This insight, confirmed through Galileo's inclined plane and free-fall experiments, explains why falling objects accelerate downward but maintain uniform horizontal motion. Understanding this unidirectional nature of gravity is the key to comprehending all physical motion.

6. Gravity is a Quantitative Force

Gravity's intensity is directly proportional to mass. A 10-kilogram body exerts gravitational pull proportionate to 10 kg; a 100-

kilogram body exerts pull proportionate to 100 kg. More mass means more gravitational force. Yet this increase is proportional, not exponential.

7. **Gravity Depends on Two Variables: Mass and Radial Distance**

The gravitational force between two bodies increases with their masses and decreases with the square of the distance between them.

$$F = \frac{GMm}{r^2}$$

This radial distance dependence explains variations in gravitational strength across different orbits and altitudes.

8. **Gravity Creates Mass-Proportionate Acceleration and Momentum**

Galileo showed that all bodies, regardless of weight, fall with equal acceleration. This occurs because gravity provides a force proportional to each body's mass, resulting in the same acceleration for all. By contrast, pressure impulse creates greater momentum in smaller bodies and struggles to move larger ones.

9. **Gravity is Distinct from Magnetism and Electricity**

Gravity is purely attractive, and it applies to all matter. Magnetism and electric forces, by contrast, can both attract and repel, and apply only to specific substances. Gravity does not behave like a magnetic or electric force and cannot be unified with them without losing its physical distinctiveness.

10. Newton's Law of Universal Gravitation Confirms All These Features

Newton's law captures gravity's nature with precision:

$$F = GMm/r^2$$

Where F is the gravitational force, and M and m are the masses, r is the radial distance, and G is the universal gravitational constant.

This law—refined by Cavendish's measurement of G = **6.6743 × 10^{-11} N·m²/kg²**—remains one of the most successful and foundational equations in science.

Closing Reflection

In sum, gravity is the quiet sculptor of the cosmos. It does not move matter by impulse, but by presence. It causes motion in one direction only—downward—and resists motion in all others unless another force (like pressure impulse) intervenes. Without gravity, there would be no structure; without understanding gravity, we cannot understand locomotion.

23.18 Mini-Recap: Matter and Gravity

We have now completed our study of **Matter** and **Gravity**, the two inseparable foundations of locomotion. Both are constant in their presence, yet profoundly different in their roles.

Matter is the **subject of all motion**. It is the carrier of mass, volume, density, and all other characteristics. It cannot move on its own, and it cannot stop on its own. Motion only becomes possible when matter is acted upon by an external cause. Matter is passive in itself, but active as the bearer of every force and every movement that unfolds in the universe.

Gravity is the **silent predicate of matter**. It is not episodic, not selective, and not optional—it is always present wherever matter exists. Gravity attracts, gathers, and tames. It creates no motion of its own, but it consumes and regulates all motion that has been initiated. It acts only in the normal (vertical) plane, pulling bodies toward their centers of mass, and through this single-directional action it sculpts the structure of the cosmos.

Together, matter and gravity explain why the universe is not scattered dust, but an ordered architecture of stars, planets, and galaxies. Matter provides the substance; gravity provides the bond.

But one question still remains unanswered: **what starts the motion?**

If matter is passive, and gravity only attracts, what force initiates the first step—the outward push, the separation, the dispersal that allows orbits, rotations, and trajectories to exist at all?

The answer is **Pressure Impulse**. Unlike gravity, which always pulls, pressure impulse pushes. Unlike matter, which is silent, pressure impulse speaks suddenly, in bursts, in events of energy release. It is the episodic, directional force that gives matter its first motion and the universe its locomotion.

We now turn to this most overlooked but foundational cause of motion: **Pressure Impulse, the motion-generating force of the universe.**

24. Characteristics of Pressure Impulse Force

Pressure Impulse Force is one of the two fundamental forces observed in the universe, alongside gravity. While gravity serves as the aggregating force—bringing bodies together—pressure impulse acts as the dispersing force, responsible for initiating motion and ejecting matter outward. Understanding this force is essential to any inquiry into universal locomotion, particularly in the horizontal or geodesic planes, where gravity plays no role.

Unlike gravity, which is an ever-present characteristic of matter, pressure impulse is not permanent or intrinsic. It arises only under specific conditions, particularly when there is an explosive or energetic transformation within matter. It is therefore not continuous but episodic, a force that appears, acts, and then disappears.

Pressure impulse is always a pushing-away force, never an attracting one. It can eject matter outward but has no capacity to pull it back. Once it has acted, the originating body cannot retrieve or influence the ejected matter through this force.

Its strength and direction vary according to the nature of the source. An explosion, collision, or internal transformation can generate an impulse of tremendous magnitude, yet always with a highly specific directional effect. For this reason, pressure impulse is qualitative and variable, shaped by the physical, chemical, or energetic properties of the matter involved.

The generation of pressure impulse depends entirely on the internal condition of matter. Chemical structure, physical phase, internal tension, and thermal state all determine whether and how an impulse arises. It does not exist spontaneously; it always requires a cause or a trigger.

Unlike gravity, which acts continuously and uniformly, pressure impulse acts once and then vanishes. It transfers momentum to another body and leaves the body to move on its own. This transience is crucial, for it means that pressure impulse is not a sustained background force but a momentary origin of motion.

Most decisively, pressure impulse is direction-independent. It can act at any angle—upward, sideways, or oblique. Gravity, by contrast, acts only in the normal (vertical) plane and never in the horizontal. This distinction defines the unique and complementary role of pressure impulse in the universe: where gravity gathers and restrains, pressure impulse scatters and sets free.

24.1 Pressure Impulse and Locomotion

In our study of universal locomotion, we have observed that most cosmic motions—planetary orbits, stellar revolutions, galactic rotations—occur in horizontal or geodesic planes. These motions cannot arise from gravity, since gravity does not initiate horizontal movement. Nor can gravity sustain them, for gravity acts only in the normal plane. The persistence of horizontal motion requires a different explanation.

This is where pressure impulse plays its vital role.

When a stone is thrown, the force we apply is a pressure impulse. That impulse is transferred into the stone as momentum. We may direct the stone vertically, horizontally, or at any oblique angle—demonstrating the directional freedom of pressure impulse. Gravity, however, responds only to the vertical component of that motion.

If the body is projected exactly in the normal plane—straight upward—its entire momentum is vertical. Gravity then acts to decelerate it. As the stone rises, its vertical momentum is gradually neutralized until the motion halts. Thereafter, gravity accelerates the body downward in the same vertical plane. This is a straight-line trajectory in the normal direction, not a parabola.

If the body is projected obliquely, gravity acts only on the vertical component of its motion. The horizontal velocity remains untouched. As gravity reduces the vertical momentum and eventually reverses it, the horizontal momentum persists unchanged. The resulting path of the projectile is curved—but not because gravity "bends" it. The curve is simply the combined effect of two independent motions: vertical acceleration due to gravity and horizontal persistence due to pressure impulse.

This shows with clarity: gravity cannot influence horizontal velocity. It cannot create or alter motion in that plane. The only way a body acquires horizontal or orbital motion is through a pressure impulse—whether from a physical explosion, a violent collision, or a mass ejection from a star, planet, or galactic core.

24.2 Historical Note: Strato's Insight

Strato of Lampsacus, the student of Theophrastus, was one of the first to recognize that even a bead of water falling from a height accelerates as it descends. This ancient observation affirms that both massive bodies and minute droplets obey the same principles. We will explore these dynamics further when examining the behavior of fluids and liquids under the combined action of pressure impulse and gravitational pull.

24.3 Pressure Impulse Is Not Always Present with Matter

Pressure impulse is not a constant companion of matter. Unlike gravity—which acts upon matter at all times, regardless of its state, motion, or composition—pressure impulse is intermittent and episodic. It arises only under specific circumstances, usually during internal or external transformations of matter.

Its generation depends on the physical and chemical characteristics of the body. This makes it fundamentally different from gravity's ever-present character. In living organisms, pressure impulse originates from biochemical processes such as metabolism and muscle contraction. In the physical world, it emerges through thermal, chemical, or atomic events—combustion, fusion, fission, or collision.

This episodic character makes pressure impulse a multifactorial and unpredictable force. The tectonic plates of Earth remain in constant contact, yet earthquakes occur only after sufficient stress has built up. Volcanoes erupt only when accumulated pressure within magma chambers exceeds structural resistance. Even when material conditions appear stable, the sudden release of energy into motion occurs only when a threshold is reached.

Thus, pressure impulse is not only directionally variable—it is also temporally variable. Its presence is always tied to a specific event, transformation, or imbalance within or between material bodies. It is a force that appears in moments, passes its effect to matter in the form of momentum, and then vanishes, leaving gravity and momentum to govern the motion thereafter.

24.4 Pressure Impulse Is Quantitatively Variable

One of the defining characteristics of pressure impulse is its extreme quantitative variability. It can manifest with the lightest touch or with unimaginable violence, depending entirely on the conditions of its initiation. A gentle push on a stone and the detonation of a supernova are both examples of pressure impulse, differing only in the magnitude of force delivered at the instant of release.

All momentum acquired by a body is imparted in this initial moment. Afterward, the body's motion is not sustained by continuous propulsion but is regulated solely by gravity, which acts only in the normal plane. Since gravity is itself both quantitatively and qualitatively invariable—determined only by the mass of the primary body and the radial distance—the entire future course of motion depends on the initial magnitude of pressure impulse.

This principle explains why two bodies, launched with different magnitudes of impulse but within the same gravitational field, follow distinct trajectories. It is not gravity that changes. Gravity remains constant. It is the pressure impulse at the beginning that determines the scale, speed, and reach of the motion.

A further distinction must be made between voluntary and **involuntary occurrences of pressure impulse**. In the human world, pressure impulse often arises intentionally—deliberate actions performed *for the sake of* achieving a goal. But in the natural world, most events occur involuntarily. They happen *because of* the conditions that necessarily lead to release. A volcano does not erupt for a reason; it erupts because pressure has exceeded containment. A star does not expel matter for a purpose; it does so because the buildup of energy reaches a threshold.

Most locomotion in the universe follows this principle—not deliberate, but consequential. Pressure impulse is therefore a causally driven, quantitatively variable, and event-dependent force. It shapes the universe not through permanence, but through spontaneous bursts—moments that transform still matter into motion, and into structure.

24.5 Pressure Impulse Is Direction-Independent

Pressure impulse force is direction-independent. Unlike gravity, which always acts toward the center of mass and strictly in the vertical or normal plane, pressure impulse can be generated in any direction—upward, sideways, downward, or at any oblique angle across the full 360°. It may act radially outward from a body's core or tangentially along its surface. This freedom of direction makes pressure impulse the true cause of motion in the horizontal, oblique, or geodesic planes—domains where gravity has no effect.

Once generated, a pressure impulse pushes matter away from its source. In this sense, it can appear centrifugal, but this must be carefully understood. The force does not arise from circular motion; rather, it creates the conditions that can later be shaped into circular or orbital paths by gravity.

All of the energy of pressure impulse is delivered at the moment of release. Once transmitted, the force itself is exhausted. If the conditions that produced the impulse—thermal buildup, chemical reaction, or internal tension—continue within the source body, pressure will gradually accumulate again until a new episode of dispersal occurs.

Gravity, in contrast, never requires buildup. It is constant, central, and always directed toward the gravitational core. It accelerates bodies when they move inward, decelerates them when they move outward, but only in the normal plane. There is no horizontal acceleration from gravity. All lateral motion is the product of earlier pressure impulse events, now carried forward as momentum.

Illustrative Analogy: Water in a Fountain

The spray of a fountain offers a simple yet striking demonstration of the direction-independence of pressure impulse. Water can be projected vertically upward, arched outward, or even shaped into spirals and patterns. Each motion originates from the same principle: pressure impulse released through an outlet. The water itself has no preference; it moves wherever the impulse directs it. Gravity then intervenes only in the vertical descent, pulling the droplets down as their momentum is expended. Figure 24.1

Figure 24.1Pressure Impulse is direction independent force

Cosmic Implications

This distinction—gravity's restriction to the normal plane and pressure impulse's multidirectional capacity—explains why the universe exhibits countless equatorial planes and orbital paths. We may throw a projectile in any direction, but gravity always acts upon it as if the motion were equatorial to the primary body's core. Every act of projectile motion, from a tossed stone to the orbital plane of a planet, reflects this dual reality: pressure impulse generates the motion in any chosen direction, while gravity tames it only in the vertical plane.

24.6 Pressure Impulse Causes Inversely Proportionate Velocity to Mass

The behavior of bodies under pressure impulse is fundamentally different from their behavior under gravity. Gravity imparts mass-proportionate momentum. This means that regardless of size, all bodies fall with the same acceleration and reach the same velocity over time. A feather and a stone, freed from resistance, are drawn equally in the normal plane by gravity.

Pressure impulse, however, operates on the opposite principle. When a pressure impulse is applied, the same force creates greater velocity and displacement in a smaller mass than in a larger one. In practical terms, lighter bodies are hurled farther and faster, while heavier bodies move more slowly and cover less distance. If the impulse is too weak to overcome gravitational attraction, no visible displacement occurs at all.

In this sense, momentum produced by pressure impulse is inversely related to the mass of the object. A small amount of matter requires only a modest impulse to achieve significant motion, while a large mass demands far greater force to move even slightly.

The principle can be expressed simply:

- More mass → less velocity, less distance, greater force required
- Less mass → more velocity, more distance, less force required

This distinction explains many observable phenomena: the scattering of fragments in explosions, the trajectories of ejecta in volcanic eruptions, and the dispersal of matter in stellar or galactic ejections. In each case, lighter fragments acquire high speed and travel great distances, while massive remnants remain closer, moving more slowly despite experiencing the same initiating force.

Thus, pressure impulse is not impartial like gravity. It discriminates according to mass, favoring the light over the heavy. Recognizing this principle is essential for understanding cosmic locomotion, where most observed horizontal and orbital motions begin not from gravity, but from the mass-sensitive action of pressure impulse.

Example: Explosion Pushing Two Different Masses

Suppose an explosion delivers the **same impulse** (force × time) to two bodies:

- Body A: m=1 kg
- Body B: m=10 kg

The impulse delivered is:

$$\boldsymbol{J = F \cdot \Delta t = 10\ \mathrm{N{\cdot}s}}$$

Impulse equals the change in momentum:

$$\boldsymbol{J = \Delta p = m \cdot v}$$

Therefore, velocity is:

$$\boldsymbol{v = \frac{J}{m}}$$

For Body A (1 kg):

$$v = \frac{10}{1} = 10\ \mathrm{m/s}$$

For Body B (10 kg):

$$v = \frac{10}{10} = 1\mathrm{m/s}$$

Interpretation

- Both bodies received the **same impulse** (10 N·s).
- The lighter body acquired a **much higher velocity** (10 m/s).

- The heavier body acquired only **1 m/s**, despite the same push.

This demonstrates the principle:
Less mass → more velocity, more distance.
More mass → less velocity, less distance.

24.7 Pressure Impulse Force Causes Momentum in the Secondary Body

A pressure impulse force is the true origin of momentum in a body. When matter receives an impulse—whether from an explosion, a collision, or an internal release of pressure—it begins to move. That movement is nothing more than the visible expression of momentum newly acquired from the initiating force.

Once set into motion by a pressure impulse, the body becomes the carrier of momentum. This momentum is not an inherent property like mass, nor is it a continuous field-like force such as gravity. It is a direct consequence of the impulse event and remains fully transferable. A moving body, upon striking another, can pass part or all of its momentum onward, thereby initiating motion in the secondary body. In this way, pressure impulse propagates motion through successive transfers.

But momentum is not inexhaustible. It is gradually consumed—either by the constant pull of gravity acting in the normal plane, or by resistance such as friction and drag in physical media. When the dispensable momentum imparted by the original impulse is entirely spent, the body comes to rest, unless it receives another impulse.

Thus, pressure impulse is the sole creator of momentum in natural bodies, while gravity and resistance act as regulators, tamers, or consumers of that motion.

24.8 Locomotion Is Due to Dispensable Momentum

Locomotion, in its simplest description, is the displacement of a material body from one place to another. But description is not explanation. To understand motion, we must ask: *what actually moves the body, what sustains the motion, and why does it finally end—or not end?*

24.8.1 Matter Alone Does Not Move

Matter—mass—exists whether still or moving. A stone on the ground and a stone in flight have the same mass. Mass is indispensable, but it is not the cause of locomotion. It is the carrier, the substrate, the enduring presence. It cannot initiate its own displacement.

24.8.2 Inertia Explains Nothing

The traditional notion of inertia claims that a body in motion continues "by itself." But inertia is not a force, not a variable, not a measurable quantity. It explains neither the beginning, nor the continuation, nor the end of motion. It is an abstract placeholder, not a cause.

24.8.3 The True Initiators: Gravity and Pressure Impulse

Every real motion begins with one of two forces:

- **Gravity**, the aggregating force. It acts in the *normal plane* only. When a secondary body lies away from a primary mass, gravity originates motion by pulling it inward. The momentum thus created is consumed when the body comes to rest against the primary. Gravity never pushes away; it only gathers.
- **Pressure Impulse**, the dispersing force. It arises episodically—when matter under temperature, volume constraint, and containment ruptures or explodes. Pressure impulse pushes matter outward, dispersing it in any direction. It is the universal initiator of spreading, ejection, and expansion.

These two together explain the twin realities of the cosmos: aggregation into structure, and dispersal into motion.

24.8.4 The Missing Link: Dispensable Momentum

When gravity or pressure impulse acts, they impart something to the body that was not there before. The body moves, though its mass has not changed. What has been added?

It is **momentum**—but not of one uniform kind. To resolve this, we distinguish:

- **Indispensable momentum**: the body's own mass, ever present, the substrate of all possible motion.
- **Dispensable momentum**: the insensible but real quantity imparted by impulse or gravity. This is carried *inside* the moving body, though it cannot be weighed, touched, or directly measured. It reveals itself only in effects: in the crater of a falling stone, in the recoil of a collision, in the ejection of a star.

Strato of Lampsacus first glimpsed this truth. Observing falling drops, he saw that greater height meant greater impact, even though the drops themselves looked unchanged. Something invisible was carried in them—what we now identify as dispensable momentum.

24.8.5 How Gravity Acts on Momentum

Crucially, gravity does not act on all momentum indiscriminately. It acts only on the **normal-plane component** of dispensable momentum. This explains why:

- Horizontal velocity remains unchanged in projectile motion.
- Orbits take shape from the interplay of constant horizontal motion and vertical gravitational modulation.
- Bodies curve or fall without losing their geodesic component of motion.

If gravity acted on all momentum equally, no horizontal or orbital motion could persist.

The Final Picture

- Matter, or indispensable momentum, is passive.
- Gravity and pressure impulse are the originators of locomotion.
- The actual mover within the body is **dispensable momentum**—the acquired, consumable, transferable quantity that carries motion.
- Gravity modulates this dispensable momentum in the vertical plane; pressure impulse creates and disperses it in all directions.
- When dispensable momentum is exhausted—through resistance, opposition, or gravitational consumption—motion ends.
- When it cannot be consumed, motion continues indefinitely.

Thus, locomotion is not an abstraction. It is the displacement of matter (indispensable momentum) *carrying within itself dispensable momentum.* This is the true physical cause of motion.

24.9 Pressure Impulse Force Creates Variable Velocities and Variable Accelerations

Pressure Impulse Force does not act uniformly across all bodies. Its effects depend directly on the mass of the body receiving the impulse. When the same impulse is applied to two different masses, the smaller body gains more velocity and travels farther, while the larger body gains less velocity and travels a shorter distance. This is not an anomaly but one of the defining characteristics of pressure impulse: it produces **inversely mass-dependent velocities**.

Acceleration under pressure impulse is also variable. It depends not only on the size of the impulse but also on how quickly it is delivered. A large force delivered in a very short time can cause rapid acceleration, resulting in violent or even explosive effects. The shorter the time of release, the greater the acceleration and the greater the damage. Pressure impulse is therefore both **quantitatively powerful** and **temporally sensitive**.

Unlike gravity, pressure impulse does not reverse the motion it creates. Once matter is expelled by an impulse, it does not return to its origin because of the impulse itself. Any return or reversal occurs only under the action of gravity, which operates as an attracting and taming force in the normal (vertical) plane. Pressure impulse is purely a dispersing agent: once it acts, its work is done. It does not seek to recover what it expelled.

This sharp distinction between dispersal without return (pressure impulse) and taming through attraction (gravity) is essential. One initiates and spreads motion, while the other draws matter back or slows it down. Together, they form the dual framework of locomotion in the universe: **pressure impulse gives motion its beginning, gravity gives motion its end.**

24.10 Newton's Third Law: Each action has an equal and opposite reaction

Newton's Third Law states: *"To every action there is always opposed an equal reaction: or the mutual actions of two bodies upon each other are always equal, and directed to contrary parts."*

This law, although profound, has often been misquoted or misunderstood. Later interpretations sometimes reduce it to the phrase "each force has an equal and opposite force." That phrasing suggests two separate forces acting independently, but this is not what Newton meant. He described a single **mutual interaction**—a shared event—in which motion is divided between two bodies.

This becomes clearest when we consider motion generated by pressure impulse. Take the case of a rocket: it moves forward because exhaust gases are expelled backward. There are not two independent forces battling each other. Instead, the rocket and its exhaust are part of the same pressure impulse event. Motion is distributed between them: one body goes forward, the other backward.

Gravity, in this scenario, is only a background influence. It may pull both the rocket and the gases toward the Earth, but it does not create the locomotion. The true origin of motion here is the pressure impulse generated inside the rocket system.

A further truth emerges when we look at how motion is shared:

- Both bodies move in opposite directions.
- Their velocities differ, depending on their masses.
- The lighter body gains higher velocity, while the heavier body moves more slowly.

This is not a contradiction of Newton's principle of equality—it is a redistribution of the same impulse. Equal impulse acts on both, but unequal masses respond with unequal velocities.

This principle can be summarized:

- More mass → less velocity
- Less mass → more velocity
- Always in opposite directions

Thus, Newton's Third Law is best understood not as "opposing forces," but as the rule of **reciprocal motion**. It describes how pressure impulse, when shared between two bodies, creates paired motions—equal in interaction, opposite in direction, but proportioned by mass.

24.11 Pressure Impulse Ejections as Action–Reaction Couples

In every domain, from the smallest explosion to the largest galactic eruption, pressure impulse acts through pairs of reciprocal motions. When matter is expelled in one direction, the source body recoils in the opposite direction. This is not a separate force, but a single event distributed across two masses, consistent with Newton's Third Law.

Solar-Scale Action–Reaction

When the Sun ejects material—whether through flares, coronal mass ejections, or more violent expulsions in its earlier history—the expelled plasma races outward at high speed. At the same moment, the Sun itself experiences a recoil, too small to notice in the short term due to its immense mass, but still present. Over time, repeated episodes contribute to the Sun's dispensable momentum as a secondary body within the Milky Way system.

Stellar Action–Reaction

Stars throughout the galaxy follow the same principle. Each eruption, supernova, or asymmetric jet distributes motion in two directions: one imparted to the expelled mass, the other to the stellar core. Lighter ejected fragments achieve immense velocities; heavier stars shift less but accumulate gradual displacement over countless events.

Galactic Action–Reaction

On the largest scales, the cores of galaxies undergo billions of such events over cosmic time. Each mass ejection—whether forming stars, clusters, or stellar streams—imparts recoil to the galactic core itself. Though each individual recoil may be slight, the cumulative effect over billions of years is profound. Galactic cores acquire vast dispensable momentum, gradually accelerating without any external opposition.

Why the Universe Never Slows

Gravity can regulate the motion of secondary bodies—planets around stars, stars around galactic cores—but it cannot regulate the motion of the primary body itself. A galaxy core's dispensable momentum cannot be consumed by its own gravity. Nothing pulls it back; nothing tames its flight. This means that once a galaxy core has acquired directional momentum from countless ejections, it carries it indefinitely.

The consequence is clear:

- **The universe accelerates, but never decelerates.**
- Dispensable momentum, once given, cannot be taken away by the source body's own gravity.
- Directional change requires a stronger external body, but no greater body exists to govern galactic cores.

Thus, pressure impulse is not only the trigger of local motion; it is the great driver of cosmic drift. The universe's expansion and the endless flight of galaxies are not due to the stretching of space, but to the cumulative recoil of matter itself—an unceasing record of action–reaction couples played out on a cosmic scale.

24.11.1 Worked-out Examples for Galactic Core Ejections

Example 1 — A single galactic-core ejection (one big shove)

Setup

- Core mass: $M_{core} = 1.0 \times 10^{11}\ M_{\odot}$
- Ejected mass (one event): $m_{ej} = 1.0 \times 10^{7} M_{\odot}$
- Ejection speed: $v_{ej} = 800\ \mathrm{km/s}$

Conservation of momentum (recoil speed):

$$v_{recoil} = \frac{m_{ej}}{M_{core}} v_{ej}$$

Compute:

$$\frac{m_{ej}}{M_{core}} = \frac{1 \cdot 10^{7}}{1 \cdot 10^{11}} = 1 \cdot 10^{-4}$$

$$v = 1 \cdot 10^{-4} \times 800\ \mathrm{km/s} = 0.08\ \mathrm{km/s} = 80\ \mathrm{m/s}$$

Interpretation: One large ejection gives the core a recoil of ≈ 80 m/s in the opposite direction.

Example 2 — Many ejections over time (how little kicks add up)

Use the recoil from Example 1 as the "single-event step": 80 m/s.

(a) If directions are mostly aligned (biased outflows):

$$v_{total} \approx \mathrm{N} \times v_{step}$$

For $N = 1 \cdot 10^{4}$ similar ejections:

$$v_{total} \approx 1 \cdot 10^{4} \times 80\ \mathrm{m/s} = 8 \cdot 10^{5}\mathrm{m/s} = 800\ \mathrm{km/s}$$

(b) If directions are random (random-walk accumulation):

$$v_{total} \approx \sqrt{N} \times v_{step}$$

For $N = 1 \cdot 10^{4}$:

$$v_{total} \approx 100 \times 80 \text{ m/s} = 8000 \text{ m/s} = 8 \text{ km/s}$$

Interpretation: Alignment matters enormously. A decade-thousands of biased ejections could drive hundreds of km/s; random directions still leave a lasting ~km/s-scale drift.

Example 3 — Contrast across scales (star, supernova, galaxy)

(A) Modest solar ejection (tiny recoil)

- Sun's mass: $M_{\odot} \approx 2 \cdot 10^{30}$ kg
- Ejected mass: $m_{ej} = 1 \cdot 10^{12}$kg (a large CME)
- Ejection speed: $v_{ej} = 1000 \text{ km/s} = 1.0 \times 10^6 \text{ m/s}$

$$v_{recoil} = \frac{m_{ej}}{M_{sun}} \times v_{ej}$$

$$v_{recoil} = \frac{1 \cdot 10^{12}}{2 \cdot 10^{30}} \times 1.0 \times 10^6 \text{ m/s} \approx 5 \cdot 10^{-19} \times 1 \cdot 10^6 \text{m/s}$$
$$\approx 5 \cdot 10^{-13} \text{ m/s}$$

Tiny and unobservable—good for intuition about how mass ratio controls recoil.

(B) Supernova ejection (big kick to remnant)

- Remnant (core) mass: $M_{core} = 1 \cdot 10^1 M_{\odot}$
- Ejected mass: $m_{ej} = 5 \, M_{\odot}$
- Ejection speed: $v_{ej} = 3000 \text{ km/s}$

$$v_{recoil} = \frac{m_{ej}}{M_{core}} \times v_{ej}$$
$$= \frac{5}{10} \times 3000 \text{ km/s} = 1500 \text{ km/s}$$

Large, consistent with observed neutron-star "kicks."

(C) Galactic-core scale (from Example 1, for comparison)

= 80 m/s (single event)

Moderate per event—but cumulative effects can be substantial (see Example 2)

24.12 Gravity and Pressure Impulse

Though gravity and pressure impulse are forces originating from matter, they can—and should—be studied independently of matter itself. Every act of motion in the universe involves some combination of matter, momentum, gravity, and pressure impulse, each operating to different degrees. Yet to truly understand locomotion, we must pause and analyze each element in isolation before considering how they act together.

This is why we first examined the characteristics of gravity in detail. We now turn to pressure impulse, the complementary force. By isolating their properties, we gain a sharper understanding of how they cooperate and oppose each other in shaping the structure of the cosmos.

The ancients sensed this duality long before modern science. Empedocles, for example, imagined four elements—earth, water, air, and fire—governed by two opposing forces: Love, which unites, and Strife, which separates. While poetic in language, these images reflect deeper physical realities. Gravity, we can say, is the force of Love: it aggregates, pulls inward, and tames motion. Pressure impulse is the force of Strife: it scatters, ejects, and initiates motion. Aristotle, too, advised that we should not be misled by words but seek the underlying meaning.

Yet neither Empedocles nor Aristotle described these forces with physical precision. Even in the modern era, Galileo and Newton transformed our understanding of motion, but they often treated "force" as a single general category. They did not systematically separate the aggregating power of gravity from the dispersing power of pressure impulse. This lack of differentiation has left gaps in how we explain planetary motion, cosmic architecture, and the persistence of horizontal trajectories in nature.

Still, progress in science has often been made without complete knowledge. Charles Darwin is a striking example. Without knowing about genes, DNA, or the molecular basis of inheritance, Darwin observed the patterns of life and proposed his Theory of Evolution by Natural Selection. His strength lay not in detailing mechanisms he could not yet know, but in seeing the logic of observable evidence. Later generations filled in the gaps.

We must follow the same path. Our observations tell us that gravity and pressure impulse are distinct in nature:

- One is continuous, central, and aggregating.
- The other is episodic, directional, and dispersing.
- Together they explain why matter moves, why it gathers, and why it disperses.

We do not need to wait for perfect mathematics before recognizing this truth. Logic and natural observation are enough to establish the foundations. Just as Darwin left genetics for later generations, so too can we leave finer mathematical details to physicists and future researchers. Our role is to clarify the causes and distinctions, to describe how gravity and pressure impulse create the locomotion we see everywhere in nature.

In short: one unites, one separates. Motion in the universe cannot be understood without both.

24.13 Comparison Between Gravity and Pressure Impulse Force

The two forces that govern locomotion in the universe act in completely different ways. Their differences are summarized in a table below. Table 24.1

Table 24.1Comparison: Gravity and Pressure Impulse

ASPECT	GRAVITY	PRESSURE IMPULSE FORCE
Nature	Continuous, constant, always present with matter	Episodic, arises only under specific conditions (explosions, ejections, reactions)

ASPECT	**GRAVITY**	**PRESSURE IMPULSE FORCE**
Direction	Always acts in the normal (vertical, radial) plane	Direction-independent: can act in any direction, 0–360°
Type of Action	Centripetal (pulling inward, aggregating)	Centrifugal/segregating (pushing outward, dispersing)
Cause of Motion	Does not initiate motion; only alters existing momentum	Sole initiator of motion in natural systems
Duration	Permanent, continuous presence	Short-lived, acts only at the moment of impulse
Relation to Mass	Creates proportionate acceleration; all bodies fall equally regardless of mass	Inversely related to mass: lighter bodies move faster, heavier bodies slower
Effect on Momentum	Consumes or modulates momentum (slows, curves, or binds motion)	Creates and imparts momentum to a body
Dependence on Matter	Inbuilt characteristic of matter; cannot exist without mass	Depends on physical state (temperature, pressure, volume, confinement)
Reversal of Motion	Can reverse motion (e.g., upward throw returning downward)	No reversal; once acted, the impulse does not pull back what it ejected

ASPECT	GRAVITY	PRESSURE IMPULSE FORCE
Cosmic Role	Responsible for orbits, aggregation, binding of structures	Responsible for ejections, dispersion, and initiation of trajectories

Final Note

Gravity alone cannot explain locomotion, and pressure impulse alone cannot sustain or regulate it. The two forces must be understood together:

- **Pressure impulse starts the motion.**
- **Gravity restrains, curves, or ends the motion.**

This duality explains projectile motion on Earth, planetary orbits in the solar system, and the larger dynamics of galaxies

24.14 How Pressure Impulse Force Works to Start Motion of Matter

In the universe, motion does not begin on its own. It must always be initiated. Among the two great forces of locomotion—gravity and pressure impulse—it is pressure impulse that plays the active role in setting matter into motion. Gravity holds, binds, and tames. Pressure impulse breaks, separates, and propels. Together they shape the cosmos through opposite yet complementary actions.

To begin motion, a pressure impulse must overcome gravity, which continuously pulls every body downward toward the nearest center of mass. For matter to move away from rest—especially in the horizontal or tangential (geodesic) direction—there must be a force strong enough to free it from this grip. That freeing push is pressure impulse.

Because it is a physical and not an abstract force, pressure impulse always acts in proportion to mass, but with different visible results:

- **Heavier or denser bodies** require much stronger impulses just to budge. When moved, they respond with slow velocity, but they carry great momentum.
- **Lighter or gaseous bodies** require only small impulses to achieve motion, often with striking velocity. A puff of gas can expand for kilometers, while a pebble hardly shifts under the same push.

This contrast is observable everywhere. In fountains or waterfalls, water rises or spills not because gravity is lifting it, but because a confined pressure impulse forces it upward. Once in motion, gravity immediately takes over, curving and taming the path back downward. The same logic applies to volcanoes, geysers, bursting stars, or even a thrown stone.

Velocity, therefore, is not directly tied to mass. The same pressure impulse can:

- Send gases or vapors racing outward at high speed,
- Move rocks or metals only slightly, as much of the force is consumed in overcoming their greater mass.

Locomotion initiated by pressure impulse is not just a matter of "mass moved," but of the physical qualities of matter—density, volume, cohesion, and internal resistance. The same push that disperses a gas cloud across space may move a mountain only a few centimeters.

Another defining feature of pressure impulse is its freedom of direction. Unlike gravity, which always acts vertically inward, pressure impulse can act in any direction. Unless constrained, it spreads motion outward in all directions at once. Boundaries shape the outcome: a nozzle turns it into a fountain, a mountain channel into a lateral eruption, a collapsing star into an outward spray.

In short: pressure impulse is the engine of motion. It separates matter, overcomes gravity's binding pull, and distributes motion across scales—from drops of water in a geyser to the ejection of stars from galactic cores.

24.15 The Mover and the Moved: From Philosophical Cause to Physical Motion

Aristotle, in his timeless analysis of motion, draws a crucial distinction: *"what effects motion as a physical agent can itself be moved."* This idea of *the mover and the moved* invites reflection in both philosophy and physics. Is every mover necessarily moved? Can something cause motion and yet remain untouched? These are not rhetorical questions—they probe the very nature of causality in motion.

In *Physics*, Aristotle notes: *"It is possible for a thing to cause motion, though it is itself incapable of being moved."* With this, he allows for two classes of movers: those that themselves undergo change, and those that might, at least in theory, remain unmoved.

In practice, however, most movers are themselves moved. A hammer striking a nail, or an explosion ejecting fragments, shows the rule clearly: the cause of motion also undergoes motion or change. This holds for all physical agents of locomotion—the most primary kind of motion, defined by Aristotle as a change of place.

24.15.1 Momentum: The Modern Signature of the Mover

In modern physics, this truth is carried forward by the concept of momentum, defined simply as:

$$P = m \times v$$

Where p is momentum, m is mass, and v is velocity. This relation carries three truths:

- A body in motion has momentum.
- That momentum must have had a cause.
- The cause is always a mover—a force or event—that imparted this motion.

Momentum is not a substance. It is a state that exists only because of a prior act of force, whether pressure impulse, collision, or gravitational acceleration.

24.15.2 Is the Mover Always Moved?

Aristotle left this as an open question. Modern physics, however, provides a definitive answer: **yes, every mover is also moved.**

Pressure impulse in a star or galactic core initiates outward motion, but the source itself undergoes change—recoil, redistribution, internal transformation. Even when the outward effect appears one-sided, the initiator is never left unchanged. This aligns perfectly with Newton's Third Law: *"For every action, there is an equal and opposite reaction."*

The examples are universal:

- A rocket moves forward; gases move backward.
- A gun fires a bullet, and the gun recoils.
- A person jumps from a boat, and the boat slides back.

And at cosmic scale:

- A star ejects mass, and its structure shifts.
- A galactic core releases stellar and planetary systems, and itself gains momentum in recoil.

There are no exceptions: to cause motion is to undergo motion.

24.15.3 The Myth of the Unmoved Mover

Aristotle imagined the possibility of an *Unmoved Mover*—a pure cause that initiates all motion but itself remains unchanged. But in the material universe, such a being cannot exist. Matter, force, and motion are bound together. To cause is to be altered. To move is to be moved.

Thus, in the physical cosmos:

- All movers are moved.
- All motion has a source, and that source also moves.
- No star or galaxy core is exempt from this mutual exchange.

This recognition marks a decisive break with abstract speculation. The universe, understood in terms of matter and locomotion, shows no trace of an unmoved mover. Instead, every cause is also an effect, every action carries reaction, and every motion reshapes the mover itself.

24.15.4 The Mover Is Also Moved: Extending Aristotle to the Cosmos

Aristotle recognized that what causes motion is itself also subject to change. Yet, because he placed the Earth at the center of the universe and considered it uniquely heavy, he may have treated it as an exception. Modern understanding shows that there are no exceptions. Every mover in the cosmos, from the smallest fragment to the largest galaxy, is also moved.

When a star ejects matter in a supernova, the ejection is not one-sided. The star recoils, its structure redistributes, and its future path is altered. When planets or comets are cast out by stellar or galactic pressure impulses, the core that launched them also acquires a recoil momentum, however slight. Over billions of years, the accumulation of countless such ejections gives even massive galactic cores a measurable, permanent momentum.

This principle confirms Newton's Third Law on the largest scales: every action has an equal and opposite reaction. But it also deepens Aristotle's philosophical insight. There is no body in the physical universe that can impart motion without itself being changed. No galaxy is exempt, no core immune. The universe itself is in continuous locomotion because every act of motion leaves its signature on both the mover and the moved.

Thus, the so-called "unmoved mover" has no place in physics. To move is to be moved, and to cause motion is to share in it. The galaxies themselves testify to this truth, carrying the dispensable momentum of countless ancient ejections, forever traveling along the paths they have acquired.

24.15.5 No Motion Without Recoil: Cosmic Consequences of the Mover Being Moved

Aristotle stated in his *Physics* that "what causes motion is itself also moved." This was not metaphorical but grounded in careful observation. Yet when extending his reasoning to the cosmos, he assumed a geocentric universe with an unmoved Earth at its center. Modern understanding shows that his deeper principle was correct, but it applies universally—every mover, from the smallest particle to the largest galactic core, is also moved.

Our own Sun is proof. In earlier sections we calculated that a massive mass ejection event—on the scale of a supernova—could have imparted to the Sun a recoil velocity of about **2000 m/s**. This demonstrates that the Sun was not formed passively in place, but was propelled outward by an immense pressure impulse. Newton's Third Law and the conservation of momentum confirm this: every ejection results in an equal and opposite recoil.

The same principle holds at the galactic scale. The Milky Way's core, over its long history, has ejected:

- Billions of stars and planetary systems, each carrying mass and momentum,
- Entire globular cluster cores, as early directed expulsions,
- Vast amounts of plasma and dust.

Each ejection decreased the core's mass and increased its momentum. Over billions of years, these impulses accumulated into the large-scale galactic motion we observe today. No body is exempt—not even galaxy cores.

24.15.6 Why Mathematics Alone Falls Short

While mathematics allows us to quantify momentum (mass × velocity), it cannot capture all the causes behind motion. Internal asymmetries, temperature gradients, collisions, and directional imbalances may all contribute, but cannot all be measured or modeled. Equations approximate, but they do not exhaust reality. To understand motion, physical causality must remain primary; mathematics must illustrate, not dictate.

24.15.7 The Inescapable Role of Pressure Impulse

Regardless of one's model of cosmic origins—massive mass ejection or the traditional nebular hypothesis—the requirement remains the same: motion must begin somewhere. And the only force capable of initiating directed motion is pressure impulse.

- In supernovae, extreme internal pressure ruptures the star, expelling matter outward.
- In collapsing nebulae, density gradients produce pressure differentials that drive flows.
- In stellar jets, confined pressure channels mass into narrow, high-velocity streams.

In all cases, pressure impulse is the initiator. Gravity can bind, but it cannot propel. Without pressure impulse, there is no initial velocity, no orbital momentum, no structure. Motion begins only when matter receives a directed impulse—and in giving that impulse, the mover itself is also moved.

25. Momentum: Characteristics and Foundation of Locomotion

The most misunderstood aspect of locomotion is this: *What is happening in the moving body? How is it moving? How does the motion come to an end?*

To answer these questions, Galileo and later Newton introduced the concept of inertia. Yet naming a concept is not the same as explaining it. A term must clarify the physical reality it describes. If it obscures understanding, then the term must be reconsidered and replaced.

Newton defined inertia—*vis insita*—as "*a power of resisting, by which every body, as much as in it lies, endeavours to persevere in its present state, whether it be of rest, or of moving uniformly forward in a right line.*" This definition treats inertia as an innate quality, existing in a body at rest, in motion, and even after motion ends. It does not explain variations in speed, direction, or orbit. Nor does it clarify how motion is sustained or extinguished. (Principia)

We understand the matter differently. A body is never in motion because of an innate force. It is always under the influence of gravity, and to move it requires a real, external cause: **pressure impulse**. Once applied, pressure impulse does not remain, but it leaves behind a new condition in the body—**momentum**.

So far, we have identified two fundamental forces:

- **Gravity** — a continuous, centripetal pull acting only in the normal plane.
- **Pressure impulse** — a sudden, directional force that initiates motion.

Now we introduce a third essential concept: **momentum**.

Momentum is not a force but the *physical consequence* of an applied force. It is the partner of pressure impulse—the state left in the body after the impulse has ended. Momentum sustains motion until it is overcome by gravity, friction, or collision.

Newton himself wrote that an impressed force "consists in the action only; and remains no longer in the body, when the action is over." He explained the continuation of motion by inertia, but this passive idea fails to explain the degrees, directions, and variations of real motion.

Momentum, by contrast, is measurable, causal, and directional. It explains:

- why bodies move differently depending on mass and direction,
- how motion can be transferred from one body to another,
- and why motion eventually ceases once momentum is consumed.

25.1.1 Key observations follow:

- Every object is already under gravitational control. To give it independent motion, a pressure impulse must act against gravity.
- Momentum is what remains in the body after the impulse; it sustains the motion.
- If no impulse is applied, gravity itself creates momentum, as in free fall.
- Momentum created by gravity is physically identical to momentum created by pressure impulse. Both are directional, measurable, and consumable.
- Whenever a body is projected at an angle not aligned with gravity, its path is necessarily curved, the shape determined by the interaction of momentum and gravity.
- Motion ends when momentum is fully consumed by gravity or friction. If neither can exhaust it, motion continues indefinitely.

25.1.2 In summary:

Bodies begin to move through pressure impulse. They remain in motion because of momentum. Gravity curves or moderates motion, but never initiates it. Inertia is not a physical entity but only a placeholder concept. Momentum provides the true measurable and causal framework for locomotion.

With these foundations established—material bodies, gravitational attraction, pressure impulse, and momentum as the carrier of motion—we can now examine why inertia must be formally replaced by momentum in every serious treatment of motion.

25.2 Origin of "Inertia" and the Difficulties in Understanding Locomotion

Inertia is one of the most widely accepted concepts in classical mechanics, yet its historical origin and implications have made it a barrier to deeper understanding of locomotion. To comprehend the true dynamics of motion—especially on the scale of the universe—we must question this entrenched idea and ask whether a more explanatory concept can take its place. I propose that momentum—not inertia—is the real cornerstone of locomotion. Once momentum is understood as the outcome and counterpart of pressure impulse and gravity, the entire field of motion becomes intelligible.

It is nearly impossible to understand locomotion, particularly in relation to impulse forces, without first grasping the nature of momentum. Momentum may be considered the counter-response or receiver of a pressure impulse delivered by a source body (the primary body) to a target (the secondary body). It is not the impulse alone, but the resulting momentum that determines the visible characteristics of motion. Most of what we observe in the universe—direction, persistence, velocity, resistance—is governed not by the initiating impulse, but by the momentum it generates and carries forward.

25.2.1 The Challenge of Unlearning Inertia

It is often easier to accept a new idea than to unlearn an old one based on deep misconception. Science advances not by forcefully discarding the past, but by replacing weaker concepts with stronger ones. A flawed idea persists until a better explanation appears.

The history of astronomy illustrates this clearly. The Pythagoreans speculated that the Sun was the center of the universe and that Earth revolved around it daily. Lacking observational evidence, their claim remained speculation. Aristotle observed no displacement of falling objects, no shifting of stars, and therefore proposed a geocentric model. Ptolemy later refined this into the *Almagest*, which dominated for centuries.

It was Copernicus who revived the heliocentric idea—not through new observations but by offering a more coherent mathematical framework. His success shows how a stronger conceptual model can displace a weaker one. We face a similar turning point with inertia. It is not obviously false, but it conceals more than it reveals. To move forward, we must replace it with something more physically grounded: momentum.

25.2.2 The Birth of Inertia

Aristotle, in seeking to explain why a body continues moving after its mover ceases, proposed that air in front gives way and air behind pushes it forward. In a world dominated by visible media such as air and water, this seemed logical. His idea held sway until Galileo challenged it.

Galileo observed that motion continues even in the absence of air, and that small and large bodies respond differently. He concluded that mass must possess some inherent resistance to changes in motion, and he called this property inertia. Thus, inertia arose not from first principles, but as a necessary explanation for the persistence of motion.

Newton later formalized inertia in the *Principia* as *vis insita*—"an inherent power" by which matter resists change, maintaining either rest or uniform motion in a straight line. Yet this idea, though mathematically useful, lacks explanatory power. There is no innate resisting power within matter. All bodies are already under gravity, and whether they move or remain at rest depends only on whether a sufficient pressure impulse has been applied. If the impulse overcomes gravity, the body moves; if it does not, the body remains still. No mysterious resisting power is needed.

25.2.3 The Limits of Inertia

Inertia fails to solve the real problems of locomotion. It explains neither the origin of motion nor its continuation in a satisfying way. As later sections will show, momentum—being a real, measurable, and transferable quantity—provides far greater clarity.

For me, as a medical doctor rather than a trained physicist, it may seem bold to question the legacy of Galileo and Newton. Yet it would be more embarrassing to remain silent when sensing a major shortfall in physics' conceptual foundations.

When I first began thinking seriously about motion, I assumed gravity was the driving force of locomotion. Over time, I realized gravity primarily aggregates matter—it pulls bodies together but does not initiate their movement. This became clear when I studied projectile motion. The forward and upward motion of a projectile arises not from gravity but from the initial impulse, which creates momentum. Gravity acts afterward, restraining and curving the path.

25.2.4 Toward First Principles

How do we understand all motions of all bodies in the universe? At first it seems impossible. Yet nature is not hiding. As Galileo said, the Book of Nature is open before us. The universe is not a criminal masking its trail—it is we who must observe carefully and think clearly.

When I feel lost in a concept, I return to the works of earlier philosophers—even the Presocratics. Their confidence and sincerity inspire, even when their answers prove incomplete.

My former professor, Mr. E. N. B. Sharma, once remarked: a specialist must know everything about something, while a generalist must know something about everything. To understand the locomotion of the entire universe, we must take the broader, generalist view. If a marathon runner stops to study every plant along the road, he will never reach the finish line. So too in physics: we must focus on first principles.

The first principles of the universe are unchanging: matter, gravity, pressure impulse, and momentum. We have already considered gravity, and studied pressure impulse in detail. Between them stands momentum—the bridge between cause and motion. To understand the structure and behavior of the universe, we must give momentum the central place it deserves.

As Aristotle wisely observed, "All learning is by means of premises, whether through demonstration or induction." Without correct premises, no conclusion can be sound. In physics, without correct foundations, no law—however elegant—can reveal truth.

A hypothesis that survives testing becomes a theory. But even the most beautiful theory must yield to a better one when reality demands. It is time for inertia to yield to momentum—with courage, logic, and reverence for truth.

25.3 Replacing Momentum in Place of Inertia

If we accept momentum as the true counterpart of pressure impulse, we can explain all forms of locomotion—across the universe—with far greater precision than is possible under the concept of inertia.

It is impossible to understand motion produced by pressure impulse without first understanding momentum. Momentum is not a convenient word but a fundamental physical reality. It is the effect passed from the primary (active) body to the secondary (passive) body during the act of impulse. While pressure impulse is the cause, momentum is the result. And it is momentum—not inertia—that determines the actual characteristics of motion: direction, speed, duration, and decay.

Why Replacing Inertia with Momentum Is Difficult

It is often easier to accept a new idea than to correct an old one built on long-standing misconception. In science, no concept is permanent unless it is supported by continuous observation and refinement. A concept must not merely survive; it must explain.

Historically, inertia was introduced as an improvement on Aristotle's mistaken claim that air behind a moving body sustains its motion. Galileo replaced that view with the idea of an internal property—inertia—that resists changes in motion. Newton refined it as *vis insita*, or "innate force," claiming that every body resists changes to its state of rest or uniform motion.

But here lies the problem. Inertia is not a force. It does not quantify motion, nor does it vary with time, friction, or curvature. It is passive—a placeholder—rather than a working explanation. According to Newton's own words, inertia exists before motion, during motion, and after motion ceases. How then can it explain motion itself?

This is why inertia must be superseded—not out of disrespect for its historical role, but because a better explanation exists. That better concept is momentum.

25.4 Momentum as a Quantitative and Qualitative Replacement

Unlike inertia, momentum has both direction and magnitude. It is the actual physical state of motion present in a body. It is created by an external force—either gravity or pressure impulse—and consumed by friction or gravitational pull. If neither acts, momentum persists indefinitely, and so does motion.

This replacement is not a whimsical revision. Just as Copernicus did not deny the geocentric model but replaced it with a stronger heliocentric one, supported by mathematics and observation, we replace inertia with momentum because momentum explains the observed phenomena of locomotion more clearly and completely.

In the natural world, nothing hides. As Galileo observed, nature is open and does not deceive us. The failure to replace inertia with momentum is not nature's error but our own hesitation to question what has been handed down.

25.4.1 Momentum as the Measurable Counterpart of Pressure Impulse

When a subject exerts pressure impulse on an object, the resulting momentum is what carries the object forward. This is true whether the impulse arises from a physical action or from gravitational pull. Momentum created by gravity and momentum created by pressure impulse are not different in kind; they are physically identical in effect.

Where inertia remains insensible and immeasurable, momentum can be calculated and understood through mass, velocity, and direction. It serves as a bridge between theory and observation, allowing us to analyze:

- variations in speed,
- curved versus straight motion,
- acceleration and deceleration,
- orbital behavior and spin,
- and the duration of motion until momentum is consumed.

25.4.2 Why Inertia Fails and Momentum Succeeds

The concept of inertia fails precisely because it does not vary. Whether a body is at rest, in slow motion, or moving rapidly, inertia remains the same—a vague background property. Momentum, in contrast, changes with every cause and produces observable effects.

Inertia misleads us into imagining that motion persists because of an inborn quality, when in reality motion continues because of actual momentum acquired from an external cause. Motion is not sustained by resistance, but by the persistence of transferred force stored as momentum.

25.4.3 From Concept to Foundation

The final reason to adopt momentum in place of inertia is that momentum is a first principle. It can be defined in terms of measurable relationships. It respects the realities of gravity, friction, and pressure impulse. It makes motion not a mystery but a natural consequence of interactions between physical bodies.

25.4.4 Clarification on the Nature of Dispensable Momentum

Momentum has traditionally been defined as the product of mass and velocity, and we do not reject this description. In our framework, however, it is necessary to distinguish between two aspects of momentum: **indispensable momentum**, which is the body's inherent quantity of mass itself, and **dispensable momentum**, which is the acquired impulse superimposed upon that mass.

In this light, velocity should not be mistaken for dispensable momentum itself. Rather, velocity serves as an external measure of the dispensable momentum carried by the body. The dispensable momentum exists *within the body itself*, inseparable from its mass, even though it originates from an applied impulse. It is not something that can be separated, extracted, or directly measured apart from the body; velocity merely reveals its presence in quantitative terms.

This distinction becomes especially important in understanding the action of gravity. Gravity does not act on the entire mass, nor on velocity, nor even on the whole of dispensable momentum. Instead, it acts specifically on the **vertical component of dispensable momentum**, while leaving the horizontal component untouched. This clarifies why gravitational influence modifies motion only in the normal plane, without altering the horizontal momentum that carries bodies in their geodesic paths.

Though subtle and difficult to demonstrate visually, this conceptual refinement allows a more precise understanding of motion. It ensures that dispensable momentum is recognized not simply as mass × velocity, but as an inseparable quality of matter in motion—born of impulse, measured by velocity, and acted upon selectively by gravity.

Momentum — Dispensable and Indispensable Momentum

To understand the full character of motion, momentum must be divided into two distinct but interrelated types: **dispensable momentum** and **indispensable momentum**. These terms allow us to distinguish between motion that is temporary and consumable, and the ever-present quality tied to mass itself.

Dispensable Momentum: The Active and Exhaustible Motion

Dispensable momentum is the acquired motion given to a body by an external force—either a pressure impulse or gravity. It is quantitative, directional, and transferable. Once given, this type of momentum can be altered, transferred, or gradually dissipated by opposing forces such as friction, resistance, or gravitational control.

When we throw a ball, the hand transfers dispensable momentum into it. The ball continues in motion until gravity and friction eventually consume it.

When gravity alone initiates motion, as in free fall, it also creates dispensable momentum, though only in the normal (vertical) plane.

In rebounds—whether in balls, carroms, or Newton's Cradle—the repeated exchange of energy is entirely due to dispensable momentum passing between bodies.

Games such as snooker, carroms, and billiards vividly illustrate how momentum can be transferred with minimal loss when friction is low.

In spinning bodies such as a top or coin, the initial pressure impulse produces rotational motion. That spin persists as dispensable momentum until friction with air or surface contact brings it to rest.

The key correction is this: **the dispensable momentum created in a body by gravity or pressure impulse will continue until it is dispensed—that is, until it is consumed by an external agent. A body cannot spend its own momentum.** Motion only ends when the body comes under gravitational control (as with planets and stars), or it encounters friction or collision. If the body is entirely free in space, outside the gravitational influence of another mass, its motion continues indefinitely. In such a case, momentum becomes a persistent expression of the original force that created it.

Indispensable Momentum: The Passive but Permanent Quality

Indispensable momentum refers to the intrinsic presence of mass itself. It is not consumed or transferred. Instead, it is the constant substrate that makes motion possible.

Mass has no motion of its own, but once motion is imparted, indispensable momentum reveals the body's capacity to carry that motion. Without it, dispensable momentum cannot be initiated or preserved.

This explains why motion occurs even in a vacuum. No external medium is required—the indispensable momentum inherent in mass allows a body to preserve whatever dispensable momentum it has been given.

Examples and Consequences

Why do we not feel Earth's enormous motion? Because we share it. The Earth's orbital speed around the Sun (about 29.78 km/s) and its daily rotation are not sensed, since we and everything around us carry the same dispensable momentum, stabilized by the indispensable momentum inherent in mass.

In the Earth–Moon system, both bodies exert gravity on each other, leading to measurable accelerations and exchanges of dispensable momentum. These transfers are especially evident orbital variations.

All dispensable momentum eventually dissipates through gravity, friction, or collision. Yet in a true vacuum, outside the gravitational influence of any mass, motion persists indefinitely. This continuation is not due to inertia, but due to the undiminished presence of momentum in the moving body. So, If we accept momentum as the true counterpart of pressure impulse, we can explain all forms of locomotion—across the universe—with far greater precision than is possible under the concept of inertia.

25.5 All Motion and Momentum Characteristics are Similar Everywhere

The universe runs on a single principle of locomotion: motion begins when a pressure impulse or gravitational interaction generates dispensable momentum, which is carried by the body's mass. This momentum persists until it is consumed by gravity, friction, or collision.

If no such external influence exists—if the body is in true vacuum, outside gravitational control—its motion continues eternally. This endurance of motion is not explained by inertia, but by the preservation of dispensable momentum within the body. Mass does not spend its own momentum; it only carries it.

This correction allows us to understand how celestial bodies, space probes, and even atoms move through space. No mysterious sustaining force is required. Only the momentum they were given, and the absence of anything to take it away.

25.5.1 Two Foundations of Motion

To understand the nature of motion in the universe, we must recognize two fundamental forms of momentum. Dispensable momentum is the actual motion a body acquires—whether from gravitational pull or pressure impulse. It is the quantity of motion carried forward and later diminished by external influences. Indispensable momentum, by contrast, is the inherent potential of mass to receive motion. It does not itself move the body, but without it no motion could exist. A body cannot be set into motion without mass, and that mass determines how much dispensable momentum it can acquire.

25.6 Momentum: The True Carrier of Motion

Momentum is the most fundamental expression of motion in the universe. It is the direct result of a pressure impulse force and is generated in the exact direction of that force. The pressure impulse does not merely push the body once—it imparts to it a measurable quantity of motion that becomes embedded in the body as momentum. Once given, momentum governs all subsequent locomotion, regardless of whether the original source remains active or not.

It is essential to recognize that momentum is not created continuously by any internal activity of the body. Chemical reactions, thermal excitation, or internal processes cannot generate momentum. The total quantity is imparted at the moment of the initial pressure impulse. From that instant onward, the body carries a finite, directional momentum which is gradually diminished only by external factors such as gravity, friction, or collision.

Just as gravity acts uniformly on all bodies—accelerating them irrespective of mass or composition—it also consumes momentum uniformly. Gravity does not discriminate between heavy and light bodies, nor does it adjust for chemical differences. It simply pulls in the normal plane, opposing and curving motion while gradually dispensing the momentum present in the body. The rate of this consumption is governed not by mass alone, but by the initial velocity of the body and its radial distance from the gravitational center.

Momentum is therefore a physically meaningful and observable quantity, akin to pressure itself. We observe it through two unmistakable signs:

- the pressure exerted by moving bodies during impact or collision, and

- the continuation of motion even when no further force is applied.

Bouncing objects provide simple illustrations. A light ball, when thrown to the ground, bounces repeatedly. A heavy ball may not bounce at all. The difference lies in the dispensable momentum each body carries. The lighter ball, retaining greater velocity relative to its weight, takes longer to dispense its momentum. The heavier ball, subject to stronger gravitational opposition and faster transfer upon impact, loses its dispensable momentum more quickly.

Mathematically, momentum is expressed by the classical relation:

$$P = m \cdot v$$

Where m is the indispensable mass, and v is the dispensable velocity.

Dispensable momentum cannot vanish on its own. It requires an external agent—gravity, friction, or impact—to reduce it. If no such force acts, the body will continue moving indefinitely with the momentum it originally acquired. This explains why celestial bodies that have escaped the gravitational field of any primary body continue endlessly through interstellar space, carried forward by their dispensable momentum.

25.7 Centrifugal Effects and Rotational Motion

This framework also clarifies phenomena often misunderstood as separate "forces." Centrifugal effects are not independent forces, but consequences of momentum acting outward when motion is constrained into a curve under a central pull. They are secondary expressions of momentum, not new causes.

Rotational or spinning momentum deserves special notice. Unlike linear motion, spin is generated by a torque-like pressure impulse, imparting angular velocity to the body. Once initiated, spin does not decay under gravity. Gravity, acting only in the normal plane, can alter linear motion but has no effect on spin velocity or axis. Thus, spinning motion continues largely unaffected by gravitational pull.

This explains why:

- planets maintain their axial rotations,
- comets preserve their spin across vast orbits,
- stars and galactic cores retain angular motion over immense timescales.

The persistence of spin is one of the clearest demonstrations of dispensable momentum in nature, particularly when no friction or external braking acts upon it.

25.7.1 Conclusion

Momentum is the true essence of motion—linear or rotational. It is the product of pressure impulse, the carrier of all movement, and the currency gradually spent through interactions with gravity or matter. Unlike inertia, which merely names a body's resistance to change, momentum explains both the cause and the behavior of motion in physically meaningful, observable terms.

25.8 How Does the Motion Created in a Mass Come to an End?

The essential characteristic of matter in motion is momentum. When a body moves, it becomes the carrier of momentum—a real, physical quantity inseparable from its mass. Without momentum, motion is impossible. Momentum is not generated continuously by the body's internal processes; it is always a transferred reality, the direct consequence of an external pressure impulse or a gravitational act.

When a subject acts upon an object—whether through mechanical pressure or gravitational influence—it imparts a force that is translated into momentum within the object. There is no qualitative difference between momentum generated by gravity and that generated by pressure impulse. Both produce measurable velocity in the body, and both are subject to eventual dissipation by external forces.

Unlike inertia, which neither explains nor quantifies anything, momentum is an intelligible and measurable entity. Although it cannot be sensed directly—what Aristotle would call an *insensible thing*—its presence is revealed through its effects: the velocity of a body, the shape of its path, and its capacity to transfer motion to other bodies.

Motion in a mass comes to an end only when its momentum is completely consumed. This consumption never happens spontaneously. It requires opposition: gravity pulling the body back, friction resisting its travel, or collision with another mass. If no such opposing force exists, momentum carries the body indefinitely. This principle explains the apparent perpetuity of motion in the vacuum of space, where interstellar objects free from friction and beyond the gravitational reach of larger bodies continue endlessly with their inherited momentum.

Thus, motion is never extinguished on its own. It ends only when the finite quantity of momentum acquired at the beginning is fully neutralized by external opposition. The cessation of motion, therefore, is not mysterious but the natural conclusion of dispensable momentum once spent.

25.9 Momentum on the Scale of Galaxies

The same principle extends to the largest structures in the universe. Dispensable momentum is never consumed by a body's own gravity. Instead, it persists and accumulates across cosmic time. In galaxies, this accumulation occurs in the cores, where billions of years of massive stellar ejections add to the core's stock of momentum. These repeated expulsions of mass and pressure impulse impart dispensable momentum in definite directions, and that momentum is carried forward by the entire galactic structure.

It is this accumulated dispensable momentum that drives the observed motion of galaxies. Space itself is not expanding or contracting; rather, the galaxies are moving under the momentum they acquired from their own violent histories of ejection. What has been called "dark energy" is thus a misconception. The apparent outward drift of galaxies is not the stretching of space but the straightforward continuation of momentum imparted by massive mass ejections.

In this framework, galactic locomotion is no longer mysterious. Momentum—created by real, physical events and preserved across cosmic distances—dictates the movements we observe. Just as a projectile continues its flight until its momentum is consumed, galaxies continue their journeys until acted upon by another massive gravitational influence.

25.10 Momentum Is the Cause of Bouncing

Every act of locomotion—from the first pressure impulse to the final standstill—follows a single pattern: momentum is created, carried, and ultimately dissipated. One of the clearest demonstrations of this principle is **bouncing**, the visible moment when a moving body, after impact, rises again due to its retained momentum.

Consider a simple but powerful comparison. Drop a rubber ball and a lead sphere of the same size from the same height at the same time. Both acquire equal gravitational momentum during their fall. As Strato of Lampsacus observed long ago, the greater the falling height, the greater the velocity, and thus the greater the momentum—a fact he confirmed by noting that higher falls produce deeper craters.

Yet the two bodies respond very differently upon impact. The lead sphere scarcely rebounds, while the rubber ball bounces visibly. Why? Both possessed the same downward momentum, but only one reverses its path.

This rebound is not caused by gravity—gravity has no repulsive power. Nor is it explained by invoking an abstract "normal force." The true cause lies in the momentum retained within the secondary body at the instant of impact.

To clarify, recall the two forms of momentum:

- **Indispensable momentum**: the body's intrinsic mass, constant and unconsumed during motion.
- **Dispensable momentum**: the acquired velocity, gradually opposed by gravity, friction, or collision.

At impact, the body's remaining dispensable momentum acts like a rebound impulse. Lighter bodies—such as a rubber ball—require less opposing force to redirect their momentum upward, and thus they bounce more readily. Heavier bodies—like a lead sphere—require much greater impulse to rebound and therefore tend to compress or deform rather than lift.

In this way, the bounce is a mirror image of projectile motion: a retained impulse pushes the body upward, and gravity immediately resumes its downward pull, repeating until momentum is fully spent.

The same principle explains why meteorites striking Earth form enormous craters. Their immense momentum, built over long falls under gravity, acts as a pressure impulse on impact—driving the energy downward and outward into the ground. Strato's recognition of this connection between fall height, velocity, and impact effect was an early step in analyzing acceleration and momentum.

Thus, bouncing is not a separate force but a manifestation of dispensable momentum after collision. More mass means less bounce, because greater force is required to overcome gravity; less mass means more bounce, because less force is required. In every case, it is momentum—not inertia, not a repulsive force—that explains the phenomenon.

This understanding also prepares us for a deeper question: if momentum explains rebounds and arcs, what explains spin? Why do we not feel the Earth's vast rotational motion? Why are we not flung from its surface like water from a whirling tub? These questions lead us directly to the study of **rotational momentum**, the subject of the next section.

25.11 Spinning Motion, Equatorial Bulge, and the Myth of Inertia-Based Forces

Momentum, though often hidden during uniform motion, becomes most clearly perceived at the moment of directional change. Whether in bouncing, turning, or rotating, the trajectory of a body reveals its retained momentum. What appears to be "resistance" is not due to an abstract inertia, but to the active momentum already present within the body, which resists redirection.

In spinning motion, this principle is especially visible. Spin is always initiated by a pressure impulse—a torque-like action applied to the body. Just as linear motion originates from a push or thrust, rotation begins with a torque-like impulse. Once created, spinning momentum persists until acted upon by friction or gravitational braking. In the absence of such forces, spin continues indefinitely, as we observe in celestial bodies across the universe.

25.11.1 Equatorial Bulge and Centrifugal Effects

One of the most striking demonstrations of spinning momentum is the equatorial bulge of rotating planets such as Earth. This bulge is not caused by an external centrifugal force. Rather, it is the natural expression of momentum within the rotating body, as its mass attempts to continue in a straight path while constrained to a circular one. "Centrifugal force" is not a true force, but a label for the outward effect of momentum in a rotating frame.

The same is true of the Coriolis effect. What is often taught as a "fictitious force" is in fact the visible consequence of momentum preserved within a rotating system. When a body moves across that system, its original momentum resists the redirection imposed by rotation, producing the curved trajectories we observe. Both centrifugal and Coriolis forces are not independent causes but descriptive expressions of momentum in action.

25.11.2 Gravity as the True Centripetal Force

In all circular or rotational systems, the only real centripetal force is gravity. No internal "inertia-based" force draws a body inward. Gravity alone restrains outward-moving momentum, curving paths into orbits or binding rotating bodies. Where gravity and friction are absent, momentum—once created—cannot be dissipated. Spin or rotation persists eternally unless interrupted by another force or collision.

Even everyday systems illustrate this interplay. Stirring a cup of coffee sets the liquid into rotation through pressure impulse. The surface may rise at the edges and dip at the center. With stronger spin, the opposite may occur: a dome forms in the center, showing that momentum, if unopposed, can locally overcome gravity.

25.11.3 Toward a New Understanding of Rotation

Many misconceptions in physics—centrifugal force, Coriolis deviation, orbital stability, even the equatorial shapes of planets—arise from treating inertia as a mysterious inherent property of matter. In reality, inertia explains nothing. Momentum, however, can be generated, measured, transferred, opposed, and preserved. It is the true carrier of motion—linear, angular, or oscillatory.

By replacing inertia with momentum as the active principle, we gain clarity in explaining not only why bodies move, but how they persist in motion, curve under influence, and respond to resistance. This understanding scales from the stirring of a coffee cup to the bulge of a planet—and to the vast rotational architectures of galaxies themselves.

25.11.4 Historical Insight: Anaxagoras and the Primacy of Rotation

It is worth remembering that the earliest philosophers did not fix their attention on projectiles but on rotation. Anaxagoras, with his concept of *Nous*—a cosmic Mind setting all things into a great whirl—was among the first to see rotation as the key to universal order. Though expressed in metaphysical terms, his intuition captured a profound truth: rotational motion is not accidental but fundamental to cosmic structure.

This ancient insight reminds us that the mystery of spin has long been central to human inquiry. In the sections ahead, we will examine rotational momentum in depth—most strikingly in the case of the Moon, whose lack of independent spin provides a crucial test case for understanding how rotation is created, maintained, and sometimes suppressed.

25.12 Spin of the Primary Body Has No Effect on Spin of the Secondary Body

One of the most overlooked facts in celestial mechanics is that the spin of a primary body does not influence the spin of its secondaries. Each spinning body retains its own angular momentum—created independently at the moment of pressure impulse—and this spin persists until consumed by friction or resistance. The motion of a secondary is not borrowed from the primary's rotation, but originates in the momentum within the secondary body itself.

Take Earth as an example. The planet spins on its axis, yet if we throw an object upward or horizontally, its spin—if it has one—is unaffected by Earth's rotation. The object carries its own dispensable momentum, which continues until fully spent. Only gravity modifies its path; Earth's spin exerts no influence.

The same principle holds on a larger scale. Earth orbits the Sun, but this orbital motion does not alter Earth's axial rotation. The Sun's gravity governs Earth's orbital path, not its spin. Differences in apparent spin durations—such as variations between sidereal and solar days—arise not from any direct action of the Sun on Earth's spin but from the relative interplay of orbital and rotational velocities at perihelion and aphelion.

Spin is thus an internally retained form of momentum, generated at the moment of an initiating impulse, whether torque-like or direct. It is not propagated from one body to another through gravity or through shared motion. Each body carries its own spin as its own inheritance of momentum.

Looking Ahead: Projectile Locomotion

We have not yet entered into a complete discussion of projectile locomotion, where all key variables—gravity, pressure impulse, momentum, and mass—act together. This subject will require deeper investigation, since it is only by following the interplay of these variables through every stage of a trajectory that the full truth of locomotion can be revealed.

As we prepare to enter that study, we recall that even the smallest feature of motion can reveal the deepest structure of the universe:

> *"Nature uses only the longest threads to weave her patterns, so each small piece of her fabric reveals the organization of the entire tapestry."*
> — *Richard P. Feynman, 1986 Dirac Memorial Lecture*

And we remember that truth, though often cloaked at first, is ultimately simple:

> *"Please observe, gentlemen, how facts which at first seem improbable will, even on scant explanation, drop the cloak which has hidden them and stand forth in simple beauty."*
> — *Galileo Galilei.*

25.13 Rotational vs Orbital Motion: Clarifying the Language and Challenging the Theory

In the study of planetary motion, clarity of terminology is essential. Common usage often blurs the distinction between different forms of angular motion, producing deep conceptual confusion. This book therefore adopts a strict two-term system:

Spin (Spinning Motion)

Spin refers to a body rotating about its own internal axis. For example, Earth spins once every 24 hours around its north–south axis, giving rise to day and night. Spin is initiated by a torque-like pressure impulse and preserved as rotational momentum. Once acquired, it remains independent of the spin of nearby bodies, unless acted upon by friction or internal resistance.

Orbital Motion (Revolution)

Orbital motion refers to a body moving in a curved path around an external primary body, typically under gravitational control. For example, Earth orbits the Sun once every 365 days. Orbital motion is path-based and mass-sensitive, determined by the initial direction and magnitude of momentum acquired at the moment of ejection or formation.

The term *rotational motion* is deliberately avoided, as it is inconsistently used in different contexts to mean either axial spin or orbital revolution. To prevent confusion:

- *Spin* will always mean motion around a body's own axis.
- *Orbital motion* will always mean revolution around another body.

The Peculiar Spins of Venus and Uranus: Powerful Exceptions to the Nebular Theory

The standard Nebular Theory proposes that planets formed from a rotating cloud of gas and dust, and therefore should share a common direction of spin and orbit. Yet two planets stand in stark contradiction to this idea:

- Venus spins backward, and extremely slowly.
- Uranus spins sideways, as if rolling along its orbit.

These are not minor anomalies. They are fundamental violations of the nebular hypothesis. How could a single rotating gas cloud produce such divergent spin directions and axial tilts? The very existence of these exceptions undermines the claim that spin was simply inherited from a uniformly rotating nebula.

The Power of Negative Premises in Physics

Aristotle, in *Prior Analytics*, noted that negative premises often carry greater logical force than affirmatives. A single disproof outweighs a hundred confirmations. Applied to physics:(Aristotle, 2018)

- To say "planets spin because the nebula spun" is a speculative affirmation.

- To observe "not all planets follow that spin" is a decisive negative.

This principle applies equally to gravity. To say "gravity acts downward" is an affirmation; but the negative—"there is no acceleration in the horizontal plane"—carries deeper causal weight. It forces the rejection of false models.

The Nebular Theory's Fundamental Flaws

The nebular hypothesis never explains the most basic questions:

- Where did the original motion come from?
- How could a rotating gas cloud generate distinct spin directions and axial tilts?
- Why does orbital motion exist across billions of kilometers in the first place?

The theory fails not only to predict exceptions but even to account for them. The diversity of planetary spins, eccentricities, inclinations, and spacing cannot be reconciled with the assumption of a single, inherited rotation. Indeed, the statement "planets spin because the nebula spun" is not an explanation at all, but a circular claim: it assumes what it seeks to prove.

A Better Foundation: Pressure Impulse and Momentum

This book replaces speculation with first principles:

- **Pressure impulse force** initiates motion.
- **Momentum**, both linear and rotational, carries that motion.
- The direction, magnitude, and effect of motion depend on the impulse and the mass at the moment of creation.

From this foundation, spin and orbital motion are not inherited mysteries but caused phenomena. Each planet's unique characteristics—whether ordinary or exceptional—reflect distinct physical origins.

Final Reflection

The solar system is a dynamic system of ejected, balanced, and individually endowed bodies—each with its own history. The peculiar spins of Venus and Uranus are not inconveniences to be explained away. They are decisive negations, pointing to a greater truth: motion must be explained, not assumed.

With this clarified foundation, we now turn to projectile motion—the domain where all fundamental variables of locomotion appear together: pressure impulse, gravity, momentum, and mass, all at once in motion.

PART III — DEMONSTRATIONS

Part III — Demonstrations

The *Demonstrations* form the living bridge between reasoning and reality. The ideas established in the previous parts now enter the domain of experiment, where phenomena speak in their own language of motion and measure. Through the pendulum, the projectile, the rebound, and other physical tests, the universal principles of gravity and pressure impulse reveal themselves as quantitative facts. These pages restore to physics its original dignity—the unity of thought and observation. Here, the laboratory becomes a miniature cosmos: every oscillation, every fall, and every curve mirrors the behavior of worlds. By grounding abstract reasoning in visible experiment, this part proves that the same laws govern the stone and the star.

26. Projectile Motion: A Gateway to Universal Locomotion

"He therefore who wishes to rejoice without doubt in regard to the truths underlying phenomena must know how to devote himself to experiment."
—Roger Bacon (1220–1292, English philosopher and scientist)[1]

Projectile motion is the most complete natural example of locomotion. In a single act—a stone thrown, a ball launched, a body ejected from a star or galactic core—we see **all the variables of motion working together**: pressure impulse, momentum, mass, gravity, and direction. Unlike free fall, which isolates gravity, or explosions, which isolate impulse, a projectile displays their interaction in real time. From playground tosses to planetary orbits, it shows how the universe moves.

The Three Fundamental Questions of Locomotion

To understand motion anywhere in the cosmos we must ask three inseparable questions:

1. How does motion begin in a body?
2. How is motion maintained?
3. How does motion come to an end?

Ancient thinkers such as Anaxagoras imagined a divine impulse (*Nous*) setting bodies in motion. Galileo and Newton later proposed inertia—the idea that motion persists unless acted upon. Yet there is no region of the universe truly free from gravity.

[1] Schneider, Michael S. A Beginner's Guide to Constructing the Universe: The Mathematical Archetypes of Nature, Art, and Science (p. 34). HarperCollins. Kindle Edition.

Directional change, variable speed, and cessation of motion cannot be explained by inertia alone.

This work replaces inertia with **momentum**—specifically, *dispensable momentum*—as the true carrier of motion. Pressure impulse creates it; gravity, resistance, and collisions alter it. This framework explains not only how motion begins, but also how it is sustained and how it ends.

What Is a Projectile and Why It Matters

A projectile is any body given an initial impulse and then left to nature. Pressure impulse initiates the path. Momentum carries it forward. Gravity acts only in the normal (vertical) plane, bending the motion downward, while the horizontal component persists unchanged unless another force intervenes. Mass determines how strongly a body responds to both impulse and gravity.

Because all these variables are present at once, projectile motion becomes the **key to universal locomotion**—a scaled-down model of how moons orbit planets, how planets orbit stars, and how stars move around galactic cores.

The Trajectory of a Projectile Body

A projectile always starts with two straight motions: a horizontal (or tangential) component and a vertical (or radial) component. Gravity reduces the vertical component step by step while leaving the horizontal untouched. The curve of the path arises not from any inherent "arc" but from the combination of one constant and one diminishing motion.

- **Upward:** The initial impulse gives both vertical and horizontal velocity. As the body rises, gravity opposes the vertical part, reducing it gradually, but the horizontal persists.
- **At the apex:** Vertical velocity becomes zero, but horizontal velocity continues. The body is not at rest—it is still moving forward.
- **Descent:** Gravity now accelerates the vertical component downward in the same odd-numbered pattern Galileo

found (1, 3, 5, 7…), while the horizontal continues. The arc is the visible outcome of this dual action.

Spin and bounce are secondary but real expressions of locomotion. Off-center impulses impart **rotational momentum**, like a bowler's fingers on a ball, affecting stability and path. Elasticity determines whether a body rebounds or comes to rest on impact.

Equalization: The Origin of Orbits

Every orbit, ellipse, or cometary path is born at an equalization point where acquired momentum and gravitational pull balance. The path is determined by the direction of motion at that instant:

- **Near-horizontal equalization** yields nearly circular orbits.
- **Mixed tangential and radial** components produce ellipses—the more radial, the more eccentric.
- **Near-vertical equalization** gives comet-like plunges.
- **Exceeding escape speed** leads to truly open paths.

Thus, the geometry of circles, ellipses, and cometary tracks is not an imposed abstraction but a natural consequence of how and when equalization occurs. Even small changes in projection angle produce drastically different outcomes—an insight missing from traditional accounts of orbital formation.

A Universal Principle

If the horizontal momentum of a body equals the gravitational pull acting on it, the body circles endlessly—this is orbital motion. Satellites, planets, and moons are projectiles launched at cosmic scale, where pressure impulse and gravity balance perfectly.

Earth's own spin and orbital motion feel imperceptible because we share its dispensable momentum, like passengers in a smoothly moving vehicle. Centripetal acceleration from spin is negligible compared with gravity; the atmosphere travels with the Earth, eliminating turbulence.

Scale and Continuity

From a tossed stone to a drifting star, the same principle rules:

- **No motion without impulse.**
- **No orbit without projection.**

- **No trajectory without momentum.**

Projectile motion is therefore not a trivial exercise in mechanics but the **gateway to understanding universal locomotion**. It reveals how impulse, gravity, mass, and momentum combine to produce every path—from the fall of a stone to the orbit of a planet to the drift of a galaxy. In later sections, we extend this logic to pendulum experiments and orbital mechanics, where the universe itself is seen as a vast field of projectiles.

26.1 The True Mechanism of Orbital Motion — The Dynamic Balance of Gravity and Momentum

All motion in the heavens begins as a **projectile**. A secondary body receives an initial **pressure impulse**, which becomes its **dispensable momentum**—the stored potential for motion that gravity will thereafter continuously modulate. Gravity, on the other hand, is not a cause of horizontal motion; it acts only in the **normal (vertical) plane**, altering direction but never supplying or removing tangential speed.

26.2 From Vertical Projection to Tangential Overshoot

When the initial impulse is directed purely vertically, the body rises until its upward momentum is exhausted, then falls back under gravity. If the vertical component exceeds escape velocity, the body never returns. But if the impulse has even a small **tangential component**, gravity cannot draw the body back along the same path. During the outward journey, gravity decelerates the motion; when the body turns inward, it accelerates again. If the reach of this arc is wide enough that gravity no longer pulls along the same line, the unchanged tangential momentum carries the body **past the central line**—an **overshoot**. This overshoot marks the birth of **orbital motion**.

26.3 The Star-Shaped Genesis of Orbits

In its first oscillations, the path is like a star: long outward arms where momentum dominates, short inward curves where gravity regains control. Each approach and retreat is a negotiation between **the body's inherited motion** and **the primary's constant pull**. Over countless repetitions, these oscillations smooth into the closed paths we call orbits. Where the arms are long, the orbits appear oblong; where the balance is tight, they appear circular.

26.4 The Sinuous Reality of Motion

Gravity does not weaken linearly—it diminishes with the square of distance. Thus, at far distances the acceleration is faint compared with the vast regions traversed. The secondary body travels enormous spans before gravity can bend its path again. To the primary, this motion is sinuous—a gentle wave of approach and retreat, rise and fall—like the undulations of a sea moving across a plane. Each crest and trough corresponds to one orbit for us, one wave of interaction for the two bodies. Orbit is therefore not a circle traced on space but a wave of acceleration and deceleration continually reshaped by distance.

26.5 The Universal Dialogue

At perihelion, when the body nears the primary, the gravitational acceleration strengthens, and the body's speed increases as though it overshoots the equilibrium. At aphelion, the pull weakens, the motion slows, and the body begins its return. This perpetual alternation forms the rhythm of the cosmos—the ceaseless dialogue of momentum seeking freedom and gravity restoring order.

26.6 The True Description

Traditional explanations in terms of kinetic and potential energy, angular momentum, or conic geometry are secondary descriptions.

They measure outcomes, not causes. The true mechanism of orbital motion rests only upon two real forces:

1. **Dispensable Momentum** — the inherited impulse that drives the motion tangentially.
2. **Gravity** — the centripetal influence that bends motion in the normal plane.

Every planet, moon, comet, and star moves by the same principle: Gravity bends; momentum continues. Their balance alone shapes the architecture of the universe.

27. Pendulum Experiments: Locomotion, Momentum, and Gravitational Balance

Circular Motion and Pendulum Experiment

Gravity acts exclusively in the *normal plane*—that is, it always pulls bodies in a straight line toward the center of mass. This force produces rectilinear acceleration or deceleration along the vertical axis relative to the surface of a primary body such as Earth. Gravity does not act in the *horizontal* or *geodesic* plane. On the other hand, the pressure impulse force generates motion in a straight line but in *any* direction depending on the origin and orientation of the impulse.

Both of these forces—gravity and pressure impulse—are fundamentally linear in action. Gravity pulls straight downward (normal to the surface), and pressure impulse projects matter along a straight line in the direction of force application. If this is the case, then a compelling question arises: **How is circular motion possible in nature if both primary forces act in straight lines?**

This apparent contradiction will be carefully addressed and resolved when we analyze the **pendulum experiments** in detail. In those experiments, we will uncover how the interaction and alternation of gravity and pressure impulse forces create the illusion—or rather, the reality—of circular or curved motion, even when no true curved force exists. Through this, we aim to understand not only pendulum motion but the foundations of circular motion itself.

27.1 Introduction: Pendulum as the Bridge Between Heaven and Earth

One of the most fortunate discoveries in classical mechanics is that a **single scientific experiment**—the pendulum—serves as a bridge between understanding **locomotion in the heavens** and **locomotion on Earth**. The pendulum experiment is unique in its ability to reveal the underlying unity of forces governing all motion in the universe. Figure 27.1

At its core, the pendulum illustrates how *gravity operates through momentum*. More importantly, it shows that the **momentum produced by gravity and the momentum produced by pressure impulse forces** share identical mechanical characteristics. In both cases, the resulting motion obeys the same fundamental laws—independent of the source of the force.

One of the key revelations from pendulum motion is that the **oscillation period** of the pendulum bob does **not depend on its mass**. Instead, it is directly related to the **square root of the string length**, showing an inverse relationship to the force of gravity. This mirrors the behavior of freely falling bodies, where **acceleration is also independent of mass** and follows the principle that *distance fallen is proportional to the square of time.*

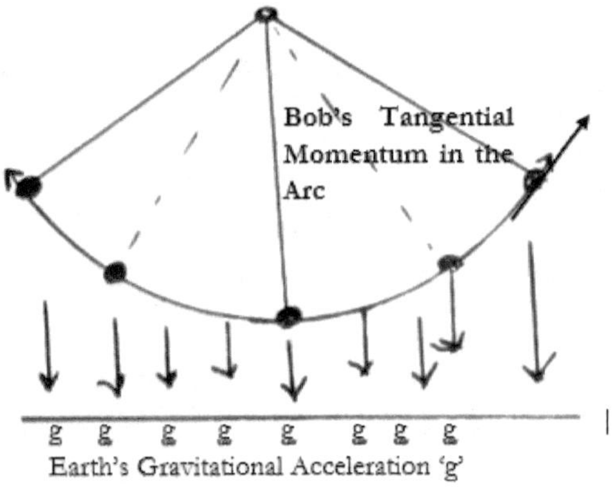

Figure 27.1Pendulum experiments and equalization of forces. At the extremes, momentum is zero while gravity acts as restoring force. At the center, momentum is maximum while gravity acts vertically. The pendulum illustrates the natural equalization between momentum and gravity, mirroring the balance that governs orbital motion.

Thus, the pendulum becomes the only known experiment that helps us **reconcile circular motion with straight-line motion,** and more importantly, it reveals the relationship between **acceleration and velocity**.

While **mass**—both of primary and secondary bodies—is essential to **quantify gravitational interaction**, it is the pendulum that enables us to understand how other parameters—**radial distance, acceleration, and velocity**—are interrelated. Without grasping these connections, any study of **cosmic locomotion** remains incomplete.

In fact, using this single experiment, we can derive much of the **mathematical evidence** required to understand the motion of the cosmos. Remarkably, even before these experimental validations, our scientific forebears—**Galileo, Newton**, and their contemporaries—intuited these relationships and formulated them as the **Law of Universal Gravitation**. Their era truly marked the golden age of classical mechanics, and the pendulum stands as one of its most enduring legacies.

27.2 From Earthly Oscillations to Universal Motion

The pendulum, one of the simplest mechanical systems on Earth, reveals first principles of locomotion across the universe. When carefully observed—as in the demonstrations of Professor Julius Sumner Miller—The Simple Pendulum, Lesson 7; available via YouTube, accessed 2025, a swinging bob becomes more than a classroom exhibit: it becomes a quantitative gateway to how gravity and momentum cooperate at every scale. Read correctly, the pendulum's swing encodes the same velocity–radius–gravity relation that governs orbital paths, planetary equilibrium, and cosmic structure.

1. The Core Observation: Acceleration and Momentum in Balance

A pendulum bob oscillates under gravitational pull and an initial pressure impulse (pull-and-release). For a given length, the local gravitational acceleration is effectively constant (in the laboratory cited, $\boldsymbol{a = 9.344\ \mathrm{m\,s^{-2}}}$, while the bob's speed adjusts so that the motion holds together. The balancing relation is shown in acceleration momentum equalization Table 27.1.

$$v = \sqrt{a\,r}, \text{ equivalently } a = \frac{v^2}{r},$$

where v is the tangential speed and r the effective radius (string length). When v falls short of $\sqrt{a\,r}$, the string tends toward slackening; when v exceeds it, the path strains the string and irregularities appear. Thus, the bob's **dispensable momentum** must match the gravitational demand set by a at radius r. This relation is not peculiar to pendulums; it is the universal kinematic condition for motion under normal-plane gravity. Pendulum shows the acceleration and velocity balance $a = v\text{^}2/r$.

Table 27.1 Pendulum Shows Acceleration and Momentum Equalization

STRING LENGTH (r) (M)	MEASURED SPEED (v) (M/S)	COMPUTED (v^2/r) (M/S²)	LOCAL (a) (M/S²)
0.10	0.9664	9.344	9.344
0.40	1.9333	9.344	9.344
0.90	2.8999	9.344	9.344

2. Gravitational Acceleration at Earth's Surface, and the Sling Analogy

From Newton's law $\boldsymbol{a = GM/r^2}$, the same uniformity that governs the pendulum governs everything near Earth's surface. Intuitively: whirl a stone in a sling—too slow and it falls inward; too fast and it strains outward; at just the right speed the inward pull and the curvature requirement balance, and the motion is smooth. The pendulum displays this balance in miniature: gravity acts continuously in the normal (vertical) plane, while the tangential component is the result of the initial pressure impulse and the momentum the bob carries.

Because the local field is nearly uniform across a swing, the measured a does not depend on amplitude (for small angles). To explore non-local regimes—Moon, Sun, or beyond—the local model gives way to the general law $\boldsymbol{a = GM/r^2}$, which bridges room-scale mechanics and cosmic dynamics by a single principle.

3. Transition to Cosmic Applications Table 27.2.

Combining the two universal relations,

$$a = \frac{GM}{r^2}, \quad a = \frac{v^2}{r},$$

Yields

$$GM = a\,r^2, \qquad v = \sqrt{\frac{GM}{r}}, \qquad r = \sqrt{\frac{GM}{a}}.$$

Using the laboratory value $a = 9.344\ \mathrm{m\,s^{-2}}$ with Earth's $\mathrm{GM} = 3.98615893 \times 10^{14}\ \mathrm{m^3\,s^{-2}}$ returns

$$r = \sqrt{\frac{GM}{a}} \approx 6{,}531{,}470\ \mathrm{m},$$

a direct readout of the lab's radial position from Earth's center. The same identities let us infer unknown masses, orbital speeds, and satellite altitudes anywhere in the cosmos.

To make the bridge unmistakable, the next table applies the identical rule to the eight planets (circular-speed idealization at each semimajor axis) using the Sun's gravitational parameter $\mu_\odot = \mathrm{GM}_\odot = 1.32712440018 \times 10^{20}\ \mathrm{m^3\,s^{-2}}$.

Table 27.2 Solar-System Circular Speeds and Gravitational Acceleration at Each Orbital radius

PLANET	RADIUS (r) (M)	SPEED ($v = \sqrt{\mu_\odot/r}$) (KM/S)	ACCELERATION ($a = \mu_\odot/r^2$) (M/S²)
Mercury	(5.7909×10^{10})	47.872	0.03957

PLANET	RADIUS (r) (M)	SPEED ($v = \sqrt{\mu_\odot/r}$) (KM/S)	ACCELERATION ($a = \mu_\odot/r^2$) (M/S²)
Venus	(1.0821×10^{11})	35.021	0.01133
Earth	(1.49598×10^{11})	29.785	0.00593
Mars	(2.27937×10^{11})	24.130	0.00255
Jupiter	(7.78412×10^{11})	13.057	0.000219
Saturn	(1.42673×10^{12})	9.645	(6.52×10^{-5})
Uranus	(2.87097×10^{12})	6.799	(1.61×10^{-5})
Neptune	(4.49825×10^{12})	5.432	(6.56×10^{-6})

The pendulum's balance $v^2/r = a$ and the planet's balance $v^2/r = \mu_\odot/r^2$ are the same equation written on two scales.

4. From Swing to Orbit

A swing is a slowed orbit anchored to a pivot; an orbit is a swing with the pivot removed and gravity alone curving the path. In a pendulum, the restoring acceleration is set by local a, while the bottom-point speed depends on the drop in height from release. In an orbit, the centripetal demand is met directly by gravity $v = \sqrt{(\mu/r)}$. The similarity is not accidental: in both cases one force pulls inward while motion along the path is maintained by the dispensable momentum imparted at initiation.

5. Orbital Pathways: Parabola, Orbit, or Escape

Let $\mu = GM$ and r be the instantaneous radial distance. The circular condition is where gravity's inward acceleration equals the curvature (momentum) requirement:

$$\frac{v^2}{r} = \frac{\mu}{r^2};\Rightarrow \quad v = \sqrt{\frac{\mu}{r}}.$$

If the tangential speed at that r is less than $\sqrt{(\mu/r)}$, gravity dominates and the body turns inward (an ellipse with the starting point at apocenter). If greater but still below escape, the ellipse opens with the starting point at pericenter. The parabolic boundary is

$$v_{esc} = \sqrt{\frac{2\mu}{r}},$$

beyond which hyperbolic escape occurs. Direction matters as much as magnitude: purely normal (vertical) impulse cannot produce an orbit; a tangential component is essential.

6. Spin, Momentum, and Gravity: Clarifying Misconceptions

These experiments reinforce a central principle of our framework: spin momentum is independent of gravity. Once imparted by a torque-like pressure impulse, a body's spin persists; apparent changes during a swing reflect changing **linear** speed along the arc, not gravity altering the axial spin or draining spin velocity. Gravity acts only in the normal plane: it curves and moderates translational motion but does not rotate the spin axis or propagate spin from one body to another.

7. Conclusion: The Pendulum as Proof of Cosmic Mechanics

From a simple swing, we recover the system of locomotion: the relation $v^2 = a\,r$ binding speed to radius under gravity; the stability condition that defines orbits; and a method to back-solve mass, radius, and speed across distant systems. To understand how a bob swings is to understand how a planet orbits. Locomotion is governed by real, measurable quantities—pressure impulse, momentum, gravity—not by passive placeholders. Wherever $v^2 = a\,r$ holds, stability follows; where it fails, motion decays or departs. The same equation speaks in the room and among the stars.

Editorial Note on Methods

This book develops a unified mechanics based on two ideas: (1) spin and linear motion are created by pressure impulse; (2) gravity acts only in the normal plane. We use accepted constants and catalog values (G, M, GM, distances) so every calculation can be independently verified. Where our interpretation differs from conventional cosmology (e.g., tidal locking, nebular theory, dark matter), we state the difference explicitly. The aim is clarity, not conformity: one set of physical principles applied consistently from pendulum to planet to galaxy.

Orbital Pathways — Worked Examples

The pendulum has already taught us that a curved path results whenever an inward pull acts continuously while motion along that path is sustained by an initial tangential cause. In celestial motion, this balance is expressed in its simplest form:

$$v = \sqrt{\frac{GM}{r}}, \quad V_{esc} = \sqrt{\frac{2GM}{R}},$$

where v is the circular orbital speed, v_{esc} the escape speed, G the gravitational constant, M the central mass, and r the radial distance from that mass.

Using accepted constants and distances keeps the numbers reproducible, while the interpretation we give them remains our own.

Earth Around the Sun

At Earth's mean distance from the Sun,

$$r \approx 1.49598 \times 10^{11}\ \mathrm{m},$$

$$GM_{\odot} \approx 1.3271244 \times 10^{20}\ \mathrm{m^3 s^{-2}},$$

the circular orbital speed is

$$v \approx 29{,}784.7\ \mathrm{m/s} \quad (29.78\ \mathrm{km/s}),$$

and the escape speed at that same distance is

$$v_{esc} \approx 42{,}121.9\ \mathrm{m/s} \quad (42.12\ \mathrm{km/s}).$$

These two numbers define the complete spectrum of outcomes at Earth's orbital radius. Below 29.78 km/s an object falls inward; at exactly that speed it maintains a circle; between 29.78 and 42.12 km/s it follows a bound ellipse; at 42.12 km/s it departs parabolically; and above that it leaves the system on a hyperbola.

Mercury's Orbit

Changing only the radius alters the speed, while the principle remains the same. Near perihelion at

$$r \approx 4.60 \times 10^{10} \text{ m},$$

the circular-equivalent speed is about 53.71 km/s. Near aphelion at

$$r \approx 6.98 \times 10^{10} \text{ m},$$

it is about 43.60 km/s. The path quickens when the Sun's inward pull is stronger and slows when it is weaker. Nothing mysterious is required beyond the same inward acceleration and tangential dispensable momentum that the pendulum demonstrates in miniature.

Near-Earth Motion

At low-Earth orbit, about 400 km above the surface, the radial distance is

$$r \approx 6.37 \times 10^{6} + 4.0 \times 10^{5} \text{ m},$$

with Earth's parameter

$$GM_{\oplus} \approx 3.986 \times 10^{14} \text{ m}^3/\text{s}^{-2}.$$

The corresponding circular speed is about 7.67 km/s, and the escape speed is about 10.85 km/s. These are the very numbers used in spacecraft planning, and they arise from the same balance that governs a pendulum's bottom-of-swing: an inward acceleration in the normal plane matched to a tangential motion created by an initiating impulse.

A Note on Interpretation

Conventional orbital mechanics uses the same relations for circular and escape speed, and explains elliptical paths through conservation of angular momentum and energy. In this framework, the numerical results remain identical, but the explanation of cause shifts: the tangential component is dispensable momentum imparted by pressure impulse events, while gravity acts only in the normal plane to curve the path. The pendulum, the planet, and the galaxy all obey this same balance. The table below shows the circular and escape speeds of Solar System planets

Constants: $GM_{\odot} = 1.3271244 \times 10^{20}\ m^3/s^{-2}$

Table 27.3 The Circular and Escape Speeds of Solar System Planets

PLANET	ORBITAL RADIUS r (M)	CIRCULAR SPEED $v = \sqrt{\frac{GM\odot}{r}}$ (KM/S)	ESCAPE SPEED $v_{esc} = \sqrt{\frac{2GM_{\odot}}{r}}$ (KM/S)
Mercury	5.7909×10^{10}	47.87	67.74
Venus	1.0821×10^{11}	35.02	49.54
Earth	1.49598×10^{11}	29.78	42.12
Mars	2.27937×10^{11}	24.13	34.13
Jupiter	7.78412×10^{11}	13.06	18.47
Saturn	1.42673×10^{12}	9.65	13.64
Uranus	2.87097×10^{12}	6.80	9.62
Neptune	4.49825×10^{12}	5.43	7.68
Pluto	5.9064×10^{12}	4.73	6.69

This table shows the same pendulum relation at work: velocity falls as radius increases, escape speed is always $\sqrt{2}$ times the circular speed, and the rule never changes. Table 27.3.

27.3 Equilibrium in Practice — From Pendulum Equality to Perihelion and Aphelion

The pendulum distilled the balance of motion into a single equality: the speed along the arc depends on the relation

$$v = \sqrt{ar}\ ,$$

where a is the inward acceleration and r the radius of curvature. In orbital motion, the same equality appears with gravity supplying the inward pull:

$$a = \frac{GM}{r^2}\ .$$

Substituting one into the other gives the standard orbital result:

$$v = \sqrt{(GM/r)}\ .$$

Nothing further is required. The pendulum's classroom balance simply changes scale, and the ceiling hook is replaced by the continuous inward action of gravity.

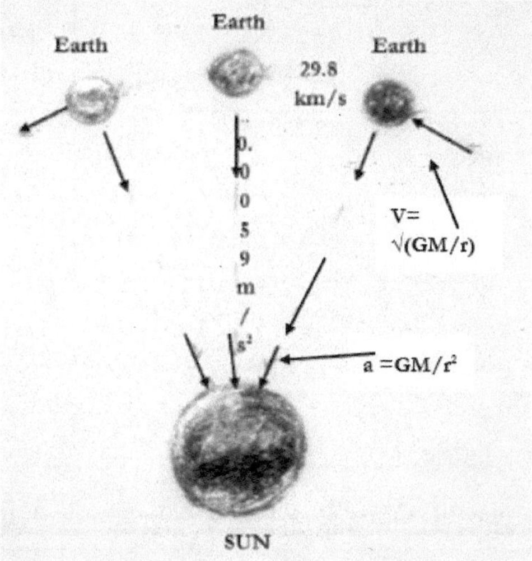

Figure 27.2 Gravitational Stability and Momentum. A stable orbit results when the inward pull of gravity balances the tangential momentum of a body, producing a curved path around the central mass.

Once this balance is understood, the variation of speed along an ellipse follows directly. Nearer to the primary body, the radius is smaller, the inward pull stronger, and the local circular-equivalent speed higher. Farther away, the radius is larger, the pull weaker, and the local circular-equivalent speed lower. A planet on an elongated path therefore moves faster near perihelion and slower near aphelion because gravity alternately augments and resists the tangential dispensable momentum it carries. Observe relation Figure 27.2.

The same arithmetic that sets the swing of a pendulum provides the numbers for planetary orbits. At Earth's mean solar distance, the circular speed is about 29.78 km/s. At Earth's perihelion the required speed rises to about 30.04 km/s; at aphelion it falls to about 29.54 km/s. Mercury, with greater extremes of distance, shows the effect more strongly: its perihelion speed exceeds 53 km/s, while at aphelion it is nearer 44 km/s. The table below shows Earth's orbital speeds at mean distance, perihelion, and aphelion. Table 27.4.

Table 27.4 Earth: Orbital Speeds at Mean Distance, Perihelion, and Aphelion

ORBITAL POSITION	DISTANCE FROM SUN (M)	ORBITAL SPEED (KM/S)
Mean Distance	1.496×10^{11}	29.78
Perihelion	1.471×10^{11}	30.04
Aphelion	1.521×10^{11}	29.54

The table below shows Mercury's orbital speeds at perihelion and aphelion. Table 27.5.

Table 27.5Mercury: Orbital Speeds at Perihelion and Aphelion

ORBITAL POSITION	DISTANCE FROM SUN (M)	ORBITAL SPEED (KM/S)
Perihelion	4.60×10^{10}	53.71
Aphelion	6.98×10^{10}	43.60

Elliptical motion therefore requires no extra machinery. If the tangential momentum at a given radius is less than the local circular requirement, the path bends inward and the present point will later be recognized as an apocenter. If the tangential momentum is greater than the local circular requirement, the path bends outward and the present point becomes a pericenter. The orbit's shape is simply a record of how the initial push compared to the ever-present normal pull of gravity.

Conventional view (for reference). Standard orbital mechanics describes these variations using energy diagrams and angular momentum conservation, and summarizes them with the vis-viva relation. Our framework keeps the same numbers but expresses the cause differently: tangential motion is created by impulse; gravity acts only in the normal plane to curve it, speeding motion when nearer, slowing it when farther.

27.4 Reading Ellipses — Where Gravity Dominates and Where Momentum Leads

An ellipse can be read like a sentence once one knows what to look for. Between the two turning points lies a mid-distance that sits roughly halfway between the near and far radii. Inside this middle stretch, the body moves faster than the circular speed at that same radius; outside it, the body moves slower. This difference is the signature of how the initial dispensable momentum compares with the local inward pull.

Closer in, gravity is strong and adds to the body's speed as it falls; farther out, gravity is weak and the body spends its stored motion against that pull and slows. The turning points themselves show which agent was stronger just before the turn. At perihelion, tangential momentum has carried the body outward until gravity reasserts control and draws it back. At aphelion, gravity has pulled the body inward until the remaining momentum is sufficient to turn the path outward again. The orbit is therefore an alternation of dominance: momentum leads while retreating from the primary, gravity leads while returning. The table below shows orbital distances and speeds of the planets NASA.(*Solar System Exploration*, 2023)

Table 27.6 Orbital Distances and Speeds of the Planets

PLANET	PERIHELION DISTANCE (M)	SPEED AT PERIHELION (KM/S)	APHELION DISTANCE (M)	SPEED AT APHELION (KM/S)
Mercury	4.60×10^{10}	58.98	6.98×10^{10}	38.86
Venus	1.075×10^{11}	35.26	1.089×10^{11}	34.79
Earth	1.471×10^{11}	30.29	1.521×10^{11}	29.29
Mars	2.067×10^{11}	26.50	2.492×10^{11}	21.97
Jupiter	7.405×10^{11}	13.72	8.166×10^{11}	12.44
Saturn	1.353×10^{12}	10.18	1.513×10^{12}	9.14
Uranus	2.742×10^{12}	7.12	3.001×10^{12}	6.49
Neptune	4.459×10^{12}	5.50	4.541×10^{12}	5.37
Pluto	4.437×10^{12}	6.10	7.375×10^{12}	3.71

(Values use $GM_{\odot} = 1.327 \times 10^{20}$ m^3/s^{2}*; distances from JPL planetary data, rounded for clarity.)*

27.4.1 Explanations by Planet Table 27.6.

Mercury — Its highly elliptical orbit shows the strongest contrast. At perihelion, gravity dominates and the planet accelerates to nearly 59 km/s. At aphelion, its momentum stretches outward, slowing to less than 39 km/s. Mercury's path is the clearest example of alternating dominance.

Venus — Nearly circular, with only slight variation. Perihelion and aphelion speeds differ by less than 2%, so the alternation is mild. Venus behaves almost like a pendulum with a very long string: steady and balanced.

Earth — Moves faster at perihelion (30.29 km/s) and slower at aphelion (29.29 km/s). The alternation is real but gentle, visible in seasonal timing.

Mars — Shows a more noticeable variation than Earth. Momentum leads the outward stretch, slowing to ~22 km/s at aphelion, then gravity accelerates it back inward to ~26.5 km/s.

Jupiter — Even at its scale, the pattern holds: perihelion speed is 13.7 km/s, aphelion 12.4 km/s. The huge mass does not change the alternating roles of momentum and gravity.

Saturn — Drops from ~10.2 km/s at perihelion to ~9.1 km/s at aphelion. Its wide ring system follows the same rule, each particle swinging between gravitational dominance and momentum lead.

Uranus — Variation is modest: 7.1 km/s at perihelion to 6.5 km/s at aphelion. The alternation is present but less dramatic.

Neptune — Nearly circular, with little change: ~5.5 km/s to 5.4 km/s. The ellipse is wide but gentle.

Pluto — The most dramatic after Mercury. From over 6.1 km/s at perihelion to only 3.7 km/s at aphelion, Pluto vividly shows how momentum and gravity alternate in control.

This way of reading an orbit avoids unnecessary abstraction. One does not need to imagine hidden reservoirs or curved space. The ellipse is simply the record of how dispensable momentum interacts with gravity's normal pull. The pendulum shows the same truth at arm's length: shorten the string and higher speed is required; lengthen it and the required speed falls. Release the bob with more or less force and the arc adjusts accordingly.

Conventional view (for reference). Traditional mechanics describes these variations with the vis-viva equation and the semi-major axis. Our account accepts the numbers but explains them more plainly: momentum is created by impulse, while gravity alternately accelerates and decelerates it along the path.

27.5 Impulse → Tangential motion (what keeps things "missing the fall")

In our framework, the Massive Mass Ejection gives each body an initial **impulse**. What survives of that impulse shows up as **tangential speed**:

- **Earth**: about **30 km/s** (29.8 km/s).
- **Sun around the Milky Way**: about **230 km/s**.

That sideways motion is what continually makes the body "miss" the center it's falling toward.

27.5.1 Gravity → Tiny radial fall each second (the "pull" 'the body' must keep up with)

At any fixed distance, gravity gives a **radial acceleration**. In one second, a freely falling body would drop a tiny amount:

- **Earth at 1 AU from the Sun**

  Solar gravity at 1 AU:

$$a_\odot = \frac{GM_\odot}{R^2} \approx \frac{(29.8\ \mathrm{km/s})^2}{1\ \mathrm{AU}}$$

$$\approx 0.0059\ \mathrm{m/s^2}$$

Radial drop in 1 s (if there were no sideways motion):

$$\Delta r = \frac{1}{2}a_\odot(1\ \mathrm{s})^2 \approx 0.003\ \mathrm{m} = 3\ \mathrm{mm}.$$

- **Sun at ~27,000 ly from the Galactic center** (≈ 8.2 kpc)

  Centripetal pull needed for a circular path:

$$a_{\text{gal}} = \frac{v^2}{R} \approx \frac{(230{,}000 \text{ m/s})^2}{2.53 \times 10^{20} \text{ m}}$$

$$\approx 2 \times 10^{-10} \text{ m/s}^2$$

Radial drop in 1 s:

$$\Delta r = \frac{1}{2} a_{\text{gal}} \approx 1 \times 10^{-10} \text{ m}$$

(about a tenth of a nanometre).

These "drops per second" are tiny, but over **billions of years** they are decisive—**unless** the tangential motion continually "carries" the body sideways.

27.5.2 The balance: when orbits hold, widen, or decay

If the **tangential speed is exactly right** for the distance (Earth's ~30 km/s at 1 AU; Sun's ~230 km/s at ~8.2 kpc), then each second's sideways motion **just matches** each second's gravitational "drop," keeping the radius essentially constant (a circular/near-circular orbit).

If the speed is **a bit higher** than the circular value, the body will **climb outward** over long times (the radius slowly increases).

If the speed is **a bit lower**, gravity **wins** a little each orbit and the body **spirals inward**.

In our view: the initial **impulse** supplies the tangential motion; **gravity** continually consumes the radial component; the **momentum** we observe is the durable remainder in the **horizontal plane** that maintains the path. These results are shown in a table below. Table 27.7

Table 27.7 Gravitational Acceleration and Tangential Speed of Major Planets

PLANET	MEAN DISTANCE FROM SUN (10^6 KM)	ORBITAL SPEED (KM/S)	SOLAR GRAVITATIONAL ACCELERATION $GM_\odot/r^2$ (M/S²)	APPROX. FREE-FALL DISTANCE PER SECOND (½ A T²)	RESULTING MOTION
Mercury	57.9	47.4	0.039	0.020 m (2 cm)	Speed slightly above circular; orbit elongated
Venus	108.2	35.0	0.011	0.005 m (5 mm)	Near-circular orbit
Earth	149.6	29.8	0.0059	0.003 m (3 mm)	Circular balance—"3 mm fall vs 30 km slide"
Mars	227.9	24.1	0.0026	0.001 m (1 mm)	Slightly slower; eccentric path
Jupiter	778.6	13.1	0.00023	0.0001 m (0.1 mm)	Heavy mass, wide orbit

PLANET	MEAN DISTANCE FROM SUN (10^6 KM)	ORBITAL SPEED (KM/S)	SOLAR GRAVITATIONAL ACCELERATION $GM_\odot/r^2$ (M/S²)	APPROX. FREE-FALL DISTANCE PER SECOND (½ A T²)	RESULTING MOTION
Saturn	1433.5	9.7	0.00010	0.00005 m (0.05 mm)	Stable circular motion
Uranus	2872.5	6.8	0.000025	0.000012 m (0.012 mm)	Very slow, nearly circular
Neptune	4495.1	5.4	0.000014	0.000007 m (0.007 mm)	Outer limit of solar binding

(Computed using $a = GM_\odot/R^2$; $GM_\odot = 1.327 \times 10^{20}$ m³ s⁻²; R from NASA Planetary Fact Sheet.)

27.5.3 Interpretation

- The farther a planet lies from the Sun, the smaller the **gravitational acceleration** and the **radial fall per second**, yet its tangential motion still exactly matches that pull.
- This microscopic balancing act, repeated each second, is what turns impulse into continuous revolution.
- The same principle holds for the Sun itself within the Milky Way—only the numbers grow more extreme and the "fall per second" shrinks to a tenth of a nanometer.

28. From Impulse to Construction: Pressure, Containment, and the Birth of Structure

Origins of Impulse in Nature

All motion begins with an impulse, but impulse itself has an origin. In every domain of nature—from volcanoes to stellar cores, from gunpowder to muscle contraction—the root cause is **pressure buildup under confinement**. Pressure arises when energy, temperature, and containment interact to store potential force within matter.

Impulse is therefore not a mystery; it is a direct consequence of physics, particularly the mechanics of gases, heat, and constrained matter. Whenever energy is confined, it seeks release. When that confinement fails, impulse is born, and motion begins.

28.1 The Preconditions of Impulse

For an impulse to arise, three factors must coexist:

1. **Energy buildup** — thermal, chemical, or nuclear.
2. **Containment or restriction** — prevention of free expansion.
3. **A release point** — rupture, fracture, or vent through which energy escapes.

Without all three, no directional motion occurs. Heat or energy alone cannot cause locomotion; only energy confined and suddenly released can.

When temperature rises within a fixed volume, pressure increases dramatically. If volume expands freely, pressure does not accumulate. Thus, **containment is the condition of direction**. This principle governs all engines, eruptions, and ejections—terrestrial and cosmic alike.

28.1.1 Natural Sources of Impulse

Thermal Expansion in Confined Spaces: Heating gas in a sealed chamber converts energy to pressure and, upon release, to motion.
Chemical Explosions: Gunpowder or nitroglycerin store chemical potential. Once triggered, confined gases expand violently, creating a single, momentary push—the pressure impulse—that launches a projectile or bullet.
Geological Eruptions: Magma and gas beneath Earth's crust accumulate pressure until containment fails, driving rocks and ash outward in impulse-driven trajectories later shaped by gravity.
Stellar and Nuclear Events: Fusion in stars begins only when immense gravitational confinement produces pressures high enough to overcome repulsion between nuclei. When the balance fails, as in supernovae, the resulting explosion expels vast quantities of matter in a single pressure impulse—the **Massive Mass Ejection (MME)** that seeds planets, comets, and other orbiting bodies.
Biological Motion: Even living systems obey the same rule. Muscle contraction converts stored chemical energy (ATP) into directed impulse through ionic and molecular confinement and release.

28.1.2 Impulse as the Bridge

Impulse represents the transition between stored energy and motion:

Impulse = Confined Energy + Pressure + Sudden Release.

It is the exact moment where stillness becomes motion—where potential energy becomes locomotion. Without confinement, energy disperses; with resistance and release, it gains direction.

28.2 Pressure Impulse and the Construction of Celestial Systems

28.2.1 From Variables to Structure

Up to this point, we have examined the universe's variables—gravity, pressure impulse, dispensable and indispensable momentum, and matter—as separate principles. We now turn to how they combine to form *structure.*

Structure arises from the union of impulse and restraint. Pressure impulse initiates motion, gravity tames it, momentum carries it forward, and matter embodies the result. The architecture of the universe—planetary systems, stellar families, and galaxies—is the enduring record of these forces acting together.

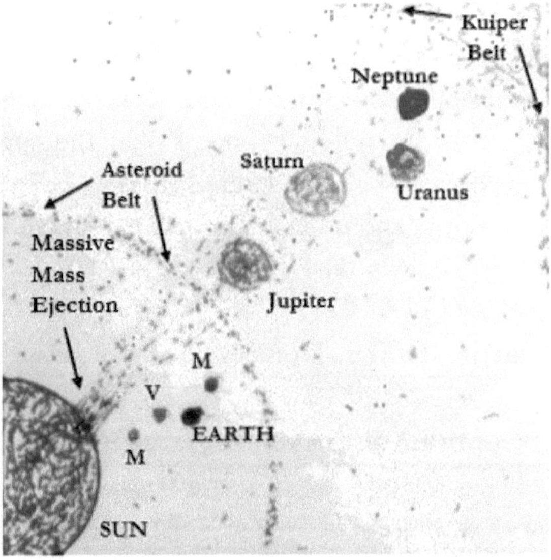

Figure 28.1Massive Mass Ejection and Solar System Formation. After the Sun's own formation, a supernova-like ejection expelled matter that condensed into the planets. Giant planets formed from large accumulations farther out, while terrestrial planets condensed closer in.

28.2.2 Mechanics of Massive Mass Ejection

Direct observation of cosmic formation is impossible within human timescales. We must reason from evidence and analogy. Figure 28.1

In the Sun, the corona's extreme temperature—millions of Kelvin compared to the photosphere's few thousand—reveals powerful internal forces. Coronal flares and coronal mass ejections (CMEs) are modern, small-scale expressions of a much greater process. Billions of years ago, when the solar envelope was less vented and more tightly confined, fusion-generated energy and plasma pressure could have accumulated to critical thresholds.

When that confinement finally failed, the release was catastrophic: **a massive mass ejection**, far greater than any present CME. Matter expelled at hundreds of kilometers per second carried enormous dispensable momentum. Gravity immediately acted on this outward-moving material, bending its straight-line paths into curved orbits. The ejected matter became the raw substance of the solar system—planets, moons, asteroids, and comets.

In this view, the solar system was not built by slow accretion but by a single physical event: a natural consequence of pressure, confinement, and release on a stellar scale.

28.2.3 Extension to Galactic Cores

The same principle applies on larger scales. Galactic cores—enormous, dense, plasma-filled regions—can likewise experience confinement and release. When pressure overcomes restraint, they eject colossal masses of matter, each carrying dispensable momentum sufficient to seed entire stellar systems, clusters, or even streams of stars.

These **galactic-scale ejections** explain the structured, disk-like arrangement of galaxies and their persistent outward motion without invoking exotic matter or cosmic expansion. Each ejection is a mechanical act of the universe's own physics, not an anomaly but a normal outcome of pressure dynamics in confined, high-energy systems.

28.2.4 Analogies and Reasoned Understanding

The process is familiar in miniature. A blocked pressure cooker vent builds force until the seal fails. An atomic bomb demonstrates how confined energy, once released, radiates shockwaves outward. Such analogies, though humble, capture the essence of cosmic events—energy confined, pressure accumulated, and release transforming potential into motion.

28.2.5 Reasonable Conclusion

Massive mass ejection is thus the mechanical foundation of cosmic structure. Straight-line ejection velocities generated by pressure impulse are curved by gravity into bounded orbits under the inverse-square law. Repeated over cosmic timescales, these events explain the disk-like form of solar systems and galaxies alike.

Though we cannot witness their original moments, we observe their living echoes in coronal ejections, supernovae, and active galactic nuclei. Together they form a coherent, testable model of cosmic formation grounded in classical mechanics rather than speculation.

29. The Moving Force of the Universe: Massive Mass Ejection Theory

29.1 Introduction

Modern astronomy often assumes that the angular momentum of planets, stars, and galaxies is an inherited trait from a rotating cloud of gas and dust This is the basis of the Nebular Theory, which suggests that cosmic structures formed through gravitational collapse of a slowly spinning nebula. But this explanation leaves one essential question unanswered:

29.2 Where did the initial motion come from?

Gravity cannot answer this. It is an aggregating force that acts only in the normal (vertical) plane—it pulls inward, but it does not push sideways. Yet every body in the cosmos—planets, stars, galaxies—shows not just mass and structure but locomotion: motion with direction and speed.

The answer lies in **Massive Mass Ejection.**

The Forgotten Impulse: Motion Begins with a Push

Every projectile, whether a stone, a ball, or a satellite, moves in a curved path because of two factors:

- A **pressure impulse force** that creates horizontal momentum.
- A **gravitational pull** that bends the path into a curve.

Galileo's parabolic motion experiments demonstrated this centuries ago. Orbital motion is nothing more than projectile motion on a cosmic scale.

Planets, moons, and stars did not inherit motion from a nebula—they were **pushed into motion** by pressure impulse forces strong enough to overcome gravity, yet balanced enough to result in stable orbits instead of escape or collapse.

29.2.1 What Is Pressure Impulse Force?

Pressure impulse is the only force that initiates motion in matter. It arises when internal pressure within a body exceeds its structural limit, forcing matter outward. In stars, this may occur through:

- Superheated plasma ruptures (e.g., coronal mass ejections),
- Explosive events such as supernovae.

This force acts only at the moment of ejection. Afterward, the expelled body carries momentum, continuing in motion until altered by gravity or resistance.

29.3 The Logic of Mass Ejection

A massive pressure-driven ejection leads to three possible outcomes:

1. **Impulse Exceeds Escape Velocity**
- The ejected body leaves the gravitational field entirely.
- Example: rogue stars, interstellar objects.
2. **Impulse Is Insufficient**
- The expelled material falls back to the source.
- Example: failed stellar eruptions or collapsing loops.
3. **Impulse Balances Gravity**
- The expelled body enters a stable orbit (circular, elliptical, or oblong).
- Example: planets, moons, asteroid belts.

This is the universal principle: **no orbital motion is possible without an initiating pressure impulse.**

29.4 Implications for Planetary Formation

The solar system is best understood as the aftermath of a massive ejection event from the early Sun. The Sun likely underwent a restructuring phase—similar to a contained supernova or a colossal coronal eruption—that expelled vast masses outward. Each fragment acquired unique momentum and spin depending on:

- Its mass,
- Its angle and direction of ejection,
- Tangential impulse at the point of release.

This explains anomalies that the Nebular Theory cannot. For example:

- **Venus** spins retrograde,
- **Uranus** spins on its side,

yet both orbit the Sun in the same direction as other planets. These irregularities make sense if planets were independent ejections, not passive condensations from a uniformly spinning cloud.

29.4.1 Angular Momentum: Consequence, Not Cause

Conventional models place angular momentum at the center of cosmic mechanics, as if it were the origin of motion. But angular momentum is not a cause. It is a **form of momentum already acquired**—a consequence of a tangential impulse.

If the Nebular Theory were correct, all planets would share aligned spins and orbits. Instead, we observe retrograde rotations, extreme axial tilts, rogue planets, and non-uniform orbital speeds. These features demonstrate that angular momentum cannot explain cosmic motion.

The only consistent explanation is that pressure impulse events—physical, directional, and varied—initiated motion individually.

29.5 Formation Hierarchy of Matter by Massive Mass Ejection

The universe organizes its visible structure through a cascade of ejective events.

Every massive mass ejection, whether from a galactic core or a stellar interior, produces successive generations of matter that differ in density, temperature, and orbital permanence. The process is not random. Each level follows naturally from the one before it—gravity shaping the outcome of pressure impulse, and pressure impulse supplying the motion that gravity later tames.

At the highest level, dense nuclei are expelled from the parent core with enormous energy. Some of these nuclei become independent gravitational systems—future galaxies or globular-cluster cores. Subsequent ejections form stellar bodies, planetary systems, and finally the finer debris that populates interplanetary and inter stellar space.

What we observe today as asteroids, comets, and diffuse dust are the long-lived remnants of those ancient eruptions. Their behavior reveals the transitional boundary between bound and unbound matter. Asteroids and short-period comets remain marginally stable, still obedient to stellar gravity but vulnerable to perturbations that may alter or erase their orbits.

Dust clouds, on the other hand, occupy the half-way state between independence and reintegration: gravitationally influenced yet not locked in steady revolution. Over millions of years they drift, merge, or fall back toward larger bodies, slowly replenishing the reservoirs from which new formations will again arise.

The following hierarchy summarizes this continuous sequence—from the densest self-bound cores to the most tenuous reintegrating matter. The hierarchy of bodies formed by massive mass ejection are shown in a table below. Table 29.1.

Table 29.1 Hierarchy of bodies produced by massive mass ejection.

EJECTION LEVEL	RESULTING BODIES	GRAVITATIONAL CONDITION	ORBITAL / EVOLUTIONARY BEHAVIOR	EXAMPLES
1 —Primary Core Ejecta	Dense nuclei retaining internal fusion	Self-bound; act as independent cores	Remain stable for billions of years	Galactic cores, globular-cluster cores

EJECTION LEVEL	RESULTING BODIES	GRAVITATIONAL CONDITION	ORBITAL / EVOLUTIONARY BEHAVIOR	EXAMPLES
	and gravity			
2 — Secondary Stellar Ejecta	Stars formed from primary core ejections	Bound to galactic core	Maintain steady orbits; centers of secondary systems	The Sun and other stars
3 — Tertiary Planetary Ejecta	Massive condensations from stellar explosions	Bound to stellar gravity	Follow stable elliptical orbits for billions of years	Planets, major moons
4 — Quaternary Boundary Bodies	Residual solid fragments from planetary or stellar ejecta	Weakly bound to stellar gravity	Some maintain long-term orbits; others perturbed into new paths	Asteroids, short-period comets (e.g., Halley)
5 — Diffuse or Reintegrating Matter	Dust, gas, ionized plasma from dispersed ejecta	Within gravitational field but not in closed orbits	Gradually accrete into larger bodies or fall back toward cores over millions of years	Interplanetary dust, zodiacal clouds, long-period comets

The upper levels represent self-sustaining gravitational systems, while the lower levels consist of marginally bound or reintegrating material. Asteroids and short-period comets remain as boundary objects—still within gravitational influence yet vulnerable to perturbations—whereas diffuse dust and plasma clouds slowly merge back into larger cores.

29.5.1 Cosmic Structures Explained by Mass Ejection

- **Galaxies**: not smooth collapses of dust clouds, but arenas of repeated ejections from their dense cores.
- **Spiral arms**: streams of matter expelled at different times and speeds.
- **Globular clusters**: possible early ejecta from galactic cores.
- **Rogue stars**: remnants of high-velocity ejections that escaped completely.
- **Gas and dust clouds**: not passive leftovers, but slowed and recaptured ejecta from earlier events.

Even **supernovae** are not annihilations but remodeling events: outbursts that expel mass and momentum while leaving a compact core behind. Our own Sun likely originated as a secondary ejection from the Milky Way's galactic core, later stabilizing as the gravitational center of its own system.

29.5.2 Summary: The Universe Moves Because It Was Pushed

- Gravity acts only in the normal plane and can only pull.
- Pressure impulse initiates motion in all planes.
- Momentum is the continuation of that impulse.
- Orbital motion is created when gravity bends momentum without consuming it.
- Spin is imparted by tangential components of the initial impulse.
- Galaxies and solar systems are built by repeated mass ejections.
- Angular momentum is not the origin of motion—it is the outcome.

Motion is not inherited. It is caused. And the cause is Massive Mass Ejection—the moving force of the universe.

We have shown comparison between Nebular Theory vs. Massive Mass Ejection Theory in a table below: Table 29.2

Table 29.2 Comparison: Nebular Theory vs. Massive Mass Ejection Theory

ASPECT	NEBULAR THEORY	MASSIVE MASS EJECTION THEORY
Origin of Motion	Assumes inherited angular momentum from a rotating gas cloud. No explanation for where the initial rotation came from.	Motion originates from pressure impulse during massive ejections (supernova-like, coronal eruptions, or galactic core events). Every orbit begins with a push.
Role of Gravity	Central force causing collapse and structure formation. Treated as if gravity alone explains orbital motion.	Gravity is an aggregating, taming force. It cannot initiate motion but bends and sustains momentum after the impulse.
Angular Momentum	Treated as a primary cause of orbits and spins.	Recognized as a consequence of tangential pressure impulses, not a cause.
Spin and Axial Tilts	Predicts planets should spin in the same direction as the nebula's rotation. Cannot explain exceptions like Venus (retrograde) or Uranus (sideways).	Variations in spin and tilt naturally explained as outcomes of different ejection angles, impulse directions, or asymmetrical impacts.
Orbital Motion	Assumed inheritance from cloud rotation.	Seen as large-scale projectile motion: initial impulse + gravitational curvature = orbit.

ASPECT	NEBULAR THEORY	MASSIVE MASS EJECTION THEORY
Irregularities	Struggles with anomalies: retrograde orbits, rogue planets, varied speeds and inclinations.	Diversity expected: each body's trajectory depends on its unique ejection impulse.
Formation of Structures	Galaxies, stars, and planets formed by smooth collapse of rotating clouds.	Galaxies and systems shaped by repeated violent ejections: spiral arms, globular clusters, rogue stars, and captured gas clouds.
Overall Picture	Passive inheritance model, relying on assumed initial rotation.	Active, physical model where pressure impulse is the true mover, and gravity is the regulator.

Nebular Theory assumes motion, but Massive Mass Ejection explains it.

PART IV — STRUCTURE

Part IV — Structure

The final part, *Structure*, brings together all that has been established. It applies the foundational principles and active variables to the great architecture of the cosmos. Here the **Massive Mass Ejection Theory** emerges as the key to formation — showing that every star, planet, and galaxy originates through impulse and is shaped by gravity.

From the solar system to the Milky Way and beyond, motion is revealed as the builder of structure. The universe is not expanding into nothingness; it is in perpetual motion, driven by the same forces that govern a falling body on Earth. This section transforms mechanics into cosmology, uniting the heavens and the laboratory under one principle: **the universe moves because it was set in motion, and that motion endures.**

***

Dr. Sayyad Masthan Vali is an independent researcher who developed the **Massive Mass Ejection Theory**, a classical-mechanics explanation of cosmic structure. His work shows that gravity acts only in the normal plane while pressure impulse drives motion in all directions, producing dispensable momentum within bodies—the true source of locomotion. *The Universe* unites observation and reasoning to reveal how these two forces alone can account for the endless motion and architecture of the cosmos.

***

30. The Solar System Read as Motion with Causes

Opening Reflection

It is an irony of the human condition that none of us can directly witness most of the essential cosmic phenomena we seek to understand. Not in a lifetime, nor even in the full span of human history, can such events be seen unfolding in their grandeur. We must rely on reasoning, constructing reality from fragments and signs.

Perhaps only one man, Tycho Brahe, was fortunate enough to see a truly live cosmic event with his own eyes. Others — Galileo, Newton, Henry Cavendish — measured, reasoned, and inferred the laws that govern such unseen phenomena. Their work gave us windows into what cannot be directly watched.

Mathematics lends confidence to our understanding; without it, we could not distinguish between propositions grounded in reality and those that are mere fancy. Yet when the true relationship between mathematics and physics is misunderstood, confidence can become misplaced.

What we attempt here is to assemble, as faithfully as possible, the pieces handed down through generations. Some may be wrong, some right. That judgment belongs to the future. Our task is to present them clearly, grounded in observation and reason, so that truth may stand or fall on its own merit. Even without full specificity, sometimes it is necessary to speak in order to keep inquiry alive.

30.1.1 Transition into Structure

The preceding sections explored the universe's **variables** — the foundational agents that govern motion and arrangement: gravity, pressure impulse, dispensable and indispensable momentum, and matter as the carrier of these forces. We treated them in isolation, examining each for its nature, limits, and scope.

Now we enter a new domain: **structure**. Here the variables no longer stand apart but act together, producing the systems we observe — from the smallest bound bodies to the largest galactic assemblies. Our task is to trace how these forces, interacting over immense scales, give rise to cosmic architecture.

Structure is not arbitrary. It is the consequence of initial conditions and subsequent taming. **Pressure impulse initiates; gravity shapes; momentum carries forward; matter anchors the process in reality.** Planetary systems, moons, stars, galaxies, and streams are not static ornaments but dynamic arrangements, constantly evolving under these same few principles.

This is the beginning of our study into the **construction of celestial systems**, where theory and observation join to tell a single, coherent story.

30.2 Construction of Celestial Systems through Matter, Gravity, Pressure Impulse, and Momentum

When we study stars, galaxies, or the solar system, direct experimental evidence is beyond human reach. We cannot recreate such systems in the laboratory, nor watch their full formation in real time. Instead, we depend on indirect observation, accumulated experience, and the reasoning that links them together.

A compelling clue to early solar system processes lies in the Sun's corona. The corona's temperature, in the millions of Kelvin, is vastly higher than the photosphere's 3,000–6,000 K. Coronal flares, coronal mass ejections (CMEs), and intense electromagnetic disturbances all signal powerful forces below. These are not surface accidents, but visible signs of deep processes in the Sun's radiative and convective zones, driven by magnetic reconnection, plasma instability, and pressure imbalance.

In today's Sun, ejections occur daily, releasing billions of tons of matter into space. But billions of years ago, conditions may have been different. If the Sun's outer layers were once more intact and resistant to venting, energy from nuclear fusion in the core, combined with immense plasma pressure, could have accumulated over long periods. By the gas laws, rising temperature, density, and confinement would drive pressure to extreme levels. When containment finally failed, the release would not resemble a modest CME, but a **massive mass ejection** — an explosive, high-velocity discharge of matter far exceeding anything we see in the Sun today.

30.2.1 Mass Ejections

Such events could have been the initiating cause of the solar system's architecture. Matter expelled at hundreds of kilometers per second carried vast **dispensable momentum**. As it traveled outward, the Sun's gravity immediately acted as the centripetal shaping force, bending trajectories into curves. Matter itself — gases, dust, molten fragments — provided the raw material for planets, moons, asteroids, and comets. The interplay of these four variables — matter, gravity, pressure impulse, and momentum — determined the structure that followed.

30.2.2 Extension to Galactic Cores

The same mechanism need not be limited to stars. Galactic cores, formed from the earliest aggregates of primordial particles, possess far greater mass, temperature, and density. If their outer layers once confined their plasma, pressure buildup could have triggered ejections on an unimaginable scale — ejecting matter sufficient to seed entire stellar systems, globular clusters, and galactic streams. Such core ejections could offer a direct, mechanical explanation for the large-scale organization of galaxies, without recourse to exotic entities or purely gravitational collapse.

Analogies in Human Experience

The dynamics are not unfamiliar. A pressure cooker with a blocked vent builds pressure until the seal fails, releasing steam explosively. An atomic bomb shows how sudden release of confined energy produces shockwaves of immense force. These analogies, though tiny in scale, help us imagine the same principle in stellar and galactic interiors.

Reasonable Conclusion

It is therefore reasonable to conclude that massive mass ejections are not anomalies but natural outcomes of pressure dynamics in confined, high-energy systems. On the cosmic stage, they may be the missing link in explaining how straight-line ejection velocities, generated by pressure impulse, are bent by gravitational attraction into circular and elliptical orbits under the inverse-square law.

Repeated over cosmic time, this mechanism could explain not only the flat, disk-like architecture of the solar system but also the planar structures of galaxies themselves.

Though we cannot witness such ancient events directly, we can observe their scaled-down analogues — modern CMEs, supernovae, and active galactic nuclei — and reason backward to formative epochs. This reasoning, supported by gas laws and gravitational mechanics, offers a coherent and testable alternative to purely accretion-based models of cosmic structure formation.

30.3 Origin of the Solar System

The Sun is not the remnant of another star's supernova. It is our own star, with its own long history. In its early life, the Sun already moved through the Milky Way as a stable star, much like those we observe today. At a certain point, however, it underwent a **massive mass ejection**—a violent release of part of its own substance. In that event, material equal to roughly **0.2% – 2% of the Sun's present mass** was expelled outward into space.

From this ejected matter every planet, moon, asteroid, and smaller body of the solar system was formed. This was not the debris of some distant catastrophe, nor the accretion of an ancient dust cloud. It was the Sun's own material, driven outward by a powerful pressure impulse yet still held in check by solar gravity. After the ejection, the Sun stabilized with its remaining mass and continued its life as a main-sequence star.

30.3.1 The Role of Impulse and Gravity

This view challenges the prevailing nebular model, which imagines planets condensing gradually from a rotating disk of dust. Instead, we propose a **single decisive event**—one that simultaneously created the raw material and imparted the motions of the solar system.

The physics is simple: when a force acts on bodies of different masses, it imparts different velocities. In symbolic form, the velocity imparted by an impulse F over a short time Δt depends on mass m:

$$v = \frac{F \cdot \Delta t}{m}.$$

Thus, **lighter fragments acquired greater speeds**, while heavier fragments moved more slowly. This natural proportionality explains the orderly structure of the solar system.

- Dense material, with smaller velocities, remained nearer the Sun, forming the **terrestrial planets**.
- Lighter material, given greater velocities, travelled farther before settling into orbits, eventually creating the **gas giants, their moons, and more distant icy bodies**.

The **asteroid belt** marks a transitional zone. Its members possess more energy than the terrestrial planets but not enough to reach the region of the giants. They are not "failed planets," but stable remnants of the same single ejection event, caught between two regimes of motion.

A Unified Origin

In this framework, all solar system bodies share one origin. None are the products of foreign stars or chance collisions. All belong to the Sun, born in the moment of its great ejection.

Material that lacked sufficient outward velocity fell back into the Sun. What remains today are those bodies whose motion reached a stable equilibrium: gravity pulling inward, momentum carrying them forward, together forming the intricate orbits we see.

Gravity Without Escape

There is no place in the galaxy entirely free of gravity. Even at the farthest reaches, gravitational influence persists, though faintly. Within the solar system, the balance of forces is exact: the Sun's gravity binds the system, while the primordial impulse preserves motion.

The solar system is therefore not the product of slow accretion or failed experiments in planet-making. It is the outcome of a **single moment of extraordinary violence**, when the Sun itself gave birth to its family of planets, moons, and countless smaller bodies. Every orbit today carries the signature of that first impulse, balanced forever against the Sun's gravitational embrace.

30.3.2 Sun's Mass Ejection as a Cause

The Sun's massive mass ejection was not the product of random chance. It was the outcome of pressure dynamics within an unstable early heliosphere. Because the Sun is a plasma body, its outer and middle layers were able to remodel after the event, leaving little visible trace today of the extraordinary violence that once occurred.

Triggering Cause

The precise trigger cannot be observed, but the most probable cause was an extreme nuclear pressure surge deep within the Sun's core. Early in its life, the heliosphere may have been less stable, allowing internal pressure to build beyond thresholds seen in ordinary solar activity.

While the Sun regularly releases energy in solar winds and coronal mass ejections, this ancient event was far greater in scale—a single, colossal release of matter in all directions.

Scale of the Event

Today, the combined mass of all planets, moons, asteroids, comets, and dust equals only about 0.2% of the Sun's present mass. This means that before the event, the Sun was only slightly more massive than it is now.

At the moment of ejection, material was expelled at velocities on the order of hundreds of kilometers per second. The upper range likely approached **615 km/s**—yet from the first instant, the Sun's gravity pulled back on the escaping matter. The solar system was born in that contest between outward impulse and inward attraction.

A Single Event, A Common Origin

Every planet, moon, asteroid, and comet arose from that one event. There were no "failed planets" and no foreign contributions from other stars. Some material was recaptured by the Sun, but what remained found equilibrium: a balance between outward velocity and solar gravity. These survivors are the bodies we see today.

Directional Characteristics

The pressure impulse was not uniform. Denser matter, destined to form the terrestrial planets, was ejected closer to the horizontal plane of the Sun's equator, where gravity quickly tamed it into tight, near-Sun orbits. Lighter matter—including gas masses and protocometary ice—was expelled with higher velocities, often along more inclined trajectories. These bodies traveled farther before slowing under solar gravity, becoming the gas giants, their moons, and the farthest icy regions.

Impulse–Gravity Balance

The mechanics of the ejection can be expressed in the simplest terms:

$$v = \frac{F \cdot \Delta t}{m},$$

where F is the pressure impulse, Δt its duration, and m the mass of the fragment. Heavier bodies received lower velocities; lighter ones higher.

From the same instant, the Sun's gravitational pull acted with equal certainty:

$$a = \frac{GM_\odot}{r^2}.$$

Bodies launched too slowly fell back into the Sun. Those launched too quickly escaped its grip entirely. Only those within the narrow band where outward momentum and inward gravity were matched settled into orbits. The present solar system is nothing more or less than this balance, frozen in motion.

The Heliosphere as Context

Even today, the Sun's heliosphere vents mass through solar winds and smaller coronal ejections. These familiar events are the miniature echoes of the same principle. The difference is scale: ordinary releases vent fractions of mass, while the massive ejection expelled material sufficient to seed an entire planetary system.

In all cases, pressure impulse is the driver; gravity the restraining force.

A Pressure-Based View of Structure

Seen in this light, the mechanics of solar system formation illustrate a universal principle: pressure buildup and release are fundamental to cosmic structure.

- Pressure impulse provides the origin of motion.
- Mass-proportionate velocity distribution determines planetary arrangement.
- Gravity transforms straight-line ejection into stable, curved orbits.

The flat shape of the solar system, and of galaxies themselves, need not be explained by inherited angular momentum in collapsing dust clouds. They can be understood as the natural result of mass ejections constrained by rotation and gravitational geometry.

The solar system was therefore not assembled gradually from chance collisions but was created in a **single decisive moment**—a balance of violent ejection and restraint that endures billions of years later.

The **prevailing nebular hypothesis** explains planetary formation as the slow condensation of a rotating gas cloud around a young star. In this view, the conservation of angular momentum prevents all material from collapsing directly into the star. Collisions and viscosity within the disk gradually produce planetesimals, which merge to form planets.

This model places angular momentum at the center of planetary stability. Yet if angular momentum were the only force at work, the outcome would not be order but dispersion or aggregation. A rotating cloud of matter, unrestrained, would spread outward indefinitely. Angular momentum alone explains neither the compact arrangement of planets nor the stability of their orbits.

30.3.3 Gravity as the Counterforce

Stability requires a balancing force. That force is **gravity**—acting from the very first moment. Gravity is not a byproduct of motion; it is inherent to matter. Without it, particles have no reason to accumulate or remain bound. Gravity alone, however, cannot explain the origin of planetary motion. It accounts for the inward pull, but not for the outward push.

The initial velocities of planets, moons, and all solar system bodies required an active cause. That cause was the **pressure impulse force** released in the Sun's massive mass ejection.

30.3.4 Pressure Impulse as the Source of Motion

In the early Sun, nuclear pressure built to extreme levels. When released in a catastrophic ejection, it expelled material outward at velocities ranging from hundreds of meters per second to hundreds of kilometers per second. The effect of this impulse can be expressed in simple form:

$$v = \frac{F \cdot \Delta t}{m},$$

where lighter masses received higher velocities and heavier masses lower.

The ejection not only imparted translational motion but also rotational motion. Variations in angle, torque, and release velocity gave each fragment its unique spin. Just as a bowler imparts spin to a cricket ball at release, the Sun's internal dynamics imprinted **spin and inclination** on each ejected body.

30.3.5 Spectrum of Trajectories

The result was a spectrum of outcomes:

- **Dense, heavy matter** remained closer to the Sun, forming the terrestrial planets.
- **Lighter material** traveled farther before solar gravity slowed it into the wide orbits of the gas giants and their satellites.
- **Moons** formed under the same principle, their orbital velocities balanced not by the Sun's pull directly but by the gravity of their parent planets.

This framework also eliminates the need for collision-based models, such as the hypothesis of a Mars-sized impact creating the Moon. A true collision would scatter debris chaotically—either into the Sun or out of the system. The observed regularity and stability of present-day orbits are far more consistent with a single ejection event in which all solar system bodies received both motion and spin together.

The True Balance

In this model, the Sun's pressure impulse was the initiating cause of planetary motion, while gravity provided the restraining force that shaped and preserved structure. The stability of the solar system arises from the equilibrium between these two realities.

Angular momentum remains present, but it is **not the architect**. It is a secondary characteristic—an inheritance of the mechanics of ejection, preserved ever after by gravity's constant balance.

30.3.6 Pressure Impulse Gravity Model Compared with Nebular Hypothesis

The **nebular hypothesis** proposes that the Sun and planets formed from the gradual gravitational collapse of a rotating gas cloud. In this view, conservation of angular momentum shaped a thin disk, and planets condensed over millions of years.

Laplace's *Celestial Mechanics* (1829) elaborated the nebular hypothesis. My own conclusions may have been partly influenced by his reasoning, though they were reached independently through classical mechanics.

Yet when examined from first principles, this model faces serious problems. A purely rotating disk of matter would not condense—it would disperse outward indefinitely. Angular momentum alone is already secondary, not the cause of motion, nor binding. The nebular hypothesis also struggles to explain why the gas giants, made of light elements, are found far from the Sun, while dense rocky planets orbit close in. Nor does it convincingly account for the asteroid belt, the Oort cloud, or the long-term stability of planetary orbits without invoking complex, untested assumptions.

30.3.7 Pressure Impulse–Gravity Framework

In contrast, the **pressure impulse–gravity model** begins with three inseparable characteristics of matter:

- **Gravity** — inherent to all mass, existing before any motion.
- **Pressure impulse** — the active cause of motion, arising when accumulated pressure is suddenly released.
- **Momentum** — the measurable, lasting effect of that impulse, preserved until acted upon by external forces.

In this framework, the early Sun underwent a **single, massive mass ejection**. All the matter of the present solar system—rock, gas, dust, ice—was expelled in that instant. Gravity acted from the first moment, resisting the outward impulse and shaping trajectories. The effect was natural: heavier, denser material received lower velocities and remained closer to the Sun, while lighter material was thrown farther. This simple sorting explains the solar system's architecture.

- Rocky planets like Mercury, Venus, Earth, and Mars stayed near the Sun.
- Lighter gases traveled outward, forming the gas giants and their moons.

- Along the way, the giants accumulated additional matter and captured smaller bodies into rings and satellites before the Sun could strip them away.

In this model, **rings, moons, the asteroid belt, and the Oort cloud** are not "leftovers" of failed formation or late collisions. They are part of the same ejected material, stabilized by planetary capture while still young. Once captured, not even the Sun's gravity could dislodge them.

30.3.8 Mathematical Consistency of Mass Ejection Model

If the Sun expelled the solar system's matter in a single event, the ejection must obey Newton's laws. We can estimate the conditions and consequences.

The Sun's present mass is:

$$M_{\odot} = 1.98847 \times 10^{30}\ \text{kg}$$

The total mass of all planets, moons, asteroids, and comets is about **0.2–2%** of the Sun's mass. This yields an ejected mass between:

$$m_{eject} \approx 3.98 \times 10^{27}\ \text{kg (0.2\%)}$$

$$m_{eject} \approx 3.98 \times 10^{28}\ \text{kg (2\%)}$$

30.3.9 Momentum of the Ejected Material

If the characteristic ejection velocity was about **616 km/s**, then the total momentum carried by the ejecta was:

$$p = m \cdot v$$

- For 0.2% ejection:

$$\boldsymbol{p \approx 2.45 \times 10^{33}\ \text{kg} \cdot m/s.}$$

- For 2% ejection:

$$\boldsymbol{p \approx 2.45 \times 10^{34}\ \text{kg} \cdot m/s.}$$

30.3.10 Reaction on the Sun

By Newton's third law, the Sun must recoil with equal and opposite momentum. Its recoil velocity is:

$$v_{recoil} = \frac{p}{M_\odot}.$$

- 0.2% case:

$$v_{recoil} \approx 1.23 \text{ km/s}.$$

- 2% case:

$$v_{recoil} \approx 12.3 \text{ km/s}.$$

For comparison, the Sun's escape velocity at its surface is:

$$v_{escape} = \sqrt{\frac{2GM_\odot}{R_\odot}} \approx 617.4 \text{ km/s}.$$

where $R_\odot = 6.9634 \times 10^8$ m.

Thus, even in the largest case, the Sun's recoil is only about **2% of its escape velocity**—far too small to unbind the Sun from its galactic orbit.

30.3.11 Interpretation

The action–reaction symmetry is crucial: the outward momentum of the planets corresponds to the Sun's recoil. This event would have shifted the Sun's position slightly within the galaxy, but not removed it.

Meanwhile, the expelled matter, with velocities in the hundreds of kilometers per second, traveled outward until checked by solar gravity. Those fragments within the right velocity band settled into orbits—forming the planets, moons, rings, and belts we see today.

This calculation demonstrates that the **pressure impulse–gravity model** is consistent with Newtonian mechanics. It explains planetary structure and stability without relying on slow condensation from a dust disk. Angular momentum is present, but only as an inherited characteristic of the initial ejection, not as the architect of creation.

30.3.12 From Straight-Line Ejection to Stable Orbits

The expelled matter began with straight-line motion, launched in the direction from the dehiscence of the Sun. The **pressure**

impulse force is direction-independent, and so matter departed along trajectories from near-equatorial to steeply inclined.

From the first instant, gravity acted as a **normal-plane force**: always inward, always bending. Gravity never canceled motion but curved it into closed paths. Depending on initial conditions, the result was a wide range of orbital forms.

30.3.13 Orbital Shapes Determined by Velocity and Direction

Near-circular orbits arose when initial speed matched the required circular velocity at that distance. Dense material, moving slowly, was captured close in to form the terrestrial planets.

Elliptical and oblong orbits occurred when speeds exceeded circular velocity but remained below escape velocity. This is typical of comets, which travel far from the Sun before being drawn back.

Inclined orbits preserved their initial tilt. Gravity bends the path but does not erase the launch plane. This explains bodies far from the solar equator, including comets and scattered asteroids.

Spin and Axial Tilt

The same impulse that launched the planets also imparted spin. Spin is not generated in flight—it is set at release. Depending on torque at ejection, a body might:

- rotate rapidly,
- turn slowly,
- or tilt at unusual angles relative to its orbital plane.

The wide diversity of planetary spins and axial tilts is therefore not accidental; it is the fossil record of the original ejection dynamics.

30.3.14 One Mechanism, Many Outcomes

Every motion in the solar system—orbital paths, rotations, tilts—arises from two forces working together:

- **Pressure impulse** — imparting linear velocity and spin at origin.
- **Gravity** — curving those motions into bound orbits.

The solar system's diversity is not evidence of multiple processes, but the natural outcome of one coherent event acting under universal law.

30.3.15 Numerical Synthesis and Context

By quantifying ejected mass, velocities, and the Sun's recoil, we see that a massive ejection is not only possible but mechanically consistent with Newtonian principles.

The solar system's variety—dense terrestrial planets, massive gas giants, distant cometary bodies—emerges from the same origin. Each orbit, spin, and tilt is a record of that first moment, when pressure impulse and gravity together forged the system, we inhabit today. The key system parameters for the Sun and ejection event are arranged in a table below. Table 30.1 and in Table 30.2.

Table 30.1Key System Parameters for the Sun and Ejection Event

PARAMETER	SYMBOL	VALUE
Solar mass	$M_\odot$	1.98847×10^{30} kg
Solar radius	$R_\odot$	6.9634×10^{8} m
Solar surface escape velocity	v_{escape}	617.4 km/s
Fraction of mass ejected (low)	—	0.2% ($m_{eject} \approx 3.98 \times 10^{27}$ kg)
Fraction of mass ejected (high)	—	2% ($m_{eject} \approx 3.98 \times 10^{28}$ kg
Characteristic ejection velocity	v_{eject}	616 km/s
Momentum of ejecta (0.2% case)	p	2.45×10^{33} kg · p m/s

PARAMETER	SYMBOL	VALUE
Momentum of ejecta (2% case)	p	$2.45 \times 10^{34}\, kg \cdot p\, m/s$
Recoil velocity of Sun (0.2% case)	v_{recoil}	1.23 km/s
Recoil velocity of Sun (2% case)	v_{recoil}	12.3 km/s

Table 30.2 Ejection Outcomes by Body Type

BODY TYPE	RELATIVE MASS	TYPICAL INITIAL VELOCITY	FINAL OUTCOME
Terrestrial planets (Mercury–Mars)	High density, heavy	Lower velocities (< 30 km/s beyond circular speed)	Curved quickly into tight, near-circular orbits close to the Sun
Gas giants (Jupiter–Neptune)	Lower density, massive by accumulation	Higher velocities (tens to hundreds of km/s above terrestrial range)	Settled farther from the Sun, broad orbits; captured rings and moons
Asteroid belt	Mixed fragments	Intermediate velocities	Stable between terrestrial and giant regimes; not "failed planets" but natural boundary products

BODY TYPE	RELATIVE MASS	TYPICAL INITIAL VELOCITY	FINAL OUTCOME
Moons	Captured fragments of varied mass	Velocities balanced against parent planet's gravity	Stable satellite orbits once captured; record of early planetary growth
Comets & Oort cloud objects	Very low density, icy	Often near escape velocity	Long-period, inclined orbits; some escaped, others remain bound in distant reservoirs

30.4 The Solar System: A Kinematic–Gravitational Explanation

30.4.1 Trigger: A Brief, Ultraluminous Ejection

The Solar System began not with a drifting cloud, but with a violent outburst from the Sun itself. In this event, a fraction of the Sun's mass was expelled quasi-radially at velocities near the escape threshold, about $v \approx 615 - 620\ \text{km/s}$.

Simple kinematics illustrates the scale:

- To reach Earth's distance ($1\ \text{AU} \approx 1.496 \times 10^{11}$ m):

$$t \approx \frac{1.496 \times 10^{11}}{6.17 \times 10^{5}} \approx 2.4 \times 10^{5}\ \text{s} \approx 2.8\ \text{days}.$$

- To reach Neptune's distance ($30\ \text{AU} \approx 4.49 \times 10^{12}$ m):

$$t \approx \frac{4.49 \times 10^{12}}{6.15 \times 10^{5}} \approx 7.3 \times 10^{6}\ \text{s} \approx 85\ \text{days}.$$

Thus, an ejection on this scale naturally produces a months-long luminous phase as the Sun's hot core becomes briefly exposed — echoing Tycho Brahe's naked-eye supernova of 1572, which remained brilliant for many weeks.

30.4.2 Ballistic Expansion and Gravitational Taming

Immediately after ejection, matter streams outward with nearly radial speed:

$$v_0 \sim 6 \times 10^5 \mathrm{m/s}.$$

As distance r grows, the Sun's gravity acts in the normal (radial) plane:

$$a_r = \frac{GM}{r^2}.$$

This decelerates the radial component, while tangential components present at launch survive — because gravity does not act horizontally.

The outcome is **equalization**:

- Radial velocity is continuously shaved away by gravity.
- Tangential velocity v_θ persists.
- When the total orbital energy

$$\epsilon = \frac{v^2}{2} - \frac{GM}{r}$$

falls below zero, bodies become bound.

This pendulum-like principle — gravity acting only vertically, not horizontally — explains how straight-line ejecta were tamed into curved orbits.

30.4.3 Emergence of a Disc and Zoning

Even small asymmetries produce shear. Over time, the ensemble of ejected matter flattens into a disc.

- **Inner hot region:** silicates and metals survive; volatiles remain gaseous → seed of terrestrial planets.
- **Outer cool region:** ices remain stable; mass accumulates quickly → giant planets and icy satellites.

Orbital speeds follow the central potential:

$$v_{circ}(r) = \sqrt{\frac{GM_\odot}{r}}.$$

Material with tangential speed close to v_{circ} circularizes; bodies with higher or lower v_θ follow ellipses until collisions and drag damp them.

30.5 From Kinematics to Bodies

- **Coagulation:** dust grains → pebbles → kilometer-scale planetesimals.
- **Runaway growth:** gravitational focusing accelerates the largest bodies.
- **Oligarchy:** a few embryos dominate regions, clearing gaps and resonances.
- **Final architecture:** scattering, captures, and resonant locks complete the system.

At every step, the forward momentum is preserved from the original ejection. Gravity's role is never to "push" but to continuously bend radial motion into orbital form.

30.5.1 Why the Months-Long Glow Matters

The months of brilliance observed in historical "new stars" find a parallel here. As outer layers thinned, the Sun's core radiated freely. For an external observer, this would appear as a supernova-like light curve.

At the same time, those months are precisely the kinematic horizon required for ejecta traveling near 615–617 km/s to fill the Solar System's volume out to Neptune — seeding the region where gravitational taming would complete the process.

30.5.2 Observable Residues Predicted

This model naturally explains the Solar System's observed features:

- **Mild eccentricities:** from surviving tangential + reduced radial velocities.
- **Rocky inner planets, icy outer planets:** from impulse-driven zoning.

- **Asteroid and Kuiper belts:** intermediate energies and incomplete captures. There is no huge core to aggregate the small asteroid bodies. Formation of planets is not an essential requirement.
- **Resonances:** long-acting gravitational refocusing, especially with Jupiter.

30.5.3 Tides, Waves, and the Moon in Scale

The Moon's gravitational pull on Earth's surface is only:

$$a_{Moon} \approx 3.3 \times 10^{-5}\ \mathrm{m/s^2},$$

tiny compared to Earth's $9.8\ \mathrm{m/s^2}$.

Tidal bulges: arise from differential pull across Earth's diameter and Earth's rotation, not wholesale lifting of oceans.

Ocean waves: dominated by winds, pressure fields, and coastal shapes, and dispensable momentum from coasts; the Moon provides timing, not amplitude.

Thus, the Moon's role is subtle and differential, not commanding.

30.5.4 Where This Leads

Having traced the Solar System's birth to a single ejection and gravitational equalization, we can now scale the reasoning upward.

- The Sun's own orbital speed around the Milky Way (~ $230\ \mathrm{km/s}$) implies an enclosed galactic mass.
- From this, we define the Milky Way's gravitational extent and compare it with its observed disc.
- We confront the mass of Sagittarius A* and the mystery of flat rotation curves, showing how the same equalization principle applies at galactic scales.

30.6 Peculiarities of the Planetary System — Causes in a Pressure Impulse Model

Every planetary system bears the imprint of the forces and conditions present at its birth. In this model, the starting point is not a drifting gas cloud that mysteriously acquires spin, but a fully formed, gravitationally stable primary — the Sun — already exerting its pull.

The decisive event is the buildup of immense internal pressure beneath an intact heliosphere. Governed by the gas laws, this pressure increased until the outer layers could no longer contain it. Instability forced a rupture, and **pressure impulse** — a directional, mass-dependent force — expelled matter into space at high velocity.

From the first instant, this matter was already under the Sun's gravitational control. Its dispersal followed a natural law: **heavier, denser material settled into nearer orbits; lighter gases and dust traveled farther before capture**. This simple principle explains the "peculiarities" of the Solar System without invoking arbitrary initial angular momentum or distant molecular clouds.

30.6.1 Planetary Orbits

All ejected matter began in straight-line motion, as dictated by the nature of impulse forces. Gravity bent these paths into circular or elliptical orbits under the inverse-square law. The degree of eccentricity depends on three variables: the ejection angle, the initial speed, and the counteracting pull of gravity.

30.6.2 Orbital Plane Alignment

Because the heliosphere rupture occurred along a structural weakness, the ejected matter was directed preferentially into a plane. That same directional bias produced the nearly flat alignment of planetary orbits observed today.

30.6.3 Rocky vs. Jovian Planets

The pressure impulse is mass-sensitive. Dense, rocky fragments lost velocity more quickly and were captured into closer orbits, forming the terrestrial planets. Lighter gases and ices traveled farther before being curved into orbits, creating the gas giants and their retinues.

30.6.4 Spin and Axial Tilt

Spin was imparted at the moment of ejection. It depended on the irregular shapes of fragments, their precise point of release, and collisions during dispersal. Axial tilt arose from the same formative chaos. No post-formation "mystery torques" are required to explain the present variety of spins and tilts.

30.6.5 Moons, Rings, and Secondary Captures

Not all matter settled into primary orbits. Some was captured by larger bodies to form moons, rings, and minor companions.

- **Moons** – Either co-ejected with their parent at slightly different velocities (co-capture), or acquired later when a fragment's velocity fell within the capture range. Their spins and orbits preserve their initial momentum.
- **Rings** – Composed of material that failed to accrete into moons within the Roche limit, or fragments shattered later and redistributed into stable belts.
- **Asteroids and Trojans** – Matter trapped in gravitational transition zones, or stabilized at Lagrange points.

30.6.6 Kuiper Belt and Oort Cloud

The most distant and loosely bound matter remains on the Solar System's edge. The **Kuiper Belt** represents the outermost cohesive plane of the original ejection. The **Oort Cloud** consists of bodies thrown into wide, loosely bound trajectories by the same impulse mechanics.

30.6.7 The Sun's Mass Dominance

The Sun retains nearly all the Solar System's mass. The ejection, though violent, released only a fraction of the Sun's total matter. Its gravity has remained the central controlling force from start.

30.6.8 Why the Solar System Is Mostly Coplanar

At first, the ejection produced a diversity of trajectories, many at steep inclinations. Over time, **orbital filtering** eliminated unstable orbits:

- Inclined paths crossed others → leading to collisions, ejections, or deflections.
- Survivors were those in non-crossing, near-equatorial paths → gradually forming today's ecliptic. Coplanarity is therefore not evidence of a uniform disk, but the **self-selection of stable orbits** over billions of years.

30.6.9 Why the Nebular Theory Fails

The Nebular Hypothesis cannot explain:

- **Origin of motion** – How stationary dust acquired orbital speeds.
- **Present orbital speeds** – Why planets move at the precise velocities required for stability.
- **Angular momentum mismatch** – Why the Sun holds nearly all the mass but only ~2% of angular momentum.

By contrast, the Massive Mass Ejection Model explains:

- **Initial motion** – Directly from pressure impulse.
- **Orbital speeds** – From mass-dependent acceleration and gravitational braking.
- **Angular momentum** – As a consequence of ejection, not an unexplained cause.

30.6.10 Conclusion

The Solar System is the coherent outcome of a single, high-energy ejection event. Its peculiarities — orbital forms, coplanarity, planetary distribution, spins, moons, rings, asteroids, and distant reservoirs — are not anomalies or debris, but the natural consequences of **matter, gravity, pressure impulse, and momentum** acting together.

This same mechanism, scaled upward, can explain stellar systems, binaries, and galaxies, providing a unified framework for cosmic structure without reliance on speculative primordial clouds

***

A Note to the Reader

The subjects discussed in this book are wide, deep, and extremely difficult. Despite sincere effort, some ideas may appear incomplete, different from present thinking, or even mistaken. If such points exist, they are not intentional. They arise from the natural limitations of working within a vast subject that nobody fully understands.

The purpose of this work is not to close questions but to open them. Every concept offered here should be examined, tested, debated, and improved by those who come after. Progress in science has never come from perfection in a single step, but from many careful corrections over generations.

I request readers—especially students and researchers—to study these ideas with patience and an open mind. If you find inconsistencies or better explanations, please see them as part of the joint journey toward clearer understanding. Let this work serve simply as one attempt to organize foundations and encourage further inquiry.

Science grows only when we learn from every effort, whether complete or incomplete. This note is offered in that spirit.

***

31. Inconsistency of Present Theories of the Solar System and Universe

Modern cosmology presents several theories about the origin of the solar system and the universe, most notably the Nebular Theory and the Big Bang Theory. Yet neither rests on a rigorous examination of first principles. Instead, both are constructed from isolated observations, around which speculative narratives are built, without answering the fundamental question of motion: how it begins, how it persists, and how it comes to an end.

The Big Bang Theory, for instance, is based primarily on the observed redshift of distant galaxies, interpreted as evidence of cosmic expansion. But this raises unresolved contradictions. If some galaxies, such as Andromeda, are approaching us while others recede, what exactly is expanding? If it is space itself, in which direction does this growth occur, and how can we speak meaningfully of space "expanding" when every galaxy carries its own independent motion? The theory also leaves unanswered how a singular point could explode and distribute matter uniformly in all directions, while simultaneously giving rise to stable galaxies with rotational dynamics, orbits, and compositional diversity. These questions remain unsettled.

The Nebular Theory suffers from similar deficiencies. It attempts to explain planetary systems as the outcome of a collapsing, rotating gas cloud. Yet it assumes angular momentum without identifying its cause, and it collapses before the anomalies it cannot absorb. Venus spins backward and Uranus spins sideways; their very existence contradicts the claim of inherited spin from a uniform nebula. The near planarity of planetary orbits, the distinct separation of terrestrial and gaseous planets, Pluto's unusual trajectory, the varied origins of moons, and the existence of structured zones such as the Asteroid Belt, Kuiper Belt, and Oort Cloud—all these features expose the incompleteness of the theory. They are not minor puzzles, but decisive failures.

31.1 A First-Principles Inquiry into Locomotion

Rather than patching these difficulties with hypothetical constructs such as dark matter or dark energy, this work begins where the ancients began: with the foundational causes of motion. The essential questions are not new: what is the nature of matter, what forces cause locomotion, how does motion begin, how is it sustained, and how does it come to an end? These questions were posed by Anaxagoras, Aristotle, Galileo, and Newton, but never answered in full.

Our approach builds on the physical realities we have established: pressure impulse as the initiating force that gives a body velocity; momentum as the acquired and internalized motion that persists within the body; and gravity as the centripetal force that modifies and constrains motion. When these are understood, projectile motion becomes the prototype of cosmic motion. The same principles explain why some bodies return along parabolic paths, why others escape entirely into hyperbolic trajectories, and why still others settle into elliptical or circular orbits.

31.2 Addressing the Knowledge Gaps of the Solar System

The orbits of planets, whether circular or eccentric, are the outcome of the direction and magnitude of the initial pressure impulse. A projection nearly perpendicular to gravity creates a circular path, while shallow angles produce elongated or elliptical orbits. In the same way, the near-planarity of planetary paths reflects a directional ejection from the Sun, with matter expelled along a consistent angular band relative to its spin axis.

The separation of terrestrial and gaseous planets follows naturally from the mass-sensitive nature of pressure impulse. Heavier materials required less velocity to settle into nearby orbits, while lighter, more diffuse matter was driven farther out, where the Sun's gravitational pull was weaker.

The peculiar spins of Venus and Uranus are not anomalies to be excused but evidence of the independence of spin from orbital inheritance. Their unique orientations point to distinct pressure impulses or collisions at the time of their creation, each imparting a specific spin that persists to this day.

Moons, in this framework, are secondary ejecta, released from the Sun during large-scale ejections, later captured into orbit around planets by gravitational control. Their irregular distribution reflects the local interactions of mass and momentum during those formative stages.

The Kuiper Belt and Oort Cloud, far from being mysterious reservoirs, are natural limits of the Sun's gravitational influence, populated by bodies too light or too obliquely ejected to be captured into planetary orbits. Likewise, the tilts of planetary axes are explained not by inherited properties, but by the orientation of the initial impulses or subsequent impacts that fixed each planet's spinning momentum.

Even the origins of the Sun find coherence in this framework. The Sun itself may be the result of a massive ejection or condensation from the galactic core. This explains its immense size and its role as a dominant gravitational presence in the solar system. The distribution of asteroids and comets is also clarified: they are not separate mysteries but the natural remains of bodies that never coalesced into planets, or fragments broken by gravitational encounters.

31.3 Conclusion: Locomotion Explains the Structure

What emerges from this perspective is not a rejection of observation but of models that fail to explain it. The Nebular and Big Bang theories attempt to explain cosmic structure without addressing the first principles of motion, and thus fall into inconsistency. By starting with locomotion itself—how motion begins, how it is preserved, how it ends, and how it is modified by gravity, impulse, and mass—we uncover natural explanations for the architecture of the solar system.

As Aristotle reminded us, *"We do not think we know a thing until we are acquainted with its first principles and carried our analysis to its simplest elements."* This is the path we have chosen. When motion is understood through its simplest causes, the solar system and the universe no longer appear as mysteries patched by speculation, but as orderly consequences of physical principles, intelligible and beautifully clear.

31.4 Clarification on the Origin of the Sun and the Planets

It is important to distinguish clearly between the origin of the Sun itself and the origin of the solar system. The Sun predates the solar system by a very long span of time. Before the planets ever formed, the Sun was already established as a mature star and was steadily orbiting the galactic core. Its origin is independent and not directly connected to the processes that created the solar system.

The entire solar system, including both the terrestrial planets and the gas giants, was produced in a single massive mass ejection from the Sun. This ejection released roughly one to two percent of the Sun's mass, expelled in a plasma state from deep within its core. The expelled matter was not uniform: some emerged as dense plasma and solid-like accumulations, while other portions were lighter gases and more diffuse plasma. These variations in density and state explain the structural division between the terrestrial and gaseous planets.

Nearer the Sun, the terrestrial planets settled into orbits where gravitational acceleration is stronger and velocity equalization is more immediate. The same initial velocities were subject to rapid gravitational adjustments, leading to the compact orbits of Mercury, Venus, Earth, and Mars. In contrast, the gas giants began with comparable initial velocities but, being composed largely of lighter and more diffuse plasma, they traveled much farther before reaching gravitational equilibrium. During that longer traversal, they lost a greater portion of their initial speed to the Sun's pull, and thus stabilized into more distant orbits with lower orbital velocities. Their larger final sizes reflect the greater amount of lighter material available to aggregate at those distances.

In this model, all planets—whether terrestrial or gaseous—share a single origin in one massive mass ejection. The Sun itself did not form in the same event and must not be confused with the planets' origin. Moreover, because the Sun was already orbiting the galaxy before the ejection, all the ejected material naturally inherited that galactic orbital velocity. Thus, the solar system as a whole shares the Sun's prior galactic motion, without requiring any separate origin for Jupiter or any other planet.

31.5 Circular, Elliptical, and Oblong Pathways: Logic of Equalization

When a body is ejected from a primary, its path is not predetermined by abstract geometry but by the balance of two realities: its acquired momentum and the gravitational pull acting upon it. Gravity operates only in the normal plane, curving motion inward, while the ejection gives the body its forward drive. The point at which these two influences find balance is what we call the **equalization point**. The nature of the orbit depends on the **direction of motion at the moment equalization is reached**.

Near-Horizontal Equalization — Circular Paths

If the secondary body arrives at equalization with its motion directed mostly tangential to the primary, the gravitational pull curves the path into a broad, nearly circular trajectory. Even if the circle lies at a great distance, as in the case of Neptune, the essential character is circular because the motion is stabilized in the tangential direction. Distance alone does not make the path oblong; the defining quality is the predominance of tangential motion at equalization.

Inclined Equalization — Elliptical Paths

When the body approaches equalization with both tangential and radial components, the result is an ellipse. The more radial the motion at that instant, the more eccentric the ellipse. Thus, planets with moderate inclinations trace elongated but still closed paths, reflecting the mixed balance of forward momentum and inward fall.

Near-Vertical Equalization — Cometary Paths

If the secondary body reaches equalization while still traveling strongly in the radial direction, the path becomes comet-like. Such bodies plunge toward the primary at steep angles and then sweep far outward again, producing highly eccentric tracks. Their equalization was not achieved in tangential motion but in near-vertical descent, and this sets the character of their orbits.

True Oblong or Open Paths

An orbit is truly oblong—not just distant—only when the body's total motion exceeds the escape condition. In that case, gravity cannot restore a bound path, and the body escapes entirely.

In this framework, the geometry of circles, ellipses, and cometary curves is not an abstract imposition but a natural consequence of how and when equalization occurs. The angle of travel at the equalization point is decisive: **tangential leads to circular stability, mixed to elliptical variation, radial to cometary plunges.**

The peculiar spins of Venus and Uranus are not anomalies to be excused but evidence of the independence of spin from orbital inheritance. Their unique orientations point to distinct pressure impulses or collisions at the time of their creation, each imparting a specific spin that persists to this day.

The Kuiper Belt and Oort Cloud, far from being mysterious reservoirs, are natural limits of the Sun's gravitational influence, populated by bodies too light or too obliquely ejected to be captured into planetary orbits. Likewise, the tilts of planetary axes are explained not by inherited properties, but by the orientation of the initial impulses or subsequent impacts that fixed each planet's spinning momentum.

The distribution of asteroids and comets is also clarified: they are not separate mysteries but the natural remains of bodies that never coalesced into planets, or fragments broken by gravitational encounters.

31.6 Massive Mass Ejection: The Tycho Brahe Analogy

The Need for an Initial Impulse

The origin of the Solar System cannot be explained by static accretion or abstract angular momentum inherited from a rotating cloud. Orbital motion demands real, measurable velocities at the moment of formation. The only physically consistent cause for such velocities is a massive mass ejection from the Sun, forceful enough to hurl material outward while keeping it gravitationally bound.

Tycho Brahe's Supernova of 1572: A Historical Record

In November 1572, Tycho Brahe witnessed a sudden, dazzling light in Cassiopeia — a "new star" that rivaled Venus and persisted for months. Modern astronomy identifies it as a supernova, but Tycho's observation, made without telescopes, carried revolutionary weight: it proved that the heavens were not immutable, as Aristotle had claimed, but dynamic.

From a physical perspective, the brightness and persistence are best explained as a **pressure-impulse event**: the sudden exposure of a stellar core, radiating immense energy while ejecting material at extraordinary speeds. The prolonged glow reflected both the expansion of plasma into space and the sustained radiation from the revealed hot core.

Applying Tycho's Lesson to Our Sun

If we imagine the young Sun undergoing a similar, though smaller, event, the Solar System's structure becomes physically coherent:

- **Ejecta speed near 617 km/s** would carry material to Earth's distance (1 AU) in ~3 days, and to Neptune's orbit (~30 AU) in ~85 days.
- These timescales mirror Tycho's months-long brilliance, when luminous plasma expanded and gradually thinned.
- The initial momentum imparted in this moment supplied every planet, moon, and asteroid with the forward velocity needed for stable orbits.

Thus, the Solar System's architecture is the fossil record of a single violent event — an ejection that set bodies in motion, while the Sun's gravity shaped their paths into long-lived ellipses.

Momentum–Gravity Equalization

The orbits themselves can be understood as the continuous exchange between two factors:

- **Dispensable momentum** — imparted at ejection, driving the outward motion.
- **Gravitational pull** — decelerating radial motion but leaving tangential momentum untouched.

At perihelion, momentum peaks and carries a planet outward; at aphelion, gravity dominates and draws it back. This alternating exchange creates the elliptical orbits described by Kepler, but now explained in mechanical terms.

31.7 The Jupiter–Sun Barycenter Misconception

Popular descriptions often claim that Jupiter is "so massive that the Sun orbits their shared center of mass." While mathematically valid in a two-body system, this is dynamically misleading:

- Jupiter is <0.2% of the Sun's mass.
- The Sun's galactic orbit (~230 km/s) is determined solely by the Milky Way's central core.
- The barycentric wobble is a small internal oscillation, not a fundamental displacement of the Solar System's center.

The **Sun remains the Absolute Primary Body** of the Solar System; no planet redefines its central gravitational role.

Conclusion: Tycho's Event as a Cosmic Blueprint

Tycho's "new star" was not only a turning point in human thought but also a living demonstration of the type of event that shaped our Solar System. A massive pressure-impulse ejection from the Sun:

- Supplied the initial velocities that planets still carry.
- Distributed matter by density and speed.
- Fixed spins, tilts, and orbital inclinations at birth.
- Allowed gravity to tame but never originate the motion.

The Solar System is thus the enduring consequence of one coherent, violent, but natural process: a massive mass ejection, governed by the same physical laws that illuminate the sky in supernovae.

32. Why Don't We Feel the Earth's Motion?

The question of why we do not feel Earth's motion is ancient. Aristotle himself raised it: *If the Earth were spinning or moving, should we not feel it?* In his reasoning, the absence of sensation proved that Earth must be stable and fixed.

Today we know Earth both spins and orbits the Sun, yet the question remains natural: if Earth is racing around the Sun at nearly **30 km/s** and spinning once every day, why do we feel no such motion?

Smooth Motion and Shared Momentum

A simple analogy helps. When you ride in a car at 100 km/h, or fly in an airplane at ten times that speed, you feel calm motion as long as the ride is smooth. Only acceleration, braking, or turbulence creates a sensation of movement.

Earth behaves like the smoothest possible vehicle. It moves through space together with its atmosphere and everything on its surface. There is no resistance, no turbulence, no external force that would shake us into awareness. Every object—land, ocean, air, and ourselves—shares the same momentum uniformly. That is why we feel nothing of Earth's enormous speed around the Sun.

The Spin of the Earth

At the equator, Earth's spin produces a surface speed of about 463 m/s (over 1,600 km/h). This seems gigantic—over 40 million meters of rotation per day—yet it remains imperceptible.

To understand why, consider the inward pull of gravity compared with the outward push of rotation. The spin produces a small outward "centrifugal" acceleration of only **0.0337 m/s^2**, while gravity pulls inward at **9.81 m/s^2**. Gravity is therefore about **290 times stronger** than the spin's outward effect.

In simple terms: Earth would need to spin almost three hundred times faster before the outward force even balanced gravity. Only then would we begin to feel weightless at the equator. Since Earth spins far more slowly, gravity overwhelms the effect, and we remain securely grounded.

The Deeper Lesson

We do not feel Earth's motion because:

- All matter on Earth shares the same momentum.
- Space offers no resistance to create turbulence.
- Earth's spin is far weaker than the pull of gravity.

What felt to Aristotle like proof of Earth's stillness is, in fact, the opposite: it is evidence of smooth, balanced locomotion governed by physical law. The stillness beneath our feet is not the absence of motion, but the perfection of it.

33. Origin of the Moon: Dynamics Beyond Impact Theory

The Moon's origin has long been debated, often framed through two traditional models: the Giant Impact Hypothesis and the Nebular Hypothesis. Both appear persuasive in their simplicity, but neither survives when tested against the fundamental laws of motion, gravity, and energy.

33.1.1 Why the Giant Impact Hypothesis Fails

The Giant Impact Hypothesis imagines a Mars-sized body, Theia, colliding with early Earth, with debris coalescing into the Moon. But this scenario collapses under closer scrutiny:

- **Relative velocity problem** – If Theia came from behind Earth in its orbit, their relative speeds would be too small, producing a low-energy collision more likely to merge than to eject a Moon's worth of mass. If it came from the outer solar system, it would orbit the Sun rather than strike Earth. If interstellar, its velocity would be so high that it would pass through without capture.
- **Earth's solar orbit problem** – An impact powerful enough to eject one-sixth of Earth's mass would also alter Earth's velocity around the Sun, destabilizing its orbit. The Giant Impact model ignores this consequence.
- **Solar gravity problem** – Debris around Earth would be strongly influenced by the Sun's gravity; most would escape long before forming a stable Moon.

The hypothesis therefore depends on a sequence of improbable conditions—perfect impact angle, perfect timing, perfect retention of debris—making it physically implausible.

33.1.2 Why the Nebular Hypothesis Fails for Moons

The Nebular Hypothesis imagines moons forming from smaller "mini-nebulae" around each planet. But such disks could not persist in the Sun's strong gravitational field; solar pull would strip them away before they condensed. Thus, the model cannot explain the origin of moons in the solar system, including our own.

33.1.3 Velocity as the Decisive Factor

The Moon's existence is best explained by **capture mechanics**. At the Moon's present distance, Earth's escape velocity is about **1.44 km/s**. The Moon's current orbital velocity is **1.02 km/s**—comfortably below escape speed, yet high enough to avoid falling inward.

If the Moon's velocity at encounter had exceeded ~12 km/s (Earth's escape velocity near its surface), it would have escaped entirely. If much lower, it would have been drawn into the Sun. Capture was possible only within a **narrow velocity window**—a balance between binding to Earth and resisting solar pull.

Importantly, Earth itself has no internal process capable of ejecting a Moon-sized body into perfect orbit. The Moon could not have been "born" from Earth; it must have been captured.

33.2 Rings and Moons: A Wider Pattern

The Moon's capture is not unique. The gas giants exhibit the same principle: many of their moons and rings are captured fragments.

Planetary rings in particular orbit at speeds that do not synchronize with the planet's orbital motion around the Sun. This shows that once captured, their dynamics are governed almost entirely by the planet, not by the Sun. Jupiter's system illustrates this clearly: some moons orbit faster than Jupiter itself moves around the Sun, yet remain bound.

Our Moon follows the same logic. Once captured, it became fully Earth's satellite. The Sun, while dominant at cosmic scales, acts only as a distant perturbation here.

33.2.1 The Moon's Special Case

The Moon's capture required a precise balance. Its speed had to be low enough for Earth to bind it, yet high enough to avoid falling sunward. Without this exact balance, the Moon would not exist today—it would have been lost into the Sun or into interplanetary space.

Its composition reflects the same solar origin as all solar system bodies—born of the Sun's great mass ejection—but its **dynamical history is unique**. The Moon endures not because it formed from Earth, but because Earth became its gravitational master at just the right moment.

The Moon's origin is best understood as the product of **celestial mechanics**: a captured body whose velocity fell within a narrow, life-permitting range. Once bound, it became independent of the Sun's control and has traveled with Earth ever since.

33.3 Earth–Moon Orbital Dynamics and Gravitational Interactions

The orbital motion of the Moon around Earth is governed by the balance between Earth's gravitational pull and the Moon's horizontal momentum. Newton's law of universal gravitation gives the acceleration due to Earth's gravity at a distance r:

$$\boldsymbol{a = \frac{GM_{\oplus}}{r^2}},$$

where

$\boldsymbol{G = 6.6743 \times 10^{-11}\ \mathrm{m^3\,kg^{-1}}s^{-2}}$ is the gravitational constant, $\boldsymbol{M_{\oplus} = 5.9724 \times 10^{24}\ \mathrm{kg}}$ is Earth's mass.

For a body in circular orbit, the required orbital velocity is given by

$$v = \sqrt{a \cdot r} = \sqrt{\frac{GM_{\oplus}}{r}}$$

The Moon's radial distances vary because its orbit is elliptical:

- Average distance:

$$r_{avg} = \mathbf{3.84 \times 10^8\ m}$$

- Perigee (closest approach):

$$r_{per} = \mathbf{3.63 \times 10^8\ m}$$

- Apogee (farthest distance):

$$r_{apo} = \mathbf{4.06 \times 10^8\ m}$$

At perigee:

$$a_{per} = \frac{GM_\oplus}{r_{per}^2} \frac{(6.6743 \times 10^{-11})(5.9724 \times 10^{24})}{(3.63 \times 10^8)^2}$$
$$\approx 3.02 \times 10^{-3}\text{m/s}^2$$
$$v_{per} = \sqrt{a_{per} \cdot r_{per}} = \sqrt{(3.02 \times 10^{-3})(3.63 \times 10^8)}$$
$$\approx 1048\ \text{m/s}.$$

At apogee:

$$a_{apo} = \frac{GM_\oplus}{r_{apo}^2} = \frac{(6.6743 \times 10^{-11})(5.9724 \times 10^{24})}{(4.06 \times 10^8)^2}$$
$$\approx 2.42 \times 10^{-3}\text{m/s}^2$$
$$v_{apo} = \sqrt{a_{apo} \cdot r_{apo}} = \sqrt{(2.42 \times 10^{-3})(4.06 \times 10^8)}$$
$$\approx 991\ \text{m/s}.$$

At average distance:

$$a_{avg} = \frac{GM_\oplus}{r_{avg}^2} \approx 2.70 \times 10^{-3}\text{m/s}^2$$
$$v_{avg} = \sqrt{a_{avg} \cdot r_{avg}} \approx 1023\ \text{m/s}.$$

Thus, the Moon's velocity varies from about **1048 m/s** at perigee to about **991 m/s** at apogee. This variation fully accounts for the elliptical form of its orbit.

33.4 Earth's Gravitational Pull on the Moon vs. Moon's Pull on Earth

The Earth exerts a gravitational force on the Moon, but by Newton's Law of Universal gravitation the Moon also exerts an attractive force on Earth. The accelerations differ, however, because of the different masses.

The Moon's mass is

$$\boldsymbol{M_m = 7.346 \times 10^{22}\ \text{kg}}.$$

At perigee ($\boldsymbol{r_{per} = 3.63 \times 10^{8}\ \text{m}}$):

- **Earth's acceleration on the Moon:**

$$\boldsymbol{a_{\oplus} \to \text{m} = \frac{GM_{\oplus}}{r_{per}^2} \approx 3.02 \times 10^{-3}\ \text{m/s}^2}$$

- **Moon's acceleration on Earth:**

$$a_m \to \oplus = \frac{GM_m}{r_{per}^2} = \frac{(6.6743 \times 10^{-11})(7.346 \times 10^{22})}{(3.63 \times 10^{8})^2}$$

$$\approx 3.33 \times 10^{-5}\ \text{m/s}^2$$

Thus, the Moon's pull on Earth is about **90 times weaker** than Earth's pull on the Moon, and nearly **300,000 times weaker** than Earth's own surface gravity ($\boldsymbol{9.81\ \text{m/s}^2}$)

This illustrates why the Moon cannot significantly alter Earth's orbital path or spin, though over very long durations its influence can lead to subtle synchronization effects.

33.5 Spin, Tides, and Earth–Moon Interactions

At the equator, Earth's surface rotates with linear velocity

$$v_{eq} = \frac{2\pi R_{\oplus},}{T}$$

where

$\boldsymbol{R_{\oplus} = 6.371 \times 10^{6}\ \text{m}}$ (Earth's radius),

$\boldsymbol{T = 86,164\ \text{s}}$ (sidereal day).

Thus,

$$v_{eq} \approx \frac{2\pi(6.371 \times 10^{6})}{86{,}164} \approx 463\ \text{m/s}.$$

The centripetal acceleration required is

$$a_{eq} = \frac{v_{eq}^2}{R_{\oplus}} = \frac{(463)^2}{6.371 \times 10^{6}} \approx 0.0337\ \text{m/s}^2.$$

This is about **297 times weaker** than Earth's surface gravity ($\boldsymbol{9.81\ \text{m/s}^2}$), so Earth's rotation only reduces effective weight by

~0.3%. That is why we remain firmly grounded despite the high surface speed.

Yet this rapid spin imparts (lag) momentum to Earth's oceans. The ocean water lags slightly behind the spinning surface, creating oscillations. These oscillations are only partially corrected by Earth's gravity, and the residual imbalance produces tides. Momentum is also created in oceans by activities like rivers inflow and atmospheric conditions all the time. This inflow of momentum creates momentum at oceans basins which is not controlled by the normal plane activity of the gravity.

The Moon's own gravitational acceleration on Earth (~ $\mathbf{3.3 \times 10^{-5}\ m/s^2}$) is real but minuscule, incapable of directly producing the magnitude of ocean tides. Instead, it plays a role in modulating and phase-locking tidal cycles rather than generating them outright.

33.6 Understanding Orbit Shape from Momentum Balance

The Moon's orbital form is a direct result of momentum balance:

- If its horizontal velocity is exactly equal to the circular value

  $$v = \sqrt{\frac{GM_{\oplus}}{r}},$$

  the orbit is circular.
- If its velocity is slightly less, the orbit becomes elliptical.
- If much less, the orbit becomes highly elongated (as in comets or meteoroids).

Thus, orbital shapes are not mysterious—they are the mechanical outcomes of imparted momentum interacting with gravitational control. At every point along the orbit, the instantaneous velocity and acceleration fully determine the path.

Conclusion

The Earth–Moon system demonstrates the fundamental principles of celestial locomotion:

- The Moon remains in orbit because its imparted horizontal momentum balances Earth's gravitational pull.
- The Moon's gravitational influence on Earth is real but extremely weak compared with Earth's own gravity.
- Tides arise primarily from the momentum and lag of the ocean water relative to Earth's spin, with lunar gravity contributing as a secondary modulating effect.
- All orbital forms—circular, elliptical, or elongated—are determined by the balance between initial momentum and gravitational control.

These relationships reinforce the principle that **motion is not an inherent property but an imparted reality, quantified and governed by pressure impulse, momentum, and gravity**.

33.7 The Moon's Motion and the Misconception of Tidal Locking

One of the most persistent claims in astronomy is that the Moon is "tidally locked" to Earth—rotating once per month so that the same face always points toward us. At first glance this seems consistent with observation, but closer reasoning shows that this explanation introduces unnecessary complexity to describe a much simpler reality.

If the Moon Were Truly Spinning

If the Moon rotated on its own axis once every month, then over two weeks we should gradually see half of its far side, and over a full month we should see all of its surfaces. This never happens. Instead, the same hemisphere faces Earth continuously—night after night, year after year. This is not evidence of rotation, but of its absence.

Straight-Line Motion Curved by Gravity

The Moon's motion is better understood as straight-line momentum continually bent into a curve by Earth's gravity. Gravity does not generate spin; it acts in the normal plane, pulling a moving body toward the attracting center and curving its path.

Because the Moon maintains the same orientation in space while traveling along this curved orbit, we always see the same face. What is often described as "rotation" is simply the geometry of curved motion without intrinsic spin.

This principle echoes Newton's first law: a body in motion continues in a straight line unless acted upon. In the Moon's case, Earth's gravity provides the inward pull that curves the path while leaving the Moon's orientation unchanged.

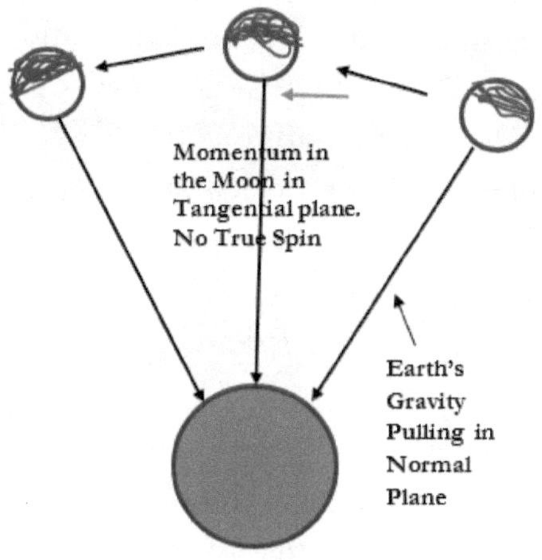

Figure 33.1Moon Orbit Around the Earth — Straight Line Motion of Impulse Momentum curved by Earth's Gravity; No True Spinning.

Why "Tidal Locking" Is Misleading. Figure 33.1.

The term "tidal locking" assumes that the Moon actively spins and that its spin has slowed to match its orbital period. But no such spin exists to match. The constant orientation of the Moon is not the product of braking or synchronization but of the absence of rotation altogether.

Spin Is Created by Pressure Impulse, Not Gravity

True rotation about an axis occurs only when a body receives a pressure impulse that imparts torque. Planets like Earth, Jupiter, and Saturn spin because they were struck by powerful torque like impulses during their birth.

A body that never receives such an impulse will not rotate. Gravity cannot start spin—it curves motion, it does not twist bodies. The Moon does not rotate because it was never given that original impulse.

A Universal Principle for All Motion

The Moon's behavior reflects a universal law:

- **All motion begins with a pressure impulse.**
- **Gravity curves that motion in the normal plane.**

This principle explains not only moons and planets but also the long-term stability of comets, asteroids, and stars in galaxies. Space itself contributes nothing—it is a passive stage. Matter interacts only with matter, through momentum and gravity.

Minor wobbles in a body's orientation are better explained by irregularities in its mass distribution or internal structure, not by mysterious effects of "space."

Gravity Pulls in the Normal Plane: The Universal Geometry of Motion

One of the most overlooked truths about gravity is its unwavering directionality. Gravity always acts along the line joining the centers of mass of two bodies. This is the normal plane—perpendicular to the tangential direction of motion.

- For a planet orbiting a star, the force vector points to the star's center.
- For a droplet falling to Earth, the vector points to Earth's center.
- For a star orbiting a galactic core, the pull points to the core's center.

This makes gravity a **centripetal force**: it governs curvature, not forward speed.

Every orbit has its own equatorial plane, defined not by some universal ecliptic but by the unique relationship between body and primary. From Earth, we see the Moon's orbit relative to Earth's equator. From the galactic core, each star's orbit is measured relative to its own orbital plane. The geometry is always local and precise.

Why This Matters

Astronomy diagrams often flatten everything into one reference plane, masking the individuality of each orbit. In truth, gravity works on each body with absolute precision, curving motion without disturbing tangential speed. This universality is what makes orbital stability possible, from Saturn's rings to galactic spiral arms.

Matter shapes matter. Space itself is empty; it neither resists nor generates motion. The ordered paths we observe over centuries and millennia are not maintained by "tidal locking" or "spatial resistance," but by the geometry of gravity pulling in the normal plane on bodies endowed with momentum from their original impulses.

Conclusion

The Moon does not spin. It travels along a straight-line path that Earth's gravity continually bends into an orbit, keeping the same face toward us. Spin never arises from gravity; it always requires a pressure impulse. What astronomers call "tidal locking" is not a special gravitational trick, but the natural outcome of unspun motion in a curved path.

Recognizing this corrects a long-standing misconception and unifies the mechanics of all motion—from moons and planets to comets and galaxies—under the same fundamental principles: **impulse, momentum, and gravity acting in the normal plane**.

34. Satellite Systems and Rings: Small Laboratories of the Same Rule

The families of moons and rings around giant planets are small, neat laboratories. They obey the same equality as everything else: at any radius r from the primary, the circular speed is $v = \sqrt{GM/r}$, and the inward pull is $a = GM/r^2$. Nothing new is required. What changes is the scale.

In our view, these systems record two steps. First came **pressure impulse** events (ejections, breakups, impacts) that gave fragments their straight-line motion and, in some cases, true spin. Then **gravity**—acting only in the normal (radial) direction—curved those lines into the tight, fast paths we see near massive planets. Because impulse is mass-sensitive, fine material travels farther and spreads more easily; heavy clumps stay nearer unless they were strongly pushed. The result is a sorted family: inner dense moons, faint wide rings, and many small pieces that follow the direction and strength of their first push.

34.1 Jupiter's rings — the same equality on display

This table shows how the **required circular speed** falls as radius grows. The match to our earlier values is the point: it's the same rule, just closer to home. Table 34.1.

Table 34.1 The Same Rule: Acceleration Velocity Equalization

ZONE / RADIUS FROM JUPITER'S CENTER (M)	$a = GM/r^2$ (M/S²)	$v_{circ} = \sqrt{GM/r}$ (M/S)
Main ring inner: 1.230×10^8	8.3738	32,093.17

ZONE / RADIUS FROM JUPITER'S CENTER (M)	$a = GM/r^2$ (M/S²)	$v_{circ} = \sqrt{GM/r}$ (M/S)
Main ring outer / Amalthea inner: 1.2894×10^8	7.6200	31,345.23
Amalthea outer / Thebe inner: 1.8135×10^8	3.8521	26,430.57
Thebe outer: 2.219×10^8	2.5729	23,893.87

How to read this table

Near Jupiter, gravity's inward pull is strong, so the required circular speed is high. As r increases, the inward pull weakens and the required speed falls. Dust and small fragments that were given enough tangential motion during ejection or breakup can occupy these paths; heavier pieces need stronger impulse to be this far out.

Why this matters for our story

Rings and moon families make the pendulum → orbit bridge easy to see. The same equality $v = \sqrt{GM/r}$ that timed a swing and set our Solar-System table also sets the speeds in these tight laboratories. The cause is the same, too: pressure impulse creates the tangential motion; gravity curves it. Spin shows up where torque was applied; where there was no torque, fragments do not gain true spin even though they move around the primary.

Conventional view (for reference): Standard explanations treat rings as debris disks shaped by collisions, tides, and shepherd moons, with motions described by Kepler's law. We keep the same measured speeds but read their origin as **impulse first, gravity after**, and we treat spin as a created state, not a by-product of gravity.

34.2 Small Bodies: Asteroids, Comets, and the Edges of Control

Small bodies keep the same acceleration and momentum equivalence. In our view, a strong ejection from the Sun gave fragments straight-line motion. Gravity then curved those lines into paths. Because pressure impulse is mass-sensitive, small pieces gained higher speeds and could travel farther before gravity turned them. Heavy pieces stayed closer unless they received a very strong push. This is why we find dense rocky populations inward, broad belts and families outward, and finally a very distant, slow population on the edge of the Sun's effective control.

The same equality holds everywhere: at distance r from the Sun, the circular speed is $v = \sqrt{((GM_\odot)/r)}$, and the inward pull is $a = GM_\odot/r^2$. Nothing else is required to read any belt or cloud. Where the given tangential motion is less than the local circular value, paths tighten and sink inward; where it exceeds that value, paths stretch outward and can enter slow escape.

Comets show the pressure impulse even more clearly. This is exactly our story: impulse creates or modifies spin; impulse creates or modifies tangential motion; gravity curves whatever motion exists in the normal (radial) direction.

Reading the belts with one glance

Closer in, the required circular speed is large; far out, it becomes small. Our earlier tables already showed this for the Kuiper Belt and Oort Cloud. Here is a compact summary that matches those numbers and is easy to see. Table 34.2.

Table 34.2 Circular speeds for major planets and belts

ZONE	REPRESENTATIVE RADIUS r (M)	$a = GM_\odot/r^2$ (M/S^2)	$v_{circ} = \sqrt{GM_\odot/r}$ (M/S)	v_{circ} (KM/S)
Earth's orbit (for scale)	1.496×10^{11}	5.93×10^{-3}	29 784.7	29.78
Jupiter's orbit (for scale)	7.785×10^{11}	2.19×10^{-4}	13 056.7	13.06
Kuiper inner edge (~30 AU)	4.488×10^{12}	6.59×10^{-6}	5 437.9	5.44
Kuiper outer edge (~50 AU)	7.479×10^{12}	2.37×10^{-6}	4 212.4	4.21
Oort inner shell (~2 000 AU)	2.992×10^{14}	1.48×10^{-9}	666.0	0.666
Oort far shell (~100 000 AU)	1.496×10^{16}	5.93×10^{-13}	94.19	0.094

How to read this table

As r grows, the inward pull a falls as $1/r^2$, and the circular-equivalent speed falls as $1/\sqrt{r}$. If a fragment out near 30–50 AU still carries tangential motion above the local circular value, it will not tighten into a small circle. It will keep almost the same speed for a long time — a flat segment in a speed–radius plot — and it may be in slow escape if the Sun's pull is no longer strong enough to bend it back on realistic timescales.

What belts and clouds tell us

The main asteroid belt records modest pushes and heavy material: many short and moderate ellipses, organized by the same equality $v = \sqrt{(GM/r)}$. The Kuiper Belt records lighter material driven farther before turning, with low required speeds and gentle curvature. The Oort Cloud marks the outer limit of effective control: speeds are very low, curvature is extremely gentle, and a small extra push can change a path from bound to slow escape.

Conventional view (for reference): Standard cosmology treats belts as leftovers from a cooling protoplanetary disk and explains comet jets as surface outgassing with small "non-gravitational" forces. We keep the same measurements but read the system as **impulse first, gravity after**: mass-sensitive ejection sorted material by how far it could go before the Sun's pull curved it; jets are present-day examples of pressure impulse altering spin and path.

Table 34.3Mean Distances and Speeds of the Planets

PLANET	DISTANCE R (AU)	SPEED V (KM/S)
Mercury	0.387	47.87
Venus	0.723	35.02
Earth	1.000	29.78
Mars	1.524	24.13
Jupiter	5.204	13.06
Saturn	9.583	9.63

PLANET	DISTANCE R (AU)	SPEED V (KM/S)
Uranus	19.218	6.80
Neptune	30.11	5.43
Pluto	39.48	4.74

Table 34.4Planets' Velocities at Perihelion (Closest Point)

PLANET	r_{peri} (AU)	v_{peri} (KM/S)
Mercury	0.308	53.77
Venus	0.718	35.17
Earth	0.983	30.03
Mars	1.381	25.33
Jupiter	4.951	13.38
Saturn	9.048	9.90
Uranus	18.33	6.97
Neptune	29.81	5.46
Pluto	29.66	5.47

Table 34.5Planets' Velocities at Aphelion (Farthest Point)

PLANET	r_{aphe} (AU)	v_{aphe} (KM/S)
Mercury	0.467	43.61

PLANET	r_{aphe} (AU)	v_{aphe} (KM/S)
Venus	0.728	34.91
Earth	1.017	29.55
Mars	1.666	23.07
Jupiter	5.459	12.75
Saturn	10.12	9.36
Uranus	20.11	6.65
Neptune	30.33	5.41
Pluto	49.31	4.24

How to read

Using one rule, $v = \sqrt{(GM/r)}$, the required circular speed falls as distance grows. The perihelion/aphelion tables show the same rule at the near and far points (kept in this simple "local circular" form so the numbers stay consistent with our model).

35. Captured Moons and Ring Systems: Dynamics of Secondary Companions

The origin of moons and rings throughout the Solar System follows the same mechanical principles that govern the Earth–Moon system. Once a body is captured by a planet, its motion is dictated almost entirely by the planet's gravity. The Sun's gravitational field remains present as a background influence, but it does not actively control or dislodge the captured body. This simple but decisive fact applies equally to massive moons and to the smallest ring particles.

35.1 Velocity and Capture

Capture is always a matter of velocity. A moon or ring particle must have a speed low enough, relative to the planet, to remain bound, but high enough to avoid falling directly into the planet or being drawn away by the Sun. For Earth, the upper limit for capture at the Moon's distance is an orbital speed of about 1.44 km/s. If a body exceeds the escape velocity at its encounter distance, it will depart into independent solar orbit. If its speed is much lower, it risks falling toward the Sun before capture is complete.

These thresholds apply to every planet. Jupiter, for example, has moons that orbit at speeds far greater than Jupiter's own orbital speed around the Sun. If the Sun's gravity controlled their motion, those velocities would have been forced into synchronization over time. The fact that these moons retain their speeds is proof that they are dynamically independent of the Sun's acceleration and are governed solely by Jupiter's gravity.

35.2 Rings as High-Speed Captures

Planetary rings often contain particles that orbit faster than the planet's own orbital speed around the Sun. This means the ring material was captured when the planet was still in transit to its final orbital position. During that migration, the planet intercepted debris whose velocity exceeded its own but still fell within the limits for capture. Once bound, the ring particles, like moons, became immune to solar acceleration in the sense that their orbital motion is now a closed system under the planet's gravity.

Because planets lack the immense internal energy sources of stars, they cannot generate the pressure impulses necessary to create ring systems from their own mass in place. The only realistic origin for such systems is capture. The same is true for many moons—especially those whose sizes and orbital dynamics show no signs of having formed alongside their parent planet.

35.3 Earth's Moon Capture

Earth's Moon is an example of capture under highly specific conditions. Its velocity at the time of encounter was low enough for Earth to hold it, yet high enough to avoid a slow fall into the Sun. Without this balance, the Moon could not exist in its present orbit. This makes the Moon's case unusual—not because of its composition, which, like all Solar System material, comes from the same solar core ejection—but because of the precise dynamic conditions that allowed its long-term stability.

The principle is the same for moons of other planets. Whether captured early in the Solar System's history or much later, the decisive factor is not chemical similarity to the host planet, but whether the body's motion met the narrow velocity requirements for permanent capture.

35.4 Independence from Solar Control

Once a moon or ring system is captured, the Sun's gravitational acceleration no longer dictates its motion. The planet becomes the primary gravitational master. While solar perturbations can cause small variations in orbits, they cannot strip a stable moon or ring from a planet under normal conditions. This independence explains why ring particles and inner moons can orbit their planets at speeds that seem disproportionate when compared directly to the planet's own orbital velocity around the Sun.

35.5 Conclusion: One Rule for All Captures

From the largest moons to the finest ring particles, the same rule applies: Capture occurs only when a body's velocity relative to the planet falls within a narrow, stable range. Once captured, the body's motion is governed by the planet's gravity, with the Sun reduced to a distant perturbing influence.

The Moon, the moons of the outer planets, and every ring system in the Solar System are variations on this same physical theme. The origin stories differ in detail, but the underlying mechanics—velocity thresholds, gravitational dominance, and the absence of solar control post-capture—are universal. This dynamic unity binds the smallest ice fragment in Saturn's rings to the largest captured moon of Jupiter, and it is the same unity that holds our own Moon as Earth's steadfast companion.

35.6 Tides, Day Length, and What Only Appears to Change

In our view, gravity acts in the normal (radial) direction and does not create spin. Spin comes from pressure impulse and torque. This single idea helps to sort out three common topics that are often mixed together: tides, day-length variations, and the illusion of changing spin near and far from the Sun.

Tides as a contest of motions

Earth's solid body spins once a day. At the equator that means about 463 m/s of sideways motion. The oceans are not rigid; large water masses lag slightly behind this spin and slosh under gravity's inward pull. Earth's own inward acceleration near the surface is about 9.8 m/s^2. The Moon's inward pull at Earth's distance is tiny by comparison—roughly one part in a few hundred thousand of Earth's own pull. The Sun's inward pull at Earth's distance is stronger than the Moon's but still small compared to Earth's pull on its oceans. In our reading, tides are mainly the result of oceans trying to keep up with the spinning solid Earth while gravity pulls inward; the slight leads and lags create the bulges and phase offsets that we call tides. The Moon's and Sun's pulls modulate this slosh but do not dominate it. The main reason tides continue for billions of years is dispensable momentum. There is continuous inflow of momentum from rivers flow, environmental and atmospheric pressure impulses.

Conventional view (for reference): Standard explanations attribute tides primarily to the Moon's differential (tidal) gravity across Earth, with the Sun providing a secondary modulation, and they model phase lags with friction and basin geometry. We keep the observed schedules but emphasize the spin-led ocean response under Earth's own strong inward pull and the dispensable momentum as the main causes of tides.

Day length: real stability, apparent changes

The daily spin of Earth is set by the torque history of the planet, not by the changing Sun–Earth distance during the year. When Earth is nearer the Sun (perihelion), we move faster along our path around the Sun. From our viewpoint, that can make the spin look "quicker"; at aphelion, it can look "slower." But the axial spin itself remains set by past impulse at the time of origin of the earth and internal balances. What changes is the way we *perceive* the timing because our orbital speed changes with distance. The pendulum analogy helps: the bob's spin does not change; what changes is how fast the bob passes a mark when the path geometry changes. In space, the same equality that sets orbital speed, $v = \sqrt{(GM/r)}$, tells us why the near part of the path feels faster and the far part slower even if the spin state itself is steady.

Conventional view (for reference): Standard geophysics acknowledges small, long-term changes in Earth's rotation from internal mass shifts and tidal friction; seasonal "length-of-day" signals are explained by exchanges of angular momentum with the atmosphere and oceans. Our emphasis here is the reader's intuition: the yearly near–far change alters *appearance* through orbital speed, not by gravity "turning the spin knob."

Why gravity cannot create spin

A uniform inward pull produces no torque. It bends straight-line motion inward but does not twist a body about its axis. Only an applied torque—a pressure impulse with a lever arm—can start true spin. That is why a bowled ball or a jetting comet can begin to rotate, and why planets with obvious rotation must have received torque in their history. Where no such torque was applied, there is no independent spin to change. In these cases, any "rotation" we think we see is a way of describing the path, not a separate axial motion.

Conventional view (for reference): Many texts explain spin histories with angular momentum inherited from a spinning protodisk and later tidal torques. We keep the observed spins but attribute each to an actual torque event (pressure impulse or encounter), not to gravity acting alone.

A quick coin-toss picture

Toss a coin upward with a steady spin. At the top it *seems* to spin more quickly because it lingers near you; near your hand it *seems* slower because it whizzes by. The spin didn't change; your vantage and the coin's path did. Planets near and far from the Sun provide the same visual trick for day length: the orbital speed changes with distance, so the passage of surface features looks different, even when the underlying spin is steady.

36. Escape, Capture, and Orphan Bodies

In our framework, one rule governs all outcomes. At a given distance r from a primary of mass M, gravity pulls inward with $a = GM/r^2$. A body keeps the tangential motion it was given by pressure impulse. If its tangential speed equals the local circular value $v = \sqrt{(GM/r)}$ it traces a circle. If it has less, the path bends inward; if it has more but still below escape, the path stretches into an ellipse. At the threshold $v_{esc} = \sqrt{2GM/r}$ the path opens and the body begins a slow departure.

36.1 Efficient reach and slow escape

Gravitational extent has no sharp edge, but its *efficient reach* is limited in practice by mass and distance. Past some radius, the inward pull is too weak to bend the path on realistic timescales. In this book we use a practical cutoff we named the **G-limit**: the distance where the inward acceleration g of the primary body falls to the numerical value of G. For the Sun this comes out near **~64 light-days**. Beyond that, the Sun can no longer effectively curve motion; a body with residual tangential speed behaves as if it is in **slow escape**, keeping nearly the same speed and showing a flat segment on a speed–radius plot.

36.2 Comets stay local to their star

By this reading, comets belong to their **resident star**. For the Sun, even the most distant solar comets remain far *inside* ~64 light-days, while **nearby stars** sit **3–4 light-years** away—orders of magnitude beyond the Sun's efficient reach. So, in our model the answer is **no**: nearby stars do **not** control or significantly perturb solar comets.

What does change a comet's path are causes *inside* the Sun's reach: small pressure impulses from jets (which can also change spin). The same holds for comets of other stars: they remain under their own star's control and are not pulled off course by distant neighbors.

Conventional view (for reference): Standard astronomy often attributes long-period comet injections to **passing stars** and **galactic tides** perturbing an extended Oort Cloud. We keep the observations (long periods, wide spreads) but assign the cause to **local impulse and encounters within the primary's efficient reach**, not to distant stars.

Capture is rare without a brake

To capture a body that arrives with excess tangential motion, something must *remove* that motion. In empty space there is no friction. Capture therefore needs a momentum sink: a pressure impulse opposite the motion, a collisional loss, or a multi-body exchange that hands momentum to a third body. Without such a brake, gravity can only curve the path; it cannot by itself make a fast passerby settle into a bound circle.

Orphan bodies

When an impulse is very strong—core ejections, close encounters—the body can exceed escape speed relative to its parent. It then travels between systems with almost constant speed, because far from any core the inward pull is tiny. These orphan bodies (planets, stars, even compact remnants) are simple consequences of the same rule: impulse first; gravity after.

How to read an outcome with one glance

Pick the controlling mass and the radius. Compute the local circular value $v_{circ} = \sqrt{(GM/r)}$.

– If the body's tangential speed is below that value, gravity dominates and the path tightens.

– If it matches, the path is circular.

– If it exceeds but is below v_{esc}, the path is a long ellipse.

– Near or above v_{esc}, the body is in **slow escape**; beyond the G-limit the primary's pull is no longer efficient and the speed looks flat with radius.

37. Reading a Path from One Snapshot

You often have only a single picture: a body at some distance r from a primary and a measured speed v. From that alone you can tell whether the path is tight and bound, a long ellipse, or already opening into escape.

The key is the **local circular value**—the speed gravity would "ask for" to make a circle at that radius:

$$v_{circ} = \sqrt{\frac{GM}{R}}$$

and the **escape value** at the same radius:

$$v_{esc} = \sqrt{\frac{2GM}{r}} = \sqrt{2}\, v_{circ}$$

Now form one simple ratio:

$$\chi = \frac{v}{v_{circ}}$$

Read it like this—just one glance:

- $\chi < 1$: gravity is stronger than the body's tangential motion at that radius; the path bends inward. You are seeing the body near or moving toward an **apocenter** of an ellipse.
- If$\chi = 1$: the path is **circular** at that radius.
- If $1 < \chi < \sqrt{2}$: the body has more tangential motion than a circle needs but not enough to leave; the path is a **long ellipse** and you are near or moving away from a **pericenter**.
- If $\chi \geq \sqrt{2}$ the body is in **escape** (an open path). Far from any strong core this shows up as a **flat speed** with radius—slow escape with nearly constant v.

That is all you need. No extra system—just the local circular value as a ruler, and the same equality the pendulum taught us.

Direction still matters

If the original push is mostly normal (radial) to the primary, the body rises and falls on a very oblong track. Many comets look this way because their projection was close to the normal direction. A purely normal push never makes an orbit; some tangential component is required to "wrap" the path.

On capture and "from other stars."

In our framework, **capture** without a brake is rare. Empty space has no friction. To capture a passerby, you must remove tangential motion—by a pressure impulse opposite the motion, by a collision, or by a three-body trade. Likewise, the common tale that comets arrive from nearby stars is, in our view, a misconception. Each star's comets live well **inside** that star's efficient reach; nearby stars are **far** outside it. So, the comet you see belongs to its **resident star**, with its very long, slender path set by a near-normal push and then curved by the resident star's gravity.

Conventional view (for reference): Standard mechanics reads the same outcomes using "specific energy" and "specific angular momentum," and it often ascribes long-period comets to distant stellar or galactic tugs. We keep the observed paths but read them with a single ruler: compare v to v_circ; impulse creates the tangential motion, gravity curves it.

A quick mental check.

At Earth's distance from the Sun, v_{circ} is about $29.8\ \mathrm{km/s}$. A body seen there moving $35\ \mathrm{km/s}$ has $\chi \approx 1.17$: a long ellipse, still bound. At the same place, v_{esc} is about $42.1\ \mathrm{km/s}$. Anything at or above that value is in escape; far from the Sun, its speed will look almost constant.

37.1 Putting It All Together (One Rule Across Scales)

Everything in this book reduces to one comparison we can do from a single snapshot. Pick the primary body and the distance r.

Compute the local circular value $v_{circ} = \sqrt(GM/r)$. If the body you are looking at has speed v, form the ratio $\chi = v/v_{circ}$. When $\chi < 1$, gravity is stronger at that radius and the path bends inward (a bound ellipse seen near apocenter). When $\chi = 1$, the path is circular at that radius. When $1 < \chi < \sqrt{2}$, the path is a longer ellipse seen near pericenter. When $\chi \geq \sqrt{2}$, the body is on an escape path and will keep nearly the same speed far from the core, because there are no brakes in empty space. The escape value at the same radius is $v_{esc} = \sqrt{\frac{2GM}{r}} = \sqrt{2}\, v_{circ}$.

Planets are the easiest place to start. At Earth's mean distance from the Sun, the circular value is about 29.8 km/s. Earth's actual speed is essentially the same, so the path is close to circular. Mercury's speed is larger when it is closer and smaller when it is farther, exactly as $v_{circ} = \sqrt{GM/r}$ demands. The ellipse is simply a record of where the given tangential motion is above or below the local circular value. Nothing more is required.

Moons and rings are the same rule in a smaller laboratory. Choose the planet's GM, pick the ring or moon distance r, compute v_{circ}, and compare with the observed speed. The numbers you already collected for Jupiter's rings fall right on $v = \sqrt{GM/r}$. The cause is still "impulse first, gravity after": a push creates tangential motion; gravity curves it in the normal direction.

Comets fit naturally. Their long, slender paths come from a projection that is close to the normal (radial) direction, plus a smaller tangential component. Near the Sun, jets can add or subtract a little speed and can add true spin because jets apply torque. But comets remain under their resident star's control. In our framework, nearby stars are far outside the Sun's efficient reach, so they do not take charge of solar comets. The same snapshot test applies: at each point, compare v with $v = \sqrt{GM_{\odot}/r}$ and you will know whether the comet is tightening, stretching, or slipping toward escape.

Clusters and streams only add one layer: the controlling mass can change with scale. Inside a globular cluster, the primary is the cluster core. Farther out, the galaxy becomes the primary. You can still read the path with the same ruler. Inside the cluster's control boundary, stars circle in the cluster's own equatorial plane. Beyond it they begin slow escape and trace a stream along the galaxy's larger path. The comparison is the same: use $M_{cluster}$ for inner stars, then use M_{gal} at the cluster's galactocentric radius. Wherever v stays above the local v_{circ}, curvature is weak and motion looks flat with radius.

Outer-galaxy stars show why flat rotation curves are not mysterious in our view. The inward pull falls as $a = \frac{GM}{r^2}$. The circular value falls as $v_{circ} \propto 1/\sqrt{r}$. If many stars far out still carry large tangential motion from earlier impulses, their v can remain roughly constant while v_{circ} falls. That means the core is no longer fully in charge at those radii. The stars are in slow escape, turning only gently. On a speed–radius plot this appears as a flat segment.

Direction completes the picture. A purely normal push never makes an orbit; it produces straight rise and fall, or escape if the speed is high enough. Orbits require a tangential component. The more tangential motion a body has at a given radius, the more the path opens; the less it has, the tighter the path. Spin, in our framework, belongs only to torque at birth or later impulse. Gravity bends lines; torque starts spin.

Conventional view (for reference) Standard mechanics uses the same numbers and writes them in the language of energy and angular momentum. It often adds dark halos to keep outer speeds flat, uses tidal locking to explain one-face moons, and traces spins to an early rotating disk. We keep the measurements but place the cause elsewhere: motion begins with pressure impulse, gravity acts only in the normal plane to curve it, and each scale has a practical reach beyond which curvature is weak and motion looks flat.

37.1.1 Putting It All Together — The One Snapshot Rule

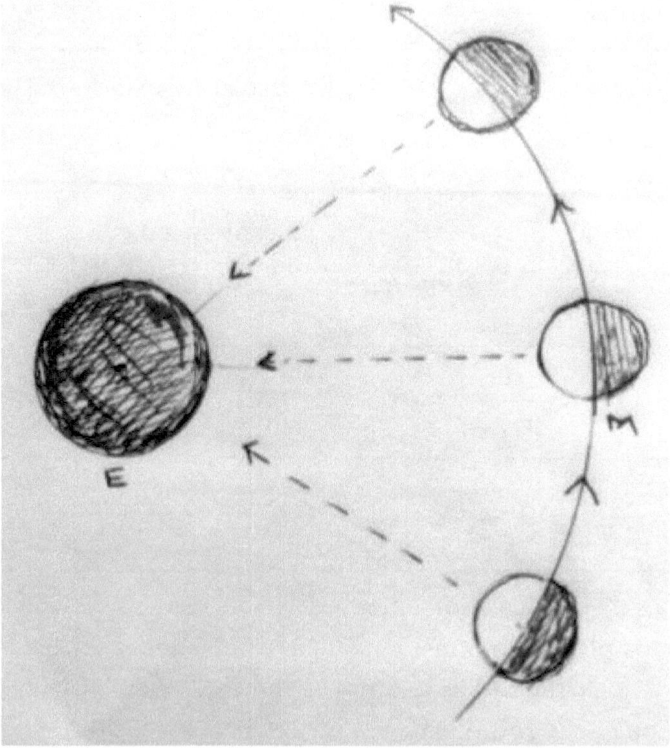

Figure 37.1Putting It All Together — The One Snapshot Rule. Each position of the secondary (M) represents a different tangential–normal balance. Gravity (dashed arrows) acts only toward the primary (E), while the initial pressure impulse provides tangential motion. Comparing the actual speed with the local circular value immediately reveals whether the body's path is closed, elongated, or escaping.

At any scale in the universe—planetary, stellar, or galactic—the path of a secondary body is determined by comparing its **actual tangential velocity** with the **local circular value** at that radius. The ratio

$$\chi = \frac{v}{v_{\text{circ}}}$$

tells the whole story. When $\chi < 1$, the motion bends inward; when $\chi = 1$, it is circular; when $1 < \chi < \sqrt{2}$, it forms an elongated ellipse; and when $\chi \geq \sqrt{2}$, the body is in escape. Figure 37.1; Table 37.1.

Table 37.1One Snapshot Rule Relation for Secondary Bodies

EQUATION	MEANING
$v_{circ} = \sqrt{\frac{GM}{r}}$	Circular (equilibrium) speed
$v_{esc} = \sqrt{\frac{2GM}{r}} = \sqrt{2}\, v_{circ}$	Escape speed at the same radius
$\chi = \frac{v}{v_{circ}}$	Snapshot ratio defining curvature
$a_{grav} = \frac{GM}{r^2}$	Local gravitational acceleration.

This "one snapshot" method is the reader's pocket tool. It works for planets, moons, comets, clusters, and galaxies. Pick the primary. Pick the radius. Compute the local circular value. Compare. The rest is vocabulary.

38. Gravitational Extent and Control Within the Solar System

Every body in the solar system has a **finite gravitational domain** — the maximum distance at which it can retain another body in a stable orbit. This boundary is defined by the point where the primary's gravitational acceleration is no longer dominant compared to competing influences. Beyond this limit, a secondary body will not be under control of the primary body.

The gravitational extent (G-limit) can be estimated by a **proportional rule**: it scales approximately with the square root of the body's mass (kg) and is measured as radial length $\sqrt{M}$m. $\sqrt{M}$m is not taken as an arbitrary value, here 'g' equals to the Universal Gravitational Constant 'G'. Within this boundary, the primary can securely bind satellites; beyond it, the satellites are lost to another center of gravity, or move independently with the dispensable momentum inside the body.

The Sun

At Earth's orbit, the Sun's gravitational acceleration is:

$$a_{\odot}(1\ \mathrm{AU}) \approx 0.00593\ \mathrm{m/s^2}$$

This exactly balances the centripetal acceleration required for Earth to maintain its orbital velocity of 29.78 km/s. At Neptune's orbit, the Sun's pull decreases to about:

$$a_{\odot}(30\mathrm{AU}) \approx 0.00059\ \mathrm{m/s^2}$$

This remains sufficient to hold Neptune, but farther out — in the Kuiper Belt and the Oort Cloud — the Sun's influence weakens. Eventually, at the outer boundary, the Sun's control gives way to the gravitational domains of nearby stars (after about 3 ly!) and, ultimately, the Milky Way core.

The Earth

Earth's gravitational acceleration at the Moon's distance is:

$$a_{\oplus}(r_{Moon}) \approx 0.00272 \text{ m/s}^2$$

This is strong enough to keep the Moon in orbit, despite the Sun's background field. Earth's gravitational domain — its **Hill sphere** — extends about 1.5 million km. Within this radius, Earth can retain satellites against the competing pull of the Sun.

The Moon: A Misunderstood Force

The Moon's gravitational acceleration on Earth's surface is only:

$$a_{Moon} \approx 3.32 \times 10^{-5} \text{ m/s}^2$$

This is about **1/300th of Earth's surface gravity** — a hundredth-of-a-meter per second squared, not meters per second squared. And yet, popular explanations of tides often present the Moon's pull as if it could lift vast volumes of water directly.

In reality, Earth's gravity overwhelmingly controls the oceans. The Moon's effect is a **tiny perturbation** superimposed upon this dominance. The height of ocean waves is governed far more by dispensable momentum in the water body, wind, atmospheric pressure, and local geography than by the Moon's acceleration.

The familiar picture of the Moon "pulling up" a bulge of water is a mathematical simplification, not a literal physical effect. Tides are better understood as the interaction of **gravitational differentials, Earth's spin, and basin momentum input** — with the Moon's weak influence modulating, not commanding, the oscillation.

Gravitational Domains in Summary

When analyzed by the square-root mass rule ($\sqrt{M}$) and by acceleration balance, ($'g'$approaches $'G'$) each primary body — the Sun, planets, and large moons — possesses a finite, measurable domain.

- Within that domain, the primary holds true orbital authority.
- Outside it, another gravitational source takes over. Or the secondary body will drift away with its dispensable momentum.

This layered arrangement defines the solar system's stability: the Sun governs the planets, planets govern their moons, and moons can govern small satellites — but always within limited, boundaries.

Recognizing these limits eliminates the illusion of **limitless gravitational dominance** and prepares us to extend the same reasoning to **star clusters, galaxies, and galactic cores**.

38.1 Milky Way Core Mass, Nature, and Gravitational Extent

Statement of the Model

We treat the Milky Way's central mass as a **sun-like plasma core** whose gravity organizes stellar orbits. The **core mass of the galaxy**—deduced from the Sun's tangential speed—sets the core's effective gravitational authority. In this view, a central black hole of only a few million solar masses (Sagittarius A*) is **dynamically negligible** at the Sun's radius and cannot by itself account for a ~100,000-light-year disc.

Core Mass from Solar Kinematics

Let the Sun's mean galactocentric radius and speed be

$$r_\odot \approx 2.57 \times 10^{20}\ \mathrm{m}\ (\approx 27{,}000\ \mathrm{ly}),$$
$$v_\odot \approx 2.30 \times 10^{5}\mathrm{m/s}.$$

Centripetal balance:

$$\frac{v_\odot^2}{r_\odot} = \frac{GM_{core}}{r_\odot^2} \Rightarrow M_{core} = \frac{v_\odot^2 r_\odot}{G}.$$

Substituting:

$$M_{core} \approx \frac{(2.30 \times 10^5)^2(2.57 \times 10^{20})}{6.6743 \times 10^{-11}} \approx 1.85 \times 10^{41}\mathrm{kg}$$
$$\approx 9.3 \times 10^{10}\ M_\odot.$$

Comparison with Sagittarius A*

Sagittarius A* has $\boldsymbol{M_{BH} \sim (4-5) \times 10^6\ M_\odot}$, over four orders of magnitude smaller than M_{core} at the Sun's position. Its gravitational dominance is confined to its immediate vicinity (light-days to light-years). The distributed core mass (hot plasma) sets the potential felt at the solar circle.

38.2 Gravitational Extent of the Galaxy

By analogy with Hill spheres, the Milky Way's **effective domain** ends where the core's inward acceleration on a test body balances competing influences (neighboring cores and the body's own tangential momentum). A core mass of order 10^{11} $M_\odot$ **comfortably supports** a disc $\sim 10^5$ ly across with bound orbits through most of that span; beyond it, bodies retain tangential momentum and drift on weakly bound or unbound paths.

Why the core glows: high surface brightness arises from **stellar crowding** and **hot plasma** in the inner kiloparsecs; no special role for Sgr A* is needed to explain luminosity at kpc scales.

Rotation Speeds Without Exotic Matter

Near-flat rotation curves outside the density peak follow naturally from:

1. **Large enclosed mass** already in the galaxy core, and
2. **Momentum retention** by stars/ejecta produced during episodic, high-energy **pressure-impulse** events.

Gravity "tames" motion within its reach but does not erase tangential momentum beyond the gravitational effective radius, yielding broad, flat curves—without invoking dark halos.

Testable Predictions and Diagnostics

- **Mass profile:** $\mathrm{M_{core}} \sim 10^{11}\ M_\odot$
- **Local field:** at $r_\odot, a = \frac{v_\odot^2}{r_\odot} \sim 10^{-10}\ \mathrm{m/s^2},$ matching the scale for long-lived near-flat speeds without a dominating point mass.
- **Event fingerprints:** past pressure-impulse ejections leave **moving groups/streams** that preserve excess tangential momentum at large r.

38.3 The Galactic Core as the Sole Source of Stellar Acceleration

38.3.1 Decisive Factor: Core Mass

Using $v_{\odot}$ and $r_{\odot}$, we infer $M_{core\prime eff} \sim 9.3 \times 10^{10}\, M_{\odot}$. Hence:

- Stellar orbits are determined by the **central core's pull.**
- Sgr A*'s few-million-$M_{\odot}$ is **negligible** at $r_{\odot}$.
- Mass within the solar radius (stars, plasma) is **co-orbiting**, not the **cause** of the Sun's acceleration.

(We therefore **reject** applying the shell theorem naively at galactic scale; in this framework only the **central core** sets the acceleration field relevant to stellar orbits.)

38.3.2 Extent of Control

The Milky Way's domain ends where the core's acceleration cannot overcome a body's tangential momentum—an effective **galactic Hill sphere**. Between galaxies, stars are essentially **independent**: each orbits the core, minimally influenced by stellar neighbors (mean separations ~4 ly vs. individual gravitational reaches of order **tens of light-days**).

38.4 Dispensable Momentum and Galactic Motion

The same ejections that endow stars with orbital momentum also give the **core itself** a net recoil (Newton's Third Law). Asymmetric ejections accumulate, so the core gains a persistent **straight-line drift** through intergalactic space. Paths change only via rare major encounters. **Thus:** flat curves reflect central binding + preserved tangential momentum; dark matter is unnecessary; galaxies are **not stationary**—they **drift endlessly**, powered by **accumulated, impulse-born motion**. Table 38.1.

Quick Reference Table

Table 38.1Galactic Core Mass and Flat Rotation Curves Relationship

QUANTITY	VALUE / RELATION	INTERPRETATION
Sun's galacto-centric radius ($r_\odot$)	($\approx 2.57 \times 10^{20}$ m) (~27.2 kly)	Orbital lever arm
Sun's speed ($v_\odot$)	($\approx 2.30 \times 10^5$ m/s)	Sets centripetal demand
Core mass M_{core}	$\frac{v_\odot^2 r_\odot}{G} \approx 9.3 \times 10^{10} M_\odot$	Core authority at $r_\odot$
Sgr A* mass	$\sim 4 - 5 \times 10^6 M_\odot$	Local influence only
Local galactic acceleration	$a = \frac{v_\odot^2}{r_\odot} \sim 10^{-10}\text{m/s}^2$	Scale of "flat" regime

39. Momentum–Gravity Dynamics in Galactic Cores and Gravitational Extent

In the standard cosmological model, the persistence of flat rotation curves in galaxies — where the velocities of stars remain nearly constant at large radial distances from the galactic core — is interpreted as evidence for *dark matter.* To sustain these velocities, theorists invoke an unseen halo of additional mass.

In the framework presented here, no hypothetical matter is required. The phenomenon emerges naturally from two interdependent realities:

Gravitational Extent Limit

Every primary body — whether star, planet, or galactic core — has a finite gravitational reach. This limit occurs where the body's gravitational acceleration (g) approaches the magnitude of the Universal Gravitational Constant (G). Beyond this threshold, the gravitational influence is too weak to bind secondaries. For the Sun, this limit is about 64 light-days; for the Milky Way's core, the limit lies near the radial edge of the visible galactic disk.

Core-Stored Dispensable Momentum

The galaxy's bulk motion arises from the dispensable momentum accumulated in its core through countless massive ejections, rebounds, and interactions. Unlike cosmological models that attribute galactic motion to "space expansion," this view asserts that galaxies move in straight-line trajectories, their stars carried with them by the core's momentum. Gravity provides structure; momentum provides transit.

Table 39.1Galactic Core Parameters and Stellar Velocities

PARAMETER	VALUE (APPROXIMATE)
Core mass (enclosed at Sun's orbit)	$9.3 \times 10^{10} M_{\odot}$
Sun's galactocentric radius	27,000 light-years
Sun's orbital velocity	230 km/s
Gravitational acceleration at Sun's radius	2.0×10^{-10} m/s^2
Effective gravitational extent of Milky Way	~100,000 light-years
Stellar velocities at outer disk	~200–220 km/s (flat profile)

Implications for Galactic Dynamics

The relationship between core mass and gravitational extent defines the true scale of a galaxy. Instead of treating the visible starlight boundary as decisive, the galaxy's domain is set by the radius where $g \approx G$. Within this region, stars remain bound in differential orbits, producing the impression of galactic "rotation."

At the periphery, where gravitational acceleration approaches the threshold, velocities stabilize. Stars no longer lose or gain significant momentum — they continue with the tangential motion they already possess. This explains the persistence of flat rotation curves without requiring dark matter.

Thus, galaxies are self-consistent dynamical systems: their **cores generate momentum through ejection events**, their **gravity organizes stars into orbits**, and their **outer regions display flat curves** as a natural consequence of the gravitational extent limit.

39.1 The Milky Way: Gravitational Reach and Flat Curves

The Milky Way can be read with the same rule we used for the Solar System: gravity pulls inward in the normal (radial) direction, while stars keep the tangential motion they were given long ago. Close to the center, gravity is strong and can bend paths tightly. Far out, gravity is weak and has less "control" over a star's path. There is no sharp edge to gravity, but there is a **gravitationally efficient extent** — a practical range where the core's pull is strong enough, on realistic timescales, to curve motion into clear, bound paths.

This efficient extent depends on two things only: the mass of the central body and the radial distance. The inward pull falls as $\mathrm{a(r) = GM/r^2}$. The tangential motion a star carries does not fade in empty space. If, at some large radius, the star's speed v is **greater** than the local circular requirement $v_{circ} = \sqrt{(GM/r)}$, gravity cannot fully bend the path. The star will not tighten into a circle; it will **slowly drift outward**, keeping almost the same speed for a very long time. On a velocity–radius plot, this shows up as a **flat rotation curve**: speed stays nearly constant instead of dropping with distance.

In this view, flat curves do not mean hidden mass; they mean **residual tangential momentum** beyond the core's efficient reach. Distant stars are not fully under the core's control — they are in **slow escape**, moving so gradually that, over human lifetimes, the paths look steady. The inequality that tells the story is simple: when $v > \sqrt{(GM/r)}$ at a given r, gravity is too weak to curve the path into a bound circle. The star keeps going, only slightly turned.

We cannot prove this today by a direct experiment in space, but the idea is testable in principle. If slow escape is true, stars far out should show small but real outward components in their motions when averaged over time, and families of stars in the same outer zones should share similar tangential directions — a memory of the pushes they received. The curve's "flatness" would then be a record of **unspent motion**, not evidence of an unseen substance.

Conventional view (for reference): Standard cosmology explains flat rotation curves by adding a massive, extended **dark matter halo** so that $M(r)$ keeps rising with r and $v = \sqrt{(GM(r)/r)}$ stays roughly constant. Some alternative models modify gravity itself at low accelerations. Our reading keeps gravity as an inverse-square pull, gives it a **practical** reach set by M and r, and reads flat curves as **slow escape with long-lived tangential motion**.

How to read the Milky Way with one glance

At small radii, compare the observed speed v with $v_{circ} = \sqrt{(GM/r)}$. If they match, gravity is fully in charge and paths are tightly bound. At larger radii, if v stays nearly constant while v_{circ} would be smaller, the star is keeping its given motion and the core's pull is no longer sufficient to bend it into a tight orbit. The pendulum taught us this balance in the room; the galaxy writes the same balance across the sky.

39.1.1 (worked example) — Milky Way Core and Flat Curves

Below is a small table. It uses **our model core mass** of $9.3 \times 10^{10} M_\odot$ and shows how the **circular-equivalent speed** falls with distance. The rule is the same as always: $v_{circ} = \sqrt{GM/r}$. If observed speeds stay flat while v_{circ} falls, we read that as **long-lived tangential motion** and **slow escape** beyond **the gravitationally efficient extent**. Table 39.2

Assumption (our model):

Core mass $M_{core} = 9.3 \times 10^{10}\ M_\odot$

Note: $v_{esc} \approx \sqrt{2} v_{circ}$ at the same radius.

Table 39.2 Circular-Equivalent Speed vs. Radius

RADIUS r (KPC)	v_{circ} (KM/S)
5	282.84
10	200.00

RADIUS r (KPC)	v_{circ} (KM/S)
15	163.30
20	141.42
30	115.47
50	89.44

How to read this table. Gravity's required circular speed drops as distance increases. If outer stars still move ≈200 km/s out to 30–50 kpc while the table says the core would "ask" for 115–90 km/s, then gravity is no longer fully in charge at those radii. The stars keep their **given** tangential motion; the core's pull is too weak to bend them into tight circles, so they are in **slow escape** with nearly constant speed.

Conventional view (for reference): Flat curves are usually explained by adding a dark-matter halo so that $M(r)$ keeps rising and $v \approx constant$. We keep gravity as an inverse-square pull but give it a **practical reach** set by core mass and radius; beyond that, persistent tangential motion dominates.

39.2 The Misconception of Galactic Rotation

Galaxies Do Not Rotate as Solid Wheels

In popular astronomy, it is often said that *galaxies rotate.* This statement, though convenient, conceals a profound misunderstanding of the true nature of motion on the cosmic scale. A galaxy is not a rigid wheel that spins as one body. It is an enormous collection of independent stellar bodies, each moving with its own acquired momentum under the gravitational influence of a single dominant galactic core.

Only the **core of the galaxy**—the condensed region of extreme density and pressure at the center—possesses genuine

rotational motion. That spin is a direct result of the internal balance between gravity and the immense pressure impulse accumulated from earlier epochs of ejection and recoil. Every other body in the galaxy—stars, clusters, and clouds—moves not because the whole galaxy spins, but because each one of them travels in its own orbit determined by the equilibrium between its dispensable momentum and the normal-plane gravitational pull of the core.

The Illusion of a Spinning Disk

When observed from a distance, the combined motion of billions of stars appears as if the entire galactic disk turns like a wheel. This is an optical and statistical illusion. Because all the stars orbit in approximately the same plane and in roughly the same direction, their independent motions produce a pattern that the eye interprets as rotation. Yet no single mechanical or material connection binds one star to another to enforce a collective spin.

If the galaxy were a true spinning solid, the stars at the periphery would have to move much faster than those near the core, just as points on the rim of a wheel travel farther per turn than points near the hub. But this is not the case. The stars do not maintain fixed angular spacing relative to one another, nor do they complete synchronized revolutions. Their orbits are independent expressions of the same governing law of motion: the balance between **gravitational acceleration** and **acquired momentum**.

The Galactic Core: The Only True Spinner

The galactic core alone possesses self-contained spin. This spin originates from the cumulative pressure impulses of earlier massive mass ejections, where recoil within the dense plasma medium imparted rotational motion to the core. This rotation is largely confined to the inner plasma region—no different in principle from the spin of a star, but on a vastly larger scale. The stars outside the core do not share this spin; they respond to its gravitational field just as planets orbit the Sun.

Therefore, the Milky Way should be understood not as a rotating wheel but as a vast family of orbiting members held by one powerful, spinning nucleus.

Why This Misinterpretation Persisted

The term *galactic rotation curve* contributed to this confusion. Early astronomers, measuring Doppler shifts along the arms of spiral galaxies, observed nearly constant velocities at different radii and concluded that the galaxy *rotates*. But what they measured were the orbital speeds of independent stars, not the rotation of a unified structure. The phrase *rotation curve* refers to the variation of orbital velocity with radial distance, not to a physical spin of the entire disk.

The misunderstanding grew because of the linguistic overlap between *rotation* (spin around one's own axis) and *revolution* (orbiting around another body). Galaxies exhibit the latter, not the former.

Orbital Motion: The Real Galactic Dynamics

Each star in the galaxy behaves like a planet in a vast, gravitationally governed system. The equality between gravitational pull and dispensable momentum determines its orbital radius. Those nearer the core experience stronger gravitational acceleration and therefore move at higher velocities; those farther out experience weaker pull but retain sufficient momentum to sustain their paths.

The visual effect of billions of independent orbits gives rise to the spiral form and apparent rotation of the disk. In truth, the spiral arms are not rotating structures but **paths traced by successive generations of stars** maintaining approximately similar momentum vectors and gravitational balance.

Consequences of Correct Interpretation

Recognizing that galaxies do not spin as wholes resolves several conceptual contradictions:

1. It eliminates the unrealistic requirement for the outer parts of the galaxy to exceed the speed of light if treated as a single rotating body.
2. It restores physical meaning to the term *flat rotation curve*: the outer stars move with nearly constant orbital speeds not

because they are tied to a wheel, but because they orbit independently under a nearly constant gravitational acceleration threshold.

3. It emphasizes the true architecture of the universe as composed of **independent but harmonized motions**, each body acting as both mover and moved, each governed by the same mechanical principles.

Conclusion

The concept of a "spinning galaxy" is therefore a visual metaphor, not a physical reality. Only galactic cores rotate; the surrounding stars and systems revolve individually. What we observe as a grand spiral wheel is, in truth, an orchestra of independent motions tuned by one gravitational conductor. Understanding this restores harmony between observation and physical causality—and reinforces the principle that all cosmic structure arises from acquired motion, not from inherited spin.

40. Globular Clusters and Stellar Streams

Globular clusters are small systems with their own centers and their own order. Each cluster is controlled by its core. The stars of the cluster move mainly in the cluster's **own equatorial plane** — the plane set by the push and torque that first organized the cluster. This local plane can be tilted any way in space. It does not have to match the plane of the cluster's larger path around the galaxy.

There is a hierarchy. The **galactic core** pulls on the cluster core; the **cluster core** pulls on its stars. Gravity acts inward (normal to the path) at each level. Tangential motion is what the system was given at birth and in later encounters. As long as the inward pull of the cluster core is strong enough at a given cluster radius, the stars there remain under cluster control and keep circling in the cluster plane. Figure 40.1.

Every system also has a **control boundary** — the distance where the local inward pull and the outside pull become comparable. For a star at cluster-centric radius r, and a cluster located at galactocentric distance R, a simple balance reads

$$\frac{G\,M_{cluster}}{r^2} \approx \frac{G\,M_{gal}}{R^2}$$

Inside this boundary, the cluster core holds the stars. Near the boundary the galaxy's pull starts to matter. Outside it, the cluster can no longer fully bend the star's path.

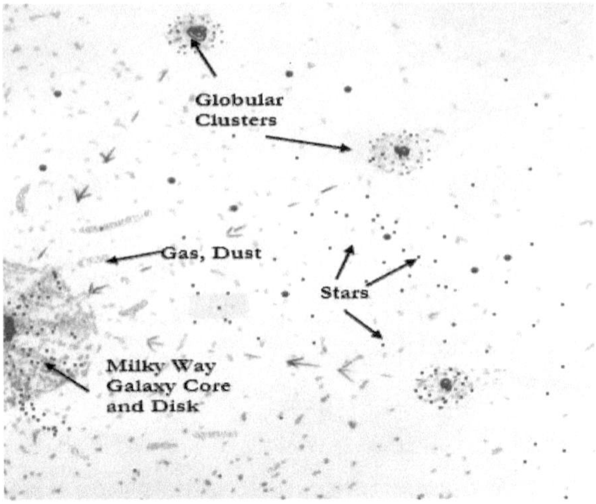

Figure 40.1 Milky Way Galaxy and Globular Clusters. The Milky Way disk and its central core are surrounded by globular clusters, which are native products of early core ejections and orbit the galactic center as independent stellar systems.

When stars drift beyond this boundary, they do not stop. They keep the **tangential motion** they already had and begin a **slow escape** along the cluster's larger path around the galaxy. Seen over time, these escaped stars form **streams** — long, thin ribbons that follow the motion the cluster already had. In our view, a stream is simply **unspent motion** that has left the cluster's control.

How to read a cluster in this framework.

Look for two planes. The first is the cluster's own equatorial plane, where most member stars move. The second is the orbital plane of the cluster around the galaxy. These planes can be different. Then look for the control boundary: inside it, stars are bound to the cluster core; outside it, they begin to trace the larger galactic path as a stream. The same equality as always guides the speeds at any radius, $v = \sqrt{(GM/r)}$ for the controlling mass at that scale.

Conventional view (for reference): Standard astronomy describes cluster stars leaving by **tidal stripping** when the galaxy's pull across the cluster exceeds the cluster's self-gravity, and it explains streams as **tidal tails** drawn out along the cluster's orbit. We keep the measurements but phrase the cause in our terms: a **local control boundary**, then **slow escape** with retained tangential motion.

Example — A Globular Cluster's Control Boundary (Simple Estimate)

We use the same idea at two scales. The **galactic core** pulls on the **cluster core** at distance R; the **cluster core** pulls on a **star** at distance r inside the cluster. A first, practical estimate of the **control boundary** is where those inward pulls are about equal:

$$\frac{G\,M_{cluster}}{r^2} \approx \frac{G\,M_{gal}}{R^2}$$

Solving this gives $r \approx R\sqrt{(M_{cluster}/M_{gal})}$. It is not exact, but it is good enough to see who controls what.

Example A (typical inner-halo cluster).

Take a cluster mass of $2 \times 10^5\ \mathrm{M_{\odot}}$. Let the cluster orbit the Milky Way core at $\mathrm{R} = 20\ \mathrm{kpc}$. Use our Milky Way core mass $\mathrm{M_{gal}} = 9.3 \times 10^{10}\ \mathrm{M_{\odot}}$.

- Control radius from the cluster core:

$$r \approx 20\ \mathrm{kpc} \times \sqrt{\frac{2 \times 10^5}{9.3 \times 10^{10}}} \approx 0.029\ \mathrm{kpc} \approx \mathrm{pc}.$$

- Typical circular speed for a star at that boundary (cluster gravity only), from $v = \sqrt{(GM_{cluster}/r)}$: about **5.4 km/s**.

Example B (lighter cluster, farther out).

Let $M_{cluster} = 1 \times 10^5 M_{\odot}$ at $R = 50$ kpc.

- Control radius:

$$r \approx 50\ \mathrm{kpc} \times \sqrt{\frac{10^5}{9.3{\times}10^{10}}} \approx 0.052\ \mathrm{kpc} \approx 52\ \mathrm{pc}$$

- Circular speed at that radius (cluster gravity only): about **2.9 km/s**.

How to read these numbers.

Inside ~30–50 pc, the cluster core's pull is strong enough to keep stars bound in the cluster's own equatorial plane. Near and beyond that radius, the galaxy's pull becomes comparable; stars can begin a

slow escape along the cluster's larger path around the galaxy. The exact boundary is not sharp, but this estimate shows the scale.

Conventional view (for reference): Astronomers often use a "tidal radius" or "Hill radius," which adds geometric factors; our estimate is the same idea written simply.

40.1 Reading Stellar Streams — Plain Rules

A **stellar stream** is the path traced by stars that have drifted beyond the cluster's control boundary. They do not lose their motion when they leave; they keep the **tangential motion** they already had, and gravity from the galaxy weakens; the escaping stars motion look like a long ribbon.

The **direction** of a stream tells us the direction of the cluster's motion around the galaxy. If we draw a line through the cluster along its orbit, the **leading side** of the stream points forward and the **trailing side** points backward along that same path. The **width** of a stream reflects how "tight" the cluster was: a tighter, colder cluster (lower internal speeds) makes a thinner stream; a hotter cluster makes a broader one. The **curvature** of the stream follows the galaxy's pull at that distance; farther out, curvature is gentle because the core's pull is weak.

Within our framework, we can read a stream with the same equality as always. At any point a star's local circular-equivalent speed is $v_{circ} = \sqrt{(GM/r)}$ for the mass that is in charge at that scale. If a stream's stars keep speeds larger than the local v_{circ}, they will not bend into tight circles; they trace **slow escape** with only gentle turning by the galaxy.

Two-plane picture

Keep two planes in mind. Each cluster has its **own equatorial plane** where its member stars move while bound. The cluster as a whole has a **larger orbital plane** around the galaxy. These planes can be different. When stars leave, they stop following the cluster plane and begin to follow the direction of the momentum inside the star, not even the galactic path. The stream, therefore, records its own escape path at that radius, not the cluster's internal plane.

Conventional view (for reference): Streams are usually described as "tidal tails" drawn out by the galaxy's varying pull across the cluster. We keep the same observations but emphasize **local control → slow escape** with retained tangential motion.

Galactic Checks (outer stars, clusters, streams)

This section shows how a general reader can "read" a galaxy with the same simple ruler used for planets. At any radius r from the galactic core, compute the **local circular value** $v_{circ} = \sqrt{GM/r}$. Then compare the star's measured speed v to v_{circ}. If v is below that value, the path tightens; if it matches, the path is circular at that radius; if it is between v_{circ} and $\sqrt{2}\,v_{circ}$, the path is a long ellipse; if it reaches or exceeds $\sqrt{2}\,v_{circ}$, the star is in **slow escape,** $v_{esc} = \sqrt{2GM/r}$, keeping nearly the same speed far out because gravity's curvature is weak.

Outer-disk stars — the flat segment as slow escape

Use one core mass for the Milky Way in our model, then see how the circular value falls with radius. We'll keep the same round number as earlier:

- Core mass $M_{core} = 9.3 \times 10^{10}\ M_{\odot}$

Table 40.1 Circular Equivalent Speeds at Specific Radial Distances for Galactic core mass $M_{core} = 9.3 \times 10^{10} M_{\odot}$

RADIUS r (KPC)	v_{circ} (KM/S)
10	200.0
20	141.4
30	115.5
50	89.4

How to read.
If you plot real star speeds at these radii and see them staying near ~200 km/s far beyond 10 kpc, then v is larger than the local v_{circ} in the outer parts. Gravity from the core is no longer fully in charge there. In our reading those stars are in **slow escape** with long-lived tangential motion, which is why the curve looks **flat** instead of falling. Table 40.1

One-snapshot test.
At $r = 30$ kpc, the table gives $v_{circ} \approx 115.5$ km/s. If a star is measured at $v \approx 200$ km/s, then $\chi = v/v_{circ} \approx 1.73$. Since $\sqrt{2} \approx 1.414$, this exceeds the escape threshold at that radius. In our view the star is already in **slow escape**; far from the core its speed will look almost constant.

40.2 Globular clusters — local control and the boundary

Each cluster has a **core** that controls its member stars out to a practical limit (the **control boundary**). A simple estimate compares the cluster's inward pull on a star at radius r to the galaxy's pull on the cluster at radius R:

$$\frac{GM_{cluster}}{r^2} \approx \frac{GM_{gal}}{R^2}$$

Solving gives$r \approx R\sqrt{M_{cluster}/M_{gal}}$. Inside r, stars stay in the cluster's **own equatorial plane**; near and beyond r, the galaxy's pull becomes comparable and stars begin a **slow escape** that traces the larger galactic path as a stream or traverse in its own momentum direction.

Worked numbers (same as earlier, for continuity). With $M_{cluster} = 2 \times 10^5 M_\odot$ at $R = 20$ kpc and $M_{gal} = 9.3 \times 10^{10} M_\odot$, the control radius is ~ 29 pc and the circular speed there (cluster gravity only) is ~ 5.4 km/s. With $M_{cluster} = 1 \times 10^5 M_\odot$ at $R = 50$ kpc, the control radius is ~ 52 pc and the boundary speed is ~ 2.9 km/s.

How to read

Inside those radii, motion aligns with the cluster's own plane. Farther out, stars that drift past the boundary no longer feel enough cluster curvature; they keep their tangential motion and slide into the galaxy's larger stream.

Stellar streams — ribbons of unspent motion

A stream is simply **cluster motion carried onward by stars that have left the boundary**. Its direction tells you the direction of the cluster's galactic path. Its width tells you how "cold" or "hot" the cluster was: tighter clusters make thinner streams. The curvature of the stream reflects the galaxy's pull at that distance. Read any point on a stream with the same ruler: compute $v_{circ} = \sqrt{GM_{gal}/R}$; if a stream star's v sits above that value, curvature will be gentle and the path will look almost straight on large scales.

A note on planes (what to expect)

Keep two planes in mind. A cluster's **own equatorial plane** organizes its bound stars regardless of how the cluster's **orbital plane** around the galaxy is tilted. Once a star passes the control boundary, it stops following the cluster plane and begins to follow the direction of its own momentum inside. If the galaxy's acceleration matches its momentum, the star follows the galaxy's plane. That is why streams trace the galaxy's path rather than the original internal plane of the cluster.

Reader checklist

Pick the controlling mass and the radius. Compute the local circular value with $v_{circ} = \sqrt{GM/r}$. Compare. If outer-disk stars keep speeds above $\mathrm{v_{circ}}$ for large r, the curve will look flat and, in our model, those stars are in slow escape. If cluster stars line up in a ribbon beyond the control boundary, that ribbon is the cluster's unspent motion being guided by the galaxy. The same two or three lines of arithmetic work at every scale in this chapter.

PART V — COSMOLOGY

Part V — Cosmology

Having traced the structure of systems great and small, we now widen the horizon to the universe itself. *Cosmology* extends the mechanical principles already known on Earth to the total motion of galaxies. It asks not only how the heavens are arranged but why they move as they do. The Massive Mass Ejection Theory provides the key: the same forces that propel a pendulum or a planet also shape the birth and destiny of galaxies. In rejecting imaginary expansions of space and focusing instead on real locomotion, this section restores the cosmos to physical law. Each phenomenon—from redshift to galactic drift—becomes a natural expression of momentum and gravity, continuing the same reasoning from terrestrial mechanics to the infinite.

41. Cosmic-Scale Structure and Motion: An Introduction

When our inquiry expands beyond the solar system, the same physical variables already studied—gravity, pressure impulse, momentum, and mass—must be re-examined on a far larger stage. At the cosmic scale these variables act not upon a single primary body and its satellites, but upon vast systems of billions of stars, nebulae, clusters, and galactic cores.

Modern astronomy has often treated this domain as if it required new laws and speculative entities—dark matter, dark energy, or the warping of spacetime—to explain large-scale motions. Yet the foundational principles of classical mechanics remain fully sufficient. What differs are the scale, the initial conditions, and the cumulative effects over immense spans of time.

The first step is to recognize that galaxies, like stars and planets, are independent gravitational systems. Each possesses a central core capable both of attracting matter and of imparting motion through massive mass ejections. These ejections, hurling plasma and heavier elements at immense velocities, endow stars and other bodies with their initial momentum—momentum that gravity by itself cannot create. Once acquired, this momentum becomes the principal determinant of large-scale motion, while gravity acts as a restraining force: guiding bodies into bounded paths, or permitting indefinite travel once they cross a gravitational boundary.

From this perspective, the "missing mass problem" of galaxies—the observed flat rotation curves—can be addressed without invoking exotic invisible halos. If the true mass of a galactic core is properly calculated, accounting for its dense plasma region and compressed heavy elements, the gravitational acceleration at different radii naturally matches the observed orbital speeds of stars.

Outer-disk velocities are thus explained not by unseen matter, but by the same balance of acquired momentum and gravitational restraint that governs the orbit of a planet in its solar system.

Cosmic motion is not an abstract stretching of space, nor the expansion of an undefined medium. It is the tangible result of matter carrying acquired momentum, continuously interacting with gravitational fields, and occasionally exchanging momentum through collisions or close encounters. At every scale, motion belongs to matter itself—not to space, not to time.

This framework prepares the way for examining the true structure of the universe: the architecture of galaxies and their interactions, the origin of globular clusters, and the overarching motions of the cosmos. The task is to preserve the unity of mechanics across all scales—resisting the temptation to replace observation and logic with speculation—and to show that the principles derived from local motion remain valid in the farthest reaches of the heavens.

41.1 Formation of Stellar Systems from Core Ejections

The birth of a stellar system is often imagined as a slow condensation of a rotating dust cloud, gradually collapsing under its own gravity. This view—the Nebular Hypothesis—assumes that motion arises spontaneously from the cloud's internal conditions. Yet motion cannot appear without cause; every velocity in the universe must be acquired through a physical impulse. A galactic core provides such an impulse through massive mass ejections, delivering both the material and the initial motion necessary for the formation of stars and their attendant systems.

When a galactic core undergoes a major ejection event, the expelled matter spans a wide range of densities, temperatures, and compositions. The heavier, metal-rich elements remain closer to the trajectory of discharge, while lighter elements disperse more widely. Within this expanding mass, regions of sufficient density undergo gravitational aggregation, giving rise to protostars. Unlike the nebular scenario, which explains all motion by an assumed "initial rotation," here the orbital paths, spin velocities, and translational speeds of emerging bodies are inherited directly from the pressure impulse of the ejection.

The mechanics unfold in a clear sequence:

Initial Ejection – The galactic core expels matter at velocities determined by the intensity of the pressure impulse.

Gravitational Capture – Denser clumps within the ejected mass collapse into primary bodies (stars), whose own gravity begins to gather surrounding matter.

Secondary Formation – Within each gravitational field, smaller bodies form or are captured, inheriting their orbital momentum from the initial ejection vector rather than from purely local processes.

Stabilization – Over time, interactions between bodies and the parent star's gravity refine their paths into relatively stable, closed orbits.

This model preserves the unity of mechanics from galactic to stellar scales and explains features that the nebular hypothesis leaves unresolved—such as why planets hold most of the angular momentum despite the Sun containing nearly all the mass, or why planetary systems display such wide variation in orbital inclinations and eccentricities. In this view, the solar system is not an isolated accident, but the direct and inevitable byproduct of galactic-scale dynamics.

The same reasoning applies throughout the galaxy. Each stellar system represents a small-scale replay of its galactic core's original act of creation—shaped by acquired momentum from ejection and tamed by the steadying hand of local gravitational restraint.

41.2 Globular Clusters and Their True Origins

Globular clusters are among the oldest and most tightly bound stellar systems in the universe, containing hundreds of thousands to millions of stars packed into a relatively small spherical volume. In standard cosmology they are often described either as remnants of early galaxy formation or as systems later captured by a galaxy's gravity. Both explanations overlook a more direct and unified possibility: that globular clusters are native to their parent galaxies, created by the same mechanical processes that form stars and planetary systems—namely, massive mass ejections from galactic cores.

In the early stages of a galaxy's life, its core undergoes cycles of intense accumulation and violent release. During the most energetic of these events, the expelled mass is not a diffuse spray but a concentrated, cohesive body—effectively a "secondary core" launched outward. This fragment retains strong gravitational control over the material ejected alongside it, and as it travels away from the galactic center, it becomes the seed of a globular cluster.

Within this traveling core, smaller-scale gravitational aggregation produces the dense star population that defines globular clusters. The stars within are not bound directly to the galaxy's main core in their immediate motion but to their own cluster core, which itself traces a long, looping orbit around the galaxy. This explains why globular clusters often have orbits highly inclined to the galactic disk and why their stars exhibit such cohesion, pointing to a deep, localized gravitational well.

Over cosmic timescales, globular clusters may lose some of their stars to the larger galaxy or to interstellar space, particularly during close passages to the galactic center or encounters with other massive objects. Yet the central pull of the cluster's own core remains the primary force shaping its structure. This stands in sharp contrast to the capture hypothesis, which would require an implausibly precise alignment of velocities and trajectories to account for the great number of clusters observed in stable galactic orbits.

Understanding globular clusters as native products of galactic core ejections not only simplifies their origin but also unifies them with the same mechanics that govern the birth of stars, planetary systems, and even outer-disk stellar motions. The galaxy thus reveals itself as a hierarchy of structures—cores within cores—each born of the same fundamental interaction between pressure impulse and gravitational restraint.

42. Intergalactic Motion and the Independence of Galaxies

At the largest visible scale, the universe appears as a web of galaxies and galaxy clusters, separated by vast stretches of intergalactic space. The prevailing cosmological model interprets their recession from one another as evidence of space itself expanding. Yet this interpretation assumes that galaxies are carried passively by a stretching fabric, rather than moving by their own momentum through static space. If we set aside this assumption and examine the mechanics of motion, a different picture emerges—one that treats each galaxy as an independent traveler.

Every galaxy, once formed, is endowed with a certain amount of dispensable momentum. This momentum originates from the asymmetrical balance of its earliest and largest mass ejection events, which act upon the galaxy as a whole. Because there is no medium in space to absorb or slow this motion, and because gravity acts only to bend or bind trajectories rather than diminish velocity in free motion, a galaxy's linear momentum can persist for billions of years without loss. Each galaxy's path through the universe is therefore an intrinsic property, not dictated by a universal flow.

Galaxies interact gravitationally only within the effective range of their cores' gravitational boundaries. Beyond this limit, the pull between galaxies becomes negligible, and their trajectories remain unaltered except in the rare case of a close encounter or collision. While such encounters can be dramatic, they are exceptions rather than the rule. The overwhelming majority of galaxies journey unimpeded, their courses determined by the impulses acquired during their formative epochs.

This perspective also reframes the observation of redshifts in distant galaxies. Rather than treating redshift as unambiguous proof of space expanding, it may be understood as a Doppler effect—the natural result of independent motion away from the observer. The apparent uniformity of galactic recession is then not a coordinated expansion but an emergent statistical pattern arising from the random distribution of acquired galactic motions.

Some may question whether massive stellar ejections, occurring over billions of years, can be established as real phenomena. The limitation lies not in their absence, but in the brevity of human observation. We have looked seriously at the heavens only since Galileo's time. Supernova events, such as the one recorded by Tycho Brahe in 1572, provide direct and lasting evidence that violent ejections of matter and energy are natural processes of stellar life. Solar system formation itself is explained more clearly by such ejections than by any static nebular collapse. The same reasoning, applied on galactic scales, gives a consistent and physically grounded account of motion across the universe.

The independence of galaxies thus preserves the unity of mechanics across all scales: from a planet orbiting a star, to a star orbiting a galactic core, to a galaxy traveling through the universe. In every case, motion belongs to matter itself, acquired through physical impulse and maintained in the absence of dissipative forces. Space is not the agent of movement—it is the stage upon which movement occurs.

42.1 Observational Anchors: Supernovae and Human Witness

Although the full drama of stellar and galactic ejections unfolds over spans of billions of years, glimpses of these processes have been witnessed within human history. Tycho Brahe's observation of the brilliant supernova of 1572 demonstrated that stars are not fixed, eternal lights but dynamic bodies capable of sudden, violent transformation. Since Galileo's time, telescopes have revealed many such cataclysms, each confirming that mass ejection is not a conjecture but a recurring feature of cosmic life cycles.

These rare yet decisive events offer direct evidence for the very mechanisms that, on larger scales, drive the motions of galaxies. Just as a single supernova can hurl matter outward with immense speed, so too can the concentrated expulsions of a galactic core endow entire stellar systems with lasting momentum. The principle is the same; only the scale differs.

42.2 Collisions, Mergers, and Rare Interactions

Although most galaxies travel for billions of years without significant interference, the immensity of cosmic time ensures that some will eventually cross paths. These encounters range from distant gravitational influences to full-scale collisions and mergers. Understanding these events through the lens of momentum and gravitational mechanics reveals why they are exceptional, and how they reshape cosmic structure when they occur.

In the vast majority of cases, the trajectories of galaxies never intersect closely enough for a collision. Their effective gravitational boundaries—determined by the mass and density of their cores—are small compared with intergalactic distances. A passing galaxy typically exerts only a mild gravitational tug, altering the path of a few outer stars or inducing minor tidal distortions, but leaving the motion and structure of both galaxies essentially unchanged.

True collisions occur when two galaxies pass within one another's core gravitational reach. In such encounters, the dynamics are governed not by exotic "space warping" but by straightforward Newtonian interaction: momentum is exchanged, velocities are altered, and mass is redistributed. Stars themselves almost never collide—the distances between them are far too great—but the interstellar gas, dust, and loosely bound systems are directly affected. These materials may be stripped, compressed, or heated, often triggering bursts of star formation where densities rise sufficiently.

Mergers, where two galaxies become gravitationally bound and eventually coalesce, are rarer still. For this to occur, their relative velocities must be low enough for mutual attraction to overcome their independent momentum. When it does happen, the process unfolds over hundreds of millions of years, with tidal forces stretching and twisting the galaxies into elaborate shapes. Their cores may ultimately spiral together, releasing immense energy and sometimes initiating new mass ejection events.

It is in these rare encounters that a galaxy can acquire new momentum. The gravitational exchange can accelerate or decelerate the merged body, altering its otherwise unchanging path through the universe. Such interactions are among the few natural mechanisms capable of modifying a galaxy's intrinsic motion after its birth.

By recognizing collisions and mergers as mechanical interactions rather than anomalies, we reinforce the principle that the same laws govern all motion—from the smallest particles to the largest cosmic structures. These events are not signs of universal expansion or contraction, but the local consequences of crossing trajectories in a cosmos of independently moving bodies.

42.3 Case Note: The Milky Way–Andromeda Encounter

The approaching path of the Andromeda galaxy (M31) toward the Milky Way is often presented as a textbook example of an inevitable galactic collision. At present, the two systems are separated by about 2.5 million light-years, and Andromeda is moving toward us at roughly 110 km/s along the line of sight. Classical estimates predict a first encounter in 4–5 billion years.

Yet the outcome is not certain. Because galaxies are vast, diffuse systems rather than solid bodies, a direct collision requires extraordinary precision in their relative trajectories. A deviation as small as a few hundredths of a degree in transverse angle, over a span of millions of light-years, can translate into an offset of tens of thousands of light-years—enough for the galaxies to pass one another without merging.

Whatever the outcome, the underlying mechanics remain the same. The approach is governed not by an expanding fabric of space, but by the independent momentum of two galaxies and the gravitational tug between their extended cores. Whether they merge or merely graze past one another, the Milky Way–Andromeda system illustrates both the rarity and the profound consequences of such encounters on cosmic timescales.

42.4 Does a tiny aim error prevent a Milky Way–Andromeda hit?

A lateral miss from a small angular offset θ over distance D is $\Delta \approx D \tan\theta \approx D\theta$ (for small angles, radians). Using $D \approx 2.5 \times 10^6\ ly$ and $\boldsymbol{\theta = 0.001^0 = 1.745 \times 10^{-5}\ rad}$:

$$\Delta \approx 2.5 \times 10^6 \text{ly} \times 1.745 \times 10^{-5} \approx 43.6 \text{ ly}.$$

To miss by **thousands** of light-years, you'd need $\theta \sim 0.02^0$ ($e.g.,$ $\boldsymbol{50{,}000/2.5 \times 10^6 \approx 0.02}$). So, a 0.001° misalignment yields only a few-dozen-ly lateral offset at today's separation—far smaller than either galaxy's $\sim$ **100,000 ly** scale. Moreover, because galaxies have extended mass, **gravitational focusing** means even non-head-on approaches can still lead to a bound encounter.

42.4.1 What do current measurements say?

Recent Hubble + Gaia re-analyses emphasize that the **fate isn't a sure thing** and depends sensitively on transverse motions and the influence of **M33** and the **Large Magellanic Cloud**. ESA summarizes a "~50–50 chance" of an actual collision within the next 10 Gyr; recent work (2025) likewise highlights large uncertainties driven by Local Group masses and proper motions. Classic estimates still place a first major encounter in the **~4–5 Gyr** range, but "collision" vs "near-miss + repeated flybys" remains model-dependent.

42.4.2 How this fits our framework

Our core point stands: galaxies are independent travelers with inherited momentum; **direct star–star impacts are rare**, and outcomes hinge on large-scale gravitational exchanges of momentum. Whether the Milky Way and Andromeda ultimately **merge** or perform **close passages** with tidal reshaping, the governing physics is the same Newtonian mechanics we are advocating—no need to invoke "space as an agent." The updated observational picture actually helps our argument: small vector differences accumulate over Mly scales, satellites perturb trajectories, and encounters are determined by extended, diffuse mass distributions rather than "solid-body" hits.

While collisions are uncommon in the lifetime of any single galaxy, they cannot be dismissed as mere curiosities. Without such rare events, galaxy cores would not have accumulated the billions of stellar masses we observe today. Each collision or merger, though separated by hundreds of millions or even billions of years, contributes to the gradual build-up of core mass and the reshaping of galactic structure. Recognizing their rarity helps preserve perspective: most galaxies will drift unimpeded through cosmic space for eons, yet the handful of encounters that do occur leave deep and lasting imprints on the universe's architecture.

42.5 Gas, Dust, and the Path to Core Assimilation

Gas and dust are among the most common products of both stellar evolution and galactic core activity, yet their roles in cosmic structure formation are often misunderstood. Not all interstellar clouds are destined to become stars; in fact, most will never achieve the density or conditions required for stellar ignition. Distinguishing their origins and mechanical fates helps explain why star formation is the exception rather than the rule.

42.5.1 Gas and Dust from Stars

Throughout their lifespans, stars shed mass in the form of stellar winds, radiation-driven outflows, and explosive events such as novae and supernovae. This material is generally low in density and widely dispersed into surrounding space. In rare cases—particularly where multiple massive stars contribute to a common medium—these ejecta can accumulate into dense enough pockets to collapse under gravity, producing new stars. More often, however, stellar-origin gas and dust simply drift through interstellar space, their motion governed by the parent star's velocity, local gravitational gradients, and interstellar turbulence.

42.5.2 Gas and Dust from Galactic Cores

Galactic cores, during major mass ejection events, expel not only condensed stellar fragments and plasma streams but also enormous quantities of loose gas and dust. This lower-density component, though launched with significant initial velocity, rarely possesses the concentration required for star formation. Instead, it spreads along trajectories defined by the pressure impulse, often dispersing into diffuse structures across thousands of light-years. Over long timescales, gravitational encounters with stars, clusters, and denser regions slow and redirect this matter, gradually drawing it back toward the core.

42.5.3 Why Most of It Does Not Form Stars

For interstellar gas and dust to condense into a star, two conditions must be met:

- **Sufficient Density** – The material must be compact enough for gravity to overcome internal pressure and dispersive motion.
- **Velocity Dissipation** – The inherited momentum from ejection must be reduced; otherwise, the matter continues to travel rather than collapse.

Most interstellar material fails one or both criteria. High-velocity gas bypasses potential aggregation sites, while low-density clouds disperse under external influences before collapse can begin. Only under rare and favorable circumstances do conditions align to create new stars.

42.5.4 Assimilation into Galaxy Cores

Material that does not ignite participates in a slower recycling process. Over thousands to millions of years, gravitational interactions deflect diffuse matter toward the galactic center. Once assimilated, it contributes to the gradual growth of the core, replenishing the reservoir of mass that will drive future ejection events. Even seemingly "wasted" interstellar gas and dust thus play a role in the long-term life cycle of galaxies, feeding the very engines that govern their large-scale motion.

By distinguishing between stellar- and core-origin material, and by recognizing the mechanical constraints of star formation, we avoid the assumption that every gas cloud is a star-in-waiting. Instead, we see a cyclical process in which much of the interstellar medium is destined not for ignition but for assimilation, sustaining the ongoing dynamics of the galactic core.

43. Volume: The Forgotten First Principle and the Question of Black Holes

Among the essential characteristics of primordial particles, **volume** has often been neglected in modern theories. Yet volume is as fundamental as mass and gravity. To deny that matter has irreducible volume is to deny its very identity. Mass cannot exist without volume, and volume cannot exist without mass; both together create gravitational affinity, the third inseparable quality.

In many black hole theories, however, matter is imagined as capable of being compressed without limit—down to a singularity of zero volume and infinite density. This notion ignores the inbuilt characteristic of volume. If every primordial particle possesses a finite, irreducible size, then no physical process can bypass it. Compression may raise density, pressure, and temperature to extraordinary levels, but it cannot erase the intrinsic volume of the particles themselves.

What then are so-called black holes? They need not be singularities at all. They may instead be **ultra-dense plasma states**, in which matter is compressed to the extreme but never beyond its primordial limit. The rise in pressure and temperature with compression ensures that such states are bounded, not infinite. The laws of mechanics remain intact, and matter retains its essential identity even in the most extreme environments.

By restoring volume to its rightful place as a first principle, we resolve the contradictions introduced by the singularity model. There is no need to imagine matter without extension or density without limit. The universe is built from particles that are indivisible in their essence—massive, voluminous, and gravitationally active—and no theory can coherently deny those characteristics without collapsing into paradox.

44. Rethinking Dark Matter: Flat Rotation Curves and the True Extent of Galactic Gravity

The idea of dark matter did not arise from direct observation of an invisible substance but from a mathematical mismatch. In the 1970s, astronomers measuring the velocities of stars in the outer regions of spiral galaxies found that these stars did not slow with distance from the galactic center, as Newtonian gravity applied to visible matter would suggest. Instead, the speeds remained nearly constant—a pattern now known as a *flat rotation curve.*

Rather than reconsider the true distribution of galactic mass or the effective extent of gravity, the prevailing response was to postulate the existence of vast halos of unseen matter extending far beyond the visible disk. This "dark matter," said to outweigh all luminous material, was invoked to provide the missing pull needed to explain the observed orbital speeds.

Yet flat rotation curves are not evidence of an exotic invisible medium but of a misinterpretation of galactic gravitational boundaries. The gravitational reach of a galactic core is not limitless; it follows a definable relationship with the square root of its mass ($\sqrt{M}$). Within this radius, the core's gravity maintains orbital motion; beyond it, bodies are no longer gravitationally bound. The difficulty lies in incomplete mass estimates—specifically, in failing to include the extremely dense plasma and heavy elements concentrated in the core.

When the true core mass is calculated—including this hidden density—Newton's universal law yields acceleration values that reproduce the observed flat rotation speeds without the need for speculative halos. Outer-disk stars are not suspended by invisible matter; they move exactly as expected, with inherited momentum balanced against the real gravitational pull of the galactic core.

The persistence of the dark matter hypothesis rests on treating galaxies as if all mass must be visible, smoothly distributed, and effective over unrealistic distances. In reality, galaxies possess finite cores with well-defined gravitational boundaries, and their flat rotation curves are the natural signature of dense cores operating within those limits.

By restoring the proper mass model and applying the √M relation for gravitational extent, we preserve the unity of classical mechanics. Galactic dynamics no longer require invisible scaffolding but follow the same physical laws that govern the orbits of planets and stars.

44.1 How "big" is 100 billion Suns at Sun-like density?

If you pack $\mathbf{10^{11}}$ solar masses at the **Sun's mean density**, the total volume is $\mathbf{10^{11} \times V_{\odot}}$ With $\mathbf{R_{\odot} \approx 6.9634 \times 10^{8}\ m,\ V_{\odot} = \frac{4}{3}\pi R_{\odot}^{3} \approx 1.414 \times 10^{27}\ m^{3}}$.

So $\mathbf{V_{total} \approx 1.414 \times 10^{38}\ m^{3}}$, giving an equivalent spherical **radius**

$$R = \left(\frac{3V_{total}}{4\pi}\right)^{\frac{1}{3}} \approx 3.23 \times 10^{12}\ \mathrm{m}$$

—that's **21.6 AU; diameter** $\approx$ **43.2 AU** (**$\approx 6.8 \times 10^{-4}$ ly).**

This is tiny compared to a spiral galaxy's stellar disc: the Milky Way's diameter is $\sim 87{,}000 - 100{,}000$ ly; Andromeda's is $\sim 152{,}000 - 260{,}000$ ly.

Takeaway: galaxies are *extremely diffuse.* "100 billion solar masses" does **not** mean a 100,000-ly-wide solid object; it's a vast, sparse system where individual stars almost never collide even in mergers.

Case Note: The Milky Way Core Mass

The Milky Way provides a clear example. Using three independent parameters—the Sun's orbital velocity, its radial distance from the galactic center, and its orbital period—the effective core mass can be calculated. Depending on the values adopted from different sources, the estimates converge within a range of roughly **85 to 115 billion solar masses**.

This scale of mass is sufficient to account for the Sun's motion around the galaxy without invoking any additional invisible matter. If the galactic core is indeed this massive, the observed flat rotation curve follows directly from Newtonian gravitation acting within the core's finite gravitational extent.

Even if the true core mass were somewhat lower, the idea of a surrounding "dark matter halo" remains mechanically inconsistent. For an orbit to be maintained, mass must reside at the center of the system, creating acceleration in the normal plane. A halo of unseen material extending outward could neither provide this centralized pull nor explain the inheritance of momentum that bodies already possess. Instead of attracting inward, such a halo would act as a diffuse exterior shell—mechanically incapable of generating the required orbital binding.

Thus, the Milky Way's own parameters highlight the central mismatch: when the true density of galactic cores is properly accounted for, there is no missing mass to explain, and the premise of a dark matter halo becomes unnecessary

To clarify how the two perspectives diverge, the following table contrasts the mainstream dark matter explanation with the core mass model. Table 44.1.

Table 44.1Competing Explanations for Flat Rotation Curves

MAINSTREAM VIEW	CORE MASS MODEL
Flat rotation curves imply *missing mass* beyond what is visible.	Flat rotation curves reflect the *true mass* of a dense galactic core.
Solution: postulate a vast, invisible **dark matter halo** extending far beyond the visible disk.	Solution: account for the **hidden density** of the plasma-rich core and heavy elements.

MAINSTREAM VIEW	CORE MASS MODEL
Mass is assumed to be smoothly distributed and gravitationally effective over unrealistic distances.	Gravitational influence has a finite radial extent, proportional to $\sqrt{M}$ of the core.
Halo provides the extra gravitational pull to "hold" fast-moving outer stars.	Outer stars move with **inherited momentum** balanced by the real gravitational pull of the core.
Requires an exotic, unobserved form of matter making up most of the universe.	Requires no new physics—Newtonian mechanics applied with corrected mass estimates.

45. Rethinking Dark Energy: Momentum, Not Expansion, Drives Galactic Recession

The idea of dark energy arose from the interpretation of distant galaxy redshifts as proof that the universe's expansion is accelerating. This interpretation assumes that space itself is stretching, carrying galaxies outward, and that some unknown form of energy must be fueling the acceleration. Yet this view rests on a fundamental misattribution: it treats observed galactic motion as a property of space, rather than as the natural outcome of galaxies' own momentum.

When a galactic core forms, it undergoes countless massive ejection events over billions of years. Each ejection imparts momentum not only to the expelled matter but also—by Newton's third law—to the core itself in the opposite direction. These tiny but repeated impulses accumulate. Over millions of such action–reaction exchanges, the core's velocity steadily increases. And because intergalactic space offers no medium to absorb momentum, the motion continues indefinitely, altered only by the rare chance of a close gravitational encounter.

This accumulated momentum is a classical property. It depends on mass, impulse, and duration, and in principle it has no upper limit. Over long timescales, repeated ejections can push a galaxy to velocities that, expressed in simple linear terms, may even appear to exceed the speed of light. This does not contradict physics, because the speed of light is not a universal speed cap on massive bodies in classical motion. Rather, it is an intrinsic property of quantum particles at the moment of their creation, fixed and unalterable by external means. Galaxies, as classical systems, are not bound by this quantum limit; their velocities reflect momentum built up over their histories.

In this framework, redshift is not the signature of expanding space but a straightforward Doppler effect: the stretching of light waves as their source recedes. The observed trend—that more distant galaxies generally show higher redshifts—reflects a statistical reality. Over cosmological distances, we are more likely to observe galaxies that have been carried farther by the accumulated impulses of their cores, and thus are receding at higher speeds. No universal "push" from dark energy is required.

The accelerating-expansion model also demands a perfectly coordinated, isotropic acceleration across the cosmos—an extraordinary claim for which there is no independent evidence beyond redshift interpretation itself. Once we recognize galaxies as independent mechanical travelers, each with its own trajectory shaped by its own history of impulses, the need for a cosmic acceleration mechanism disappears.

By reframing dark energy as a misinterpretation of momentum mechanics, we strip away yet another speculative layer from cosmology. Motion once again belongs to matter itself, not to the fabric of space. The large-scale distribution of recession velocities is not the trace of an expanding universe, but the natural outcome of billions of years of accumulated impulses in a momentum-preserving environment. Table 45.1

Table 45.1 Competing Explanations for Cosmic Redshift and Recession

MAINSTREAM VIEW: EXPANSION + DARK ENERGY	MOMENTUM MODEL: INDEPENDENT GALACTIC TRAVELERS
Redshift is evidence of the *expansion of space itself.*	Redshift is a *Doppler effect* caused by galaxies moving through space with inherited momentum.
Galaxies are passive objects carried outward by a stretching fabric of space.	Galaxies are *active travelers*, propelled by accumulated momentum (impulses) from repeated core ejections.

MAINSTREAM VIEW: EXPANSION + DARK ENERGY	**MOMENTUM MODEL: INDEPENDENT GALACTIC TRAVELERS**
To explain accelerating expansion, an unknown force—**dark energy**—is invoked as a universal "push."	No new force is required. Motion arises from the intrinsic property of momentum, inseparable from matter once imparted.
Space is treated as an agent with its own dynamics, capable of stretching, accelerating, and even determining cosmic fate.	Space is not a force but an infinite stage: boundless, without edges, limits, or alternate "multiverses." Only matter moves; space does not.
The universe's future is governed by the density of dark energy and the expansion rate of space.	The universe's future is governed by the mechanics of motion—momentum, gravity, and mass—acting on galaxies over cosmic time.

This perspective restores continuity between the physical sciences and the oldest philosophical intuitions about the cosmos. Ancient thinkers already imagined the universe as infinite—without walls, limits, or external boundaries. In our framework, this vision gains mechanical grounding: space itself is not a moving or expanding entity, but the infinite stage upon which material bodies travel. Motion belongs to matter alone, carried by the inseparable force of momentum. Galaxies do not need a universal push from dark energy; their trajectories are written in the impulses of their own cores, preserved over billions of years. Thus, the universe is both infinite in extent and unified in principle: one cosmos, governed everywhere by the same laws of mechanics, without the need for speculative forces or imagined multiverses.

Once we free cosmology from the assumption that space itself expands or accelerates, the question of destiny returns to where it belongs—not to the geometry of emptiness, but to the enduring properties of matter and the unidirectional momentum it carries.

PART VI — PRIMORDIAL PARTICLES, ORIGIN, AND FATE

Part VI — Primordial Particles, Origin, and Fate

Every reasoning about the universe must finally arrive at a boundary where imagination can no longer substitute for logic. At that threshold stand the *primordial particles*—the irreducible realities from which all later forms arise. They are not to be invented or pictured, but humbly accepted as the axiomatic beginning of existence. Beyond them there is neither proof nor need of proof; within them lies every potential cause and every future effect. From their inherent characteristics—mass, pressure, impulse, and the capacity for motion—emerge the endless structures of matter and the ceaseless rhythm of the cosmos. Here, cause and effect are no longer separate events but two aspects of the same unfolding necessity. This part therefore turns from the measurable to the inevitable, from what can be derived to what must simply *be*. It is both the starting point and the quiet conclusion of all physical reasoning: the universe begins where explanation must end.

46. The Fate of the Universe

Predictions about the universe's destiny have long been framed in terms of large-scale models of expansion, contraction, or some delicate balance between the two. In these views, the ultimate outcome is tied to the supposed dynamics of space itself—as though emptiness could stretch, accelerate, or collapse. But when we return motion to its rightful owner—matter—the picture changes fundamentally. The fate of the universe cannot be separated from the intrinsic nature of matter and the momentum it carries.

At the smallest scale, matter is composed of primordial particles whose essential properties set the possibilities for all larger structures. Through aggregation and nuclear fusion, these particles build the heavier elements that populate the cosmos. This process is naturally one-way: fusion is spontaneous and energy-releasing, while fission—splitting nuclei into lighter components—requires extraordinary external input. In nature, without intervention, matter does not revert to its primordial state. Even when all accessible nuclear energy has been exhausted, the particles themselves persist.

This permanence of matter means that the universe's mass inventory is effectively eternal. Stars will burn out, galaxies will consume their gas, and luminous processes will fade, but the underlying particles will remain. They endure as the inert building blocks for whatever structures may later emerge, awaiting only the conditions to participate in new cycles of aggregation and transformation.

Locomotion adds another dimension to this permanence. Every galaxy carries dispensable momentum acquired through countless core ejection events. This momentum is unidirectional: gravity may bend paths, but in the absence of resistance, it never erases motion. Over cosmic timescales, galaxies will continue to drift along trajectories set long ago, occasionally interacting, merging, or exchanging momentum, but never as participants in a coordinated expansion or contraction of the whole.

The combined implications of matter's permanence and the irreversibility of momentum are profound. The universe will not collapse into nothingness, nor will it thin into nonexistence. Instead, it will transform into a realm where luminous energy is rare, matter exists chiefly as cold remnants, and motion continues without universal design—driven by impulses imparted billions of years earlier.

In this view, the fate of the universe is not an end but a transformation. The fundamental realities—matter, gravity, pressure impulse, and momentum—remain constant, even if their expressions change. The cosmos becomes an endless stage upon which matter moves: sometimes colliding, sometimes aggregating, always persisting. Eternity, in this sense, is not poetic abstraction but the mechanical consequence of the indestructibility of matter and the conservation of motion.

46.1 The Origin of the Universe and the Emergence of Primordial Particles

Any discussion of the universe's origin must begin with intellectual humility. **Logic and observation** *can describe how matter behaves once it exists, but they cannot, by themselves, resolve the ultimate question of why or how something emerges from nothing.* ***At some point, an axiomatic foundation must be accepted.*** In this model, that foundation is the sudden presence of primordial particles—the first, irreducible building blocks of all matter.

From this boundary onward, the unfolding of the universe is progressive, comprehensible, and governed by principles that can be discovered through reason and observation. Each primordial particle possesses inbuilt, unchangeable characteristics: mass, volume, gravitational capacity, pressure-impulse potential, intrinsic quantum speed limit, and other essential properties. These are not later additions or arbitrary features, but the fundamental conditions that make every subsequent phenomenon possible in both quantum and classical physics.

In the quantum domain, these first principles manifest as the indivisible nature of particles, the quantization of energy levels, and the fixed, unalterable speed of light. In the classical domain, they appear as secondary yet inevitable characteristics: gravity, temperature, pressure, and momentum. These secondary realities are not separate laws imposed from outside but direct consequences of the nature of primordial particles themselves.

The Big Bang model, by contrast, begins with a hypothetical explosion of space-time. It does not explain the aggregation of matter, the segregation of forces, or the specific inbuilt properties of the particles that supposedly emerged. In that view, large-scale structures arise from density fluctuations in an expanding medium. In the particle-centered model, structure and motion follow instead from the inherent properties of matter from the very first instant, without invoking space-time expansion as a causal agent.

Key Differences Between the Models

By grounding the origin of physical behavior in the properties of primordial particles, this model preserves continuity across all scales. From the first atoms to the largest galaxies, every stage of the universe flows from the same unchanging foundation. No speculative fields or mysterious forces are required. Complexity is not an accident of fluctuations in an expanding void but the logical unfolding of the simplest, most fundamental realities.

46.2 The Inbuilt Characteristics of Primordial Particles

Once we accept the existence of primordial particles as an axiomatic starting point, the next task is to understand their intrinsic properties. These features are not acquired through interaction; they are the original, unalterable traits from which every later phenomenon in the universe arises. In this framework, these characteristics form the bridge between quantum and classical physics—the place where the absolute principles of the smallest scale dictate the possibilities of the largest.

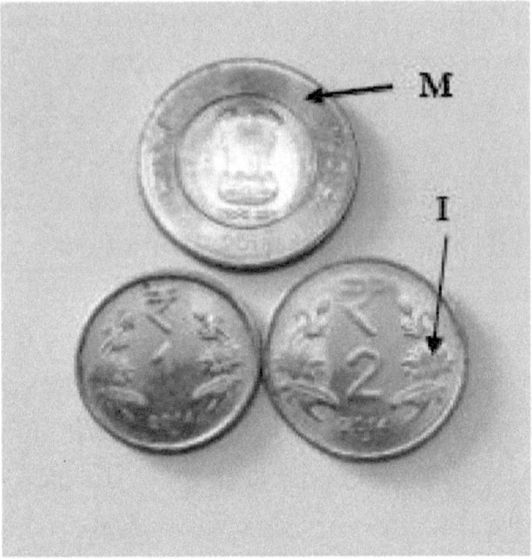

Figure 46.1 The Coin Analogy for Primordial Particles. The "M" 'metal' of the coin represents essential, inbuilt characteristics (mass, volume, gravitational affinity). The "I" 'imprints' represent variable but inbuilt traits—temperature potential, pressure impulse affinity, and electric charge.

46.2.1 Mass, Volume, and Gravity: The Essential Coin of Existence

To understand primordial particles as the true foundation of the universe, we must recognize not only their presence but their inbuilt, inseparable characteristics. These are **mass, volume, and gravitational affinity**. Together they form the essence of matter itself. Without mass there is no substance, without volume there is no extension, and without gravitational affinity there is no participation in the construction of the cosmic structure.

This unity can be understood through a simple **coin analogy**. The *metal of the coin* represents the essential and universal traits of primordial particles: mass, volume, and gravity. These qualities are always present, unchanging, and indivisible from the very being of matter. Without them, a particle could not exist, nor could it contribute to the architecture of the universe. Figure 46.1.

By contrast, the *imprints on the coin* represent the **variable but still inbuilt differentiating traits**: temperature potential and affinity for pressure impulse. These are not external additions, but expressions that vary from one particle to another, or under different conditions, much like the stamped images on otherwise identical coins. They provide diversity, allowing matter to manifest in different forms, yet always upon the same essential base of metal.

Through this analogy, we see the structure of physical reality as both unified and differentiated. Every particle shares the same essential substrate, while the variables etched upon it create the richness of cosmic phenomena.

Mass

Mass is the defining measure of a particle's material existence. It determines gravitational capacity, resistance to acceleration, and participation in momentum exchange. Mass is not created or destroyed in natural processes; it is only redistributed among structures and energy states.

Gravitational Capacity

Every primordial particle possesses inherent gravitational influence. This is not a field imposed from outside but a direct consequence of its existence as matter. Aggregation and large-scale structures become possible only because this capacity operates continuously and universally, even across vast distances.

Pressure Impulse Potential

Alongside gravity, primordial particles possess the ability to generate and respond to pressure impulses. At the cosmic scale, this manifests as the initiating force behind mass ejection events, supernova-like explosions, and the first motions of bodies in space. Unlike gravity, which bends motion, pressure impulse begins it.

Intrinsic Quantum Speed Limit

The speed of light is not an arbitrary constant. It is the maximum velocity at which the quantum expressions of these particles—such as photons—can propagate. This limit is embedded in the nature of the particles themselves and cannot be surpassed by any quantum-scale process. Crucially, it applies only to quantum phenomena, not to the large-scale motion of galaxies.

Capacity for Thermal and Kinetic States

Primordial particles inherently contain the potential for a range of energy expressions. Thermal states emerge from particle motion and interaction, while kinetic states manifest as momentum on larger scales. These are secondary, but inevitable, consequences of the particle's fundamental constitution.

Immutability

Though particles may combine into atoms, molecules, and complex structures, their essential properties remain unchanged. This permanence ensures that the fundamental rules of physics remain constant across cosmic time, enabling the universe to be understood through consistent principles.

46.3 Quantum and Classical Domains

In the quantum universe, these characteristics define absolute first principles: the indivisibility of particles, quantized energy states, and the fixed propagation speed of light. In the classical universe, the same characteristics manifest as mass, volume, gravitational attraction, momentum, temperature, and large-scale motion. The distinction lies only in scale and expression, not in underlying reality. Both domains spring from the same immutable properties of matter.

By grounding all cosmic phenomena in the inbuilt characteristics of primordial particles, we achieve a unified view in which no speculative external fields or unobservable energies are required. Every structure, from the smallest atom to the largest galaxy, is the direct, mechanical consequence of what these particles are and what they can do.

46.4 Time and Space: Not Causes, but Stages

In much of modern cosmology, time and space are treated as though they were physical entities—capable of expanding, bending, or flowing. In our framework, both are descriptive rather than causal.

Time is simply a measure of change, a way of comparing one motion or process to another. It does not flow or pass independently; without change, time has no meaning. We cannot ascribe qualities to time as if it were a substance. It is not a cause of events, nor does it act upon matter. Yet our thinking is never separate from time, for all reasoning and observation unfold against the background of motion and sequence.

Space is the stage upon which matter exists and moves. It is not a substance, nor does it possess independent powers. Without matter, space has no function; it does not push, pull, or expand. To imagine space itself as an agent of cosmic change is to mistake the setting for the play.

The true causes of all motion, energy, and transformation lie in matter itself. Matter is the subject; its properties are the predicates. Gravity, pressure impulse, temperature, momentum, and every form of energy arise from the interactions of primordial particles. Time and space describe the framework in which these interactions are observed, but they are never the origin of what occurs.

In this view, time and space are more philosophical than physical. They provide the language of description, not the mechanism of causation. The stage is vast, the sequence unending, but the actors—the primordial particles and their immutable properties—are the only sources of the cosmic existence.

46.5 Temperature and Energy Gradients in Cosmic Structure

Temperature is often treated as a passive descriptor of hot and cold regions, yet in cosmic structure it plays an active role in shaping how matter behaves. Heat is simply the kinetic energy of particles, and its distribution determines whether matter disperses or aggregates.

Near galactic cores or in active stellar nurseries, high temperatures prevent immediate condensation. Particles retain enough kinetic energy to overcome their mutual gravitational attraction, prolonging the dispersal phase after a mass ejection. In cooler, quiescent regions, particles lose energy, reducing their velocities and agitation. Under these conditions gravity prevails, leading to aggregation and the gradual build-up of new structures. This is why most star formation occurs not in the immediate blast path of an ejection, but in cooled, denser zones where velocity and thermal turbulence have diminished.

On the largest scales, the gradients of temperature observed across galaxies and intergalactic space are themselves the results of matter's own interactions—energy released through fusion, collisions, compression, and radiative processes. No external field or "background heat" drives these variations. They are entirely the mechanical consequences of matter's fundamental properties, redistributed by motion and interaction.

Temperature, therefore, is not merely a measure of comfort or contrast; it is a governing condition in cosmic architecture. It sets the balance point between dispersion and aggregation, defining when matter will remain scattered and when it will coalesce into the stars, clusters, and galaxies that populate the universe.

46.6 From Quantum to Classical: The First Stable Structures

The earliest stage of the universe, immediately following the axiomatic appearance of primordial particles, was a quantum universe—governed by indivisible particles, the fixed speed of light, and quantized interactions. But as these particles began to combine, a threshold was crossed: stable structures such as atomic nuclei emerged, and with them the rules of classical physics began to assert themselves on larger scales.

The moment a stable atom existed, it could join others to form a larger mass whose gravity influenced its surroundings. From there, collisions and compressions produced pressure impulses that generated the first macroscopic motions.

This handoff—from quantum-dominated behavior to classical gravitational and momentum mechanics—forms the bridge on which the observable universe was built. Quantum laws define the possible building blocks; classical laws govern how those blocks assemble into stars, planets, and galaxies.

46.7 Conclusion: A Mechanical and Material Universe

From the smallest primordial particle to the largest galactic system, the universe unfolds according to the same principles. The origin of all things lies in matter—not as a product of expanding space-time, but as an axiomatic reality. Matter is the subject; its characteristics—mass, volume, gravity, pressure impulse, temperature, momentum—are the predicates. Every observed phenomenon is an expression of these inherent properties.

The quantum domain embodies the absolute first principles: the indivisibility of primordial particles, the fixed quantum speed limit of light, and the quantization of energy exchange. The classical domain expresses the inevitable consequences of these principles at larger scales: gravitational binding, momentum preservation, thermal gradients, and the interplay of pressure impulse with gravity to generate motion and structure.

In this framework, galaxies are not carried outward by an expanding fabric of space. They move under their own accumulated momentum, imparted by countless core ejection events and preserved in the absence of dissipative forces. Flat rotation curves require no invisible halos of dark matter; they are the natural outcome of correctly modeled gravitational boundaries. Cosmic redshifts require no mysterious dark energy; they are the Doppler signatures of independent galactic travelers.

The permanence of matter ensures that the universe's mass inventory will never vanish. Even after stellar fuel is exhausted, the particles remain, ready to participate in new cycles of aggregation and motion. The universe will not collapse into nothingness, nor dissolve into emptiness—it will endure, endlessly reshaped by the same mechanical and material principles that have operated since the first moment matter existed.

In this view, the cosmos is not an enigma requiring exotic forces or unseen entities. It is a material universe, wholly governed by the manifestations of matter's own inbuilt properties. Time and space are not actors but the stage; the drama belongs to matter alone.

PART VII — APPLICATIONS AND REFLECTIONS

.Part VII — Applications and Reflections

The final part turns understanding into use. The principles established throughout this book find their confirmation in the coherence of phenomena and their power to predict new relations. *Applications and Reflections* revisits familiar systems—the solar neighborhood, intergalactic motion, and the limits of gravitational control—to test them against the unified framework of locomotion. Here we move from explanation to insight, from observation to foresight. The reflections that follow are not speculative but consequential: they show how two simple forces—gravity and pressure impulse—can account for the endless diversity of forms in the universe. In concluding the journey, this part returns to the same truth with which it began: matter and motion are one, and through their unity the universe eternally endures.

47. Observable Predictions You Can Check

This section states, in plain language, what our model expects to see. Each item is short, testable, and tied to the same ruler we already used: compare a body's speed v to the local circular value $v_{circ} = \sqrt{GM/r}$. No special jargon is needed.

47.1.1 Outer-disk stars: flat speeds as slow escape

Far from the galactic core, gravity's required circular speed falls with distance, but many stars keep almost the same speed. In our view they are not held tightly; they are in **slow escape**, keeping their old tangential motion while the core's pull is weak. What to look for: long stretches of nearly constant speed at large radii, plus tiny outward drift when motions are averaged over time.

47.1.2 Comets are local to their star

Comets belong to their **resident star** and live well inside that star's efficient reach. Nearby stars are far outside the Sun's reach, so they do not control solar comets. What to look for: very long, slender paths set by near-normal projection, with small changes from jets or planetary encounters, but no need for "captures from other stars."

47.1.3 No capture without a brake

Gravity curves paths; it does not remove tangential motion. Capture of a passerby needs a **brake**: a pressure impulse opposite the motion, a collision, or a three-body exchange. What to look for: whenever capture is claimed, there should be clear evidence of energy/momentum loss or a multi-body handoff.

47.1.4 Spin is a torque signature

True spin comes only from torque (pressure impulse with a lever arm). Where torque at birth (or later) was strong, spin is strong; where there was no torque, there is **no independent spin**. What to look for: bodies with unusual spins or tilts read as records of the direction and strength of the impulses they received, not as products of gravity alone.

47.1.5 Two planes in clusters

Each globular cluster has its **own equatorial plane** for member stars and a **separate orbital plane** around the galaxy. Stars remain in the cluster plane while under the cluster core's control; beyond the control boundary they join the galactic path and form a stream. What to look for: inner motion aligned with the cluster's local plane, outer motion aligned with the galaxy's larger path.

How to use this section

When you meet a new system, pick the controlling mass and the distance r. Compute the local circular value $v\_circ = \sqrt{(GM/r)}$. If the measured speed is below, the path tightens; if it matches, the path is circular at that radius; if it is above but below escape, the path is a long ellipse; if it reaches $\sqrt{2}\, v_{circ}$, the body is in escape and will keep nearly the same speed far from the core. Every prediction here follows from that one comparison.

47.2 Solar System: Simple Checks (planets, rings, comets)

This section shows quick ways a general reader can test our model with familiar objects. Each check uses the same ruler: compare the body's speed v with the local circular value $v_{circ} = \sqrt{GM/r}$. The escape value at the same radius is $vesc = \sqrt{2GM/r} = \sqrt{2}\, v_{circ}$.

47.2.1 Planets: perihelion vs. aphelion

Take any planet. At the nearer point to the Sun (perihelion), the radius r is smaller, so v_{circ} is larger; at the farther point (aphelion), r is larger and v_{circ} is smaller. If you place the observed speeds beside these two local circular values, you will see the same pattern every time: faster when nearer, slower when farther. This is simply $v = \sqrt{GM/r}$ at work. For Earth, v is about $30.03\ \mathrm{km/s}$ at perihelion and $29.55\ \mathrm{km/s}$ at aphelion; Mercury shows a stronger difference (about $53.7\ \mathrm{km/s}$ vs. $43.6\ \mathrm{km/s}$. No extra machinery is needed—just the change in r.

Reader check.

Pick a planet and its perihelion/aphelion distances from any handbook, compute $\mathrm{v_{circ}}$ for each using, and compare to the listed speeds. The match is the pendulum equality on a solar scale: inward pull stronger when nearer, weaker when farther; speeds follow.

47.2.2 Rings and close moons: a small laboratory

Near a massive planet the same rule is easy to see because distances are small and changes are sharp. Around Jupiter, the required circular speed $v_{circ} = \sqrt{GM_J/r}$ falls clearly as r grows. Inner ring material moves tens of kilometers per second; slightly farther out it is already slower. Our earlier numbers showed, for example,$\sim 31.3\ \mathrm{km/s}$ near the main ring's outer edge and $\sim 23.9\ \mathrm{km/s}$ near Thebe's outer edge. The pattern is the point: one rule, different radius.

Reader check.

Take a ring radius r (in meters) and Jupiter's GM from our constants box, compute $\mathrm{v_{circ}}$ with, and compare to any listed ring speed. It will match within rounding. This is the pendulum → orbit bridge in miniature.

47.2.3 Comets: near-normal push, long slender paths

Comets path look "very oblong" because their original projection is mostly **normal** to the Sun (radial) with only a small **tangential** component. Gravity acts inward only; it cannot create spin, and it cannot remove tangential motion. So, the path stretches where the given tangential motion exceeds the local circular need and tightens where it falls short. Jets near the Sun are tiny pressure impulses: they can change **spin** (because jets apply torque) and nudge the path by adding or subtracting a little speed. The body still remains under the Sun's control well inside the Sun's **efficient reach** (our G-limit near ~64 light-days).

Reader check.

At any point on a comet's path, compute the local $v_{circ} = \sqrt{GM_{\odot}/r}$. If the comet's v is only a little above or below that value, you are seeing a bound, very long ellipse. If v approaches $\sqrt{2}\, v_{circ}$, you are near the threshold of slow escape.

47.2.4 "Captured from other stars"? Our answer

In our framework, comets are **local** to their star. The Sun's efficient reach ends near ~64 light-days; typical "nearby" stars are ~3–4 light-years away—far beyond that reach. Gravity has no sharp edge, but its ability to **curve** a path falls with distance. Distant stars do not take charge of solar comets.

Capture without a **brake** is rare because vacuum offers no friction. To capture a passerby, something must remove tangential motion: a pressure impulse opposite the motion, a collision, or a three-body exchange. Without such a loss, gravity alone only **bends** the path.

Reader check.

When you read that a comet was "captured," look for the brake: a clear energy/momentum loss or a multi-body handoff. If none is present, in our view it was never captured; it was already local and simply curved.

47.2.5 Pluto and the outer family: gentle curvature, low circular values

Far out, the required circular speeds are low. At ~30–50 AU, v_{circ} is only a few km/s. Bodies that still carry larger tangential motion will not settle into tight circles; they keep almost the same speed for a very long time. That is why speed–radius plots in the outer family often look **flat**. It is **long-lived tangential motion** beyond the Sun's strongest reach, not a new substance.

Reader check.

Choose any distance in the Kuiper Belt, compute v_{circ} with $v = \sqrt{GM/r}$, and compare with listed orbital speeds. The low values explain the gentle curvature and long periods without adding any extra entities.

Closing note for Section 2.

Every example above uses one comparison only: the measured speed against the local circular value. That is what the pendulum taught and what the heavens repeat. In Section 3 we'll apply the same ruler to **galactic** checks the reader can do: outer-disk stars, cluster streams, and slow escape segments.

47.3 Galactic Checks (outer stars, clusters, streams)

This section shows how a general reader can "read" a galaxy with the same simple ruler used for planets. At any radius r from the galactic core, compute the **local circular value** $v_{circ} = \sqrt{GM/r}$. Then compare the star's measured speed v to $\mathrm{v_{circ}}$. If v is below that value, the path tightens; if it matches, the path is circular at that radius; if it is between $\mathrm{v_{circ}}$ and $\sqrt{2}\, v_{circ}$, the path is a long ellipse; if it reaches or exceeds $\sqrt{2}\, v_{circ}$, the star is in **slow escape,** $v_{esc} = \sqrt{2GM/r}$, keeping nearly the same speed far out because gravity's curvature is weak.

Outer-disk stars — the flat segment as slow escape

Use one core mass for the Milky Way in our model, then see how the circular value falls with radius. We'll keep the same round number as earlier:

- Core mass $M_{core} = 9.3 \times 10^{10}\ M_\odot$

For this M_{core}, the circular-equivalent speeds are:

Table 47.1Radial distance and Circular Equivalent Speeds of Stars

RADIUS r (KPC)	v_{circ} (KM/S)
10	200.0
20	141.4
30	115.5
50	89.4

How to read.

If you plot real star speeds at these radii and see them staying near ~200 km/s far beyond 10 kpc, then v is larger than the local v_{circ} in the outer parts. Gravity from the core is no longer fully in charge there. In our reading those stars are in **slow escape** with long-lived tangential motion, which is why the curve looks **flat** instead of falling like $1\sqrt{r}$.

One-snapshot test.

At $r = 30$ kpc, the table gives $v_{circ} \approx 115.5$ km/s. If a star is measured at $v \approx 200$ km/s, then $\chi = v/vcirc \approx 1.73$. Since $\sqrt{2} \approx 1.414$, this exceeds the escape threshold at that radius. In our view the star is already in **slow escape**; far from the core its speed will look almost constant.

47.3.1 Globular clusters — local control and the boundary

Each cluster has a **core** that controls its member stars out to a practical limit (the **control boundary**). A simple estimate compares the cluster's inward pull on a star at radius r to the galaxy's pull on the cluster at radius R:

$$\frac{GM_{cluster}}{r^2} \approx \frac{GM_{gal}}{R^2}$$

Solving gives$r \approx R\sqrt{M_{cluster}/M_{gal}}$. Inside r, stars stay in the cluster's **own equatorial plane**; near and beyond r, the galaxy's pull becomes comparable and stars begin a **slow escape** that traces the larger galactic path as a stream.

Worked numbers (same as earlier, for continuity).

With $\mathrm{M_{cluster}} = 2 \times 10^5 \mathrm{M_\odot}$ at $R = 20$ kpc and $\mathrm{M_{gal}} = 9.3 \times 10^{10} \mathrm{M_\odot}$, the control radius is $\sim$ 29 pc and the circular speed there (cluster gravity only) is $\sim$ 5.4 km/s.

With $\mathrm{M_{cluster}} = 1 \times 10^5 \mathrm{M_\odot}$ at R = 50 kpc, the control radius is ~52\sim52~52 pc and the boundary speed is $\sim$ 2.9 km/s.

How to read.

Inside those radii, motion aligns with the cluster's own plane. Farther out, stars that drift past the boundary no longer feel enough cluster curvature; they keep their tangential motion and slide into the galaxy's larger stream.

47.3.2 Stellar streams — ribbons of unspent motion

A stream is simply **cluster motion carried onward by stars that have left the boundary**. Its direction tells you the direction of the cluster's galactic path. Its width tells you how "cold" or "hot" the cluster was: tighter clusters make thinner streams. The curvature of the stream reflects the galaxy's pull at that distance. Read any point on a stream with the same ruler: compute $v_{circ} = \sqrt{GM_{gal}/R}$; if a stream star's v sits above that value, curvature will be gentle and the path will look almost straight on large scales.

47.3.3 A note on planes (what to expect)

Keep two planes in mind. A cluster's **own equatorial plane** organizes its bound stars regardless of how the cluster's **orbital plane** around the galaxy is tilted. Once a star passes the control boundary, it stops following the cluster plane and begins to follow the **galactic** plane at that radius. That is why streams trace the galaxy's path rather than the original internal plane of the cluster.

Reader checklist

Pick the controlling mass and the radius. Compute the local circular value with $v_{circ} = \sqrt{GM/r}$. Compare. If outer-disk stars keep speeds above v_{circ} for large r, the curve will look flat and, in our model, those stars are in slow escape. If cluster stars line up in a ribbon beyond the control boundary, that ribbon is the cluster's unspent motion being guided by the galaxy. The same two or three lines of arithmetic work at every scale in this chapter.

47.4 Pocket Calculator: One-Minute Numbers for Any Orbit

This section shows how any reader can get the three key numbers at a chosen distance r from a primary: the local circular speed v_{circ}, the escape speed v_{esc}, and the inward acceleration a. We only use the same equalities we have seen already: $v_{circ} = \sqrt{GM/r}$, $v_{esc} = \sqrt{2GM/r}$, $a = GM/r^2$.

Step 1 — Pick the primary and its *GM*.

Sun: $GM_{\odot} = 1.32712440018 \times 10^{20}\ m^3/s^2$.

Earth: $GM_{\oplus} = 3.986004418 \times 10^{14}\ m^3/s^2$

Jupiter: $GM_J \approx 1.2668653 \times 10^{17}\ m^3/s^2$

Step 2 — Pick the radius *r*.

You can use meters or AU. If using AU, remember $1\ AU = 1.495978707 \times 10^{11}\ m$

Step 3 — Compute.

Use the three equalities above. Two quick scaling tips help you work in your head:

- If we double r, v_{circ} drops by $1/\sqrt{2}$ and a drops by $1/4$.
- $v_{esc} = \sqrt{2}\, v_{circ}$ at the same r.

47.4.1 Worked examples

Example A — Sun at 1 AU (Earth's distance).

$$r = 1\,\text{AU} = 1.495978707 \times 10^{11}\text{m}$$

$$v_{circ} = \sqrt{GM_{\odot}/r} \approx 29.78\ \text{km/s}.$$

$$v_{esc} = \sqrt{2}\, v_{circ} \approx 42.1\ \text{km/s}\,.$$

$$a = \frac{GM_{\odot}}{r^2} \approx 5.93 \times 10^{-3}\text{m/s}^2$$

How to read it.

This is why Earth's orbital speed sits near $30\ \text{km/s}$ and why escape from Earth's orbit needs about $42\ \text{km/s}$. The numbers are just the pendulum equality written on a solar scale.

Example B — Sun at 30 AU (Kuiper inner edge).

$r = 30$ AU.

By scaling, v_{circ} is $29.78/\sqrt{30} \approx 5.44\ \text{km/s}$.

$v_{esc} \approx 7.69\ \text{km/s}$.

$a \approx 6.59 \times 10^{-6}\ \text{m/s}^2$

How to read it.

Far out, the circular requirement is small and curvature is gentle. A fragment that still carries larger tangential motion will look flat in a speed–radius plot and can be in slow escape in our reading.

Example C — Low Earth Orbit (LEO) around Earth.

$r \approx 6{,}700$ km from Earth's center (6.7×10^6 m)

$$v_{circ} = \sqrt{GM_{\oplus}/r} \approx 7.7\ \text{km/s}.$$

$$v_{esc} \approx 10.9\ \text{km/s}$$

$$a = \frac{GM_{\oplus}}{r^2} \approx 8.9\ \text{m/s}^2$$

How to read it.

Near Earth, the inward pull is strong and the circular value is high. This is the same story in a smaller laboratory.

Example D — Jupiter's main ring (≈1.29×10⁸ m).

$r = 1.2894 \times 10^8$ m

$$v_{circ} = \sqrt{GM_J/r} \approx 31.35\ \text{km/s}.$$

$$a = \frac{GM_J}{r^2} \approx 7.62\ \mathrm{m/s^2}$$

How to read it.

Inner ring material must move very fast; a bit farther out the required speed falls. Our earlier ring numbers follow this exactly.

47.4.2 One-snapshot classifier

Given a body's measured speed v at radius r, form $\chi = \mathrm{v}/\mathrm{v_{circ}}$. If $\chi < 1$, the path bends inward; $\chi = 1$ is circular; $1 < \chi < \sqrt{2}$ is a long ellipse; $\chi \geq \sqrt{2}$ signals escape in our reading. This works for planets, moons, comets, clusters, and outer-disk stars. It is the same single ruler everywhere.

47.5 Reading Textbooks in Our Language (Side-by-Side Guide)

This is a simple translation sheet. Left column: common textbook wording. Right column: how we say the same situation inside our framework. Keep it handy as a quick reference while reading.

Table 47.2 Reading Textbooks in Our Language

TEXTBOOK PHRASE	OUR READING
Tidal locking	**Constrained linear motion curved by gravity**: one face stays toward the primary because there is no independent spin from torque; the path geometry keeps the same side facing in.
Angular momentum from a rotating disk	**Impulse and export:** a strong ejection gave pieces tangential motion; smaller pieces carried more outward speed. Spins record applied torque, not gravity.
Dark matter halo to keep outer speeds flat	**Long-lived tangential motion beyond efficient reach**: far out, the core's pull is too

TEXTBOOK PHRASE	**OUR READING**
	weak to bend paths tightly; stars keep nearly constant speed (slow escape).
Kepler's laws (ellipses, equal areas)	**The same equality everywhere**: at each radius $v_{circ} = GM/r$ ellipses simply record where given tangential motion is above or below that value.
Centrifugal force balances gravity	**Two straight effects**: tangential motion carried from an impulse vs. inward pull GM/r^2; when they match at a radius, a circular path appears.
Spin–orbit resonance	**Torque history plus periodic tugs**: true spin comes from torque at birth; resonances are regular nudges that phase-lock angles without gravity creating spin.
Tidal forces strip stars to make streams	**Control boundary then slow escape**: beyond a cluster's practical reach, stars keep their motion and line up along the galaxy's path as a stream.
Planetary capture of comets	**Rare without a brake**: gravity alone curves paths; capture needs a loss of motion (impulse opposite the motion, collision, or a three-body handoff).
Gravitational assist (slingshot)	**Momentum exchange**: a body trades a bit of tangential motion with a moving planet; no new force, just a handoff inside the same rules.
Orbital energy increases/decreases	**Compare to the local circular value**: when v rises above $\sqrt(GM/r,)$, the path opens; when v falls below, it tightens.

TEXTBOOK PHRASE	OUR READING
Prograde/retro-grade rotation exceptions	**Torque signature**: spin direction and tilt reflect the direction and geometry of applied impulses; there is no universal spin rule from gravity.
Comets from passing stars	**Local residents**: comets remain under their own star's efficient reach; nearby stars are far outside that reach and do not take control.

How to use this page. Table 47.2

When you meet a term that isn't listed, do the one-minute check: pick the primary, take the distance r, compute $v_{circ} = \sqrt{GM/r}$, and compare with the object's speed v. If v is below, paths tighten; if it matches, the path is circular there; if it is above (but below escape), the path is a long ellipse; near $\sqrt{2}\, v_{circ}$ the motion is in slow escape. This single ruler translates most textbook language into our plain terms.

47.6 Frequently Asked Points

Where helpful, I point to the same equalities we use everywhere: $v_{circ}\, \sqrt{(GM/r)}$, $v_{esc} = \sqrt{2GM/r}$, and $a = GM/r^2$.

47.6.1 "Isn't the Moon rotating once per month?"

We observe one face of the Moon at all times. In our reading, that's **constrained linear motion curved by Earth's gravity**, not true axial spin. Without a torque at birth, there is no independent spin to change. The path geometry keeps the same side facing in.

47.6.2 "Why do outer-galaxy speeds look flat?"

Far from the core, the circular value v_{circ} falls with distance($\propto 1/\sqrt{r}$). Many stars still carry **large tangential motion** from earlier pushes, so v stays roughly constant. That's **slow escape**: gravity's curvature is too weak there to tighten the path, so the speed–radius curve looks flat.

47.6.3 "Do tides prove the Moon dominates Earth's oceans?"

Earth's own inward pull near the surface ($\sim 9.8\ \mathrm{m/s^2}$) is far larger than the Moon's pull at Earth. In our view, tides are mainly oceans **lagging/leading** the spinning solid Earth under Earth's own gravity, with the Moon and Sun modulating the slosh, and mainly because of dispensable momentum acquired all the time. The schedule matches observations; the dominant inward pull is Earth's.

47.6.4 "Can gravity create spin?"

No. A uniform inward pull bends paths but produces **no torque**. Spin needs a **pressure impulse** with a lever arm (torque). That's why a bowled ball or a jetting comet can start spinning, but a pure fall cannot.

47.6.5 "If gravity acts only inward, how do we get circles and ellipses?"

Add the **given tangential motion** to the inward pull. Where v equals v_{circ} at that radius, **a circle** appears. Where v is below, the path tightens inward; where v is between v_{circ} and $\sqrt{2}v_{circ}$, it is a long ellipse; at $\sqrt{2}v_{circ}$ the path opens (escape).

47.6.6 "Are comets captured from nearby stars?"

In our framework, **no**. Each star has a practical reach (our **G-limit**). For the Sun, we place it near ~64 light-days. Nearby stars are ~3–4 light-years away—far outside the Sun's efficient reach. Solar comets are **local residents**; their very oblong paths come from near-normal projection plus a small tangential component.

47.6.7 "But we read about 'capture' all the time."

Capture without **a brake** is rare. Vacuum has no friction. To capture a passerby you must remove tangential motion—by an opposite impulse, a collision, or a three-body exchange. Without that, gravity only **curves** the path; it doesn't make a fast body settle.

47.6.8 "Why does day length seem to change over the year?"

Closer to the Sun (perihelion) our orbital speed is higher; farther (aphelion) it is lower. That changes how surface features **appear** to pass, but the planet's **spin state** is set by past torque, not by changing distance. It is a viewpoint effect tied to $v_{circ} = \sqrt{GM/r}$.

47.6.9 "How do rings 'prove' anything?"

They are a small laboratory of the same rule. Around Jupiter or Saturn, compute v_{circ} $\sqrt{(GM/r)}$ at a few ring radii. The required speed falls exactly as $1/\sqrt{r}$. That is the pendulum equality written in a tight system.

47.6.10 "What sets a globular cluster's edge?"

A control boundary where the cluster core's inward pull on a member star ($GM_{cluster}/r^2$) is comparable to the galaxy's pull on the cluster (GM_{gal}/R^2). Inside, stars follow the cluster's own **equatorial plane**; outside, they **slowly escape** and trace the galaxy's larger path as a stream or become orphan stars to move completely escaping cluster and main galaxy.

47.6.11 "Why do some planets spin backward or sit on their sides?"

Torque history. A torque applied in the opposite sense (or obliquely) leaves a **retrograde** spin or a large **tilt.** Spin direction follows the direction of the applied impulse.

47.6.12 "What's the one test I can always do?"

At a distance r from a primary with mass M, compute $v_{circ} = \sqrt(GM/r)$.

Compare the body's speed v.

— Below v_{circ}: path tightens.
— Equal: circular there.
— Between v_{circ} and $\sqrt{2}v_{circ}$: long ellipse.
— At or above $\sqrt{2}v_{circ}$: escape; far out, speed looks flat.

47.7 Case Notes (Mercury, Venus, and the Earth–Moon system)

These three short "mini-stories" show how our single ruler works in practice. For each case, read the path by comparing the body's speed v with the local circular value $v_{circ} = \sqrt{GM/r}$. Where useful, We include the round numbers.

47.7.1 Mercury — a long ellipse and a minimal spin

Snapshot.

At perihelion r ≈ 0.308 AU Mercury moves about 53.7 km/s; at aphelion r ≈ 0.467 AU it is about 43.6 km/s. Those numbers follow $v_{circ} = \sqrt{GM_{\odot}/r}$ exactly: nearer means a larger v_{circ}; farther means a smaller one. The path is a **pronounced ellipse** because v swings well above and below the local circular value as r changes.

Reading in our framework.

Mercury's **true spin is minimal** (a "strong opponent of angular momentum," as we observe it). Its path needs no inherited disk spin to explain the ellipse; it only needs the given **tangential motion by impulse from ejection** plus the Sun's inward pull. Closer in, gravity acts more strongly in the normal direction so the speed must be higher; farther out, the required speed is lower. That is all the ellipse records.

Conventional note (for reference): Textbooks talk about a 3:2 spin-orbit resonance to describe Mercury's slow rotation. We keep the observation of slow spin but read spin as a **torque history,** not a product of gravity.

One-minute check.

At r = 0.308 AU, compute $v_{circ} = \sqrt{GM_{\odot}/r}$; you will recover a value near the listed perihelion speed. Repeat at r = 0.467 AU for aphelion.

Venus — retrograde spin as a torque signature

Snapshot.

Venus moves near 35 km/s on an almost circular path (perihelion ~ 35.17, aphelion ~ 34.91 km/s). Its slow retrograde spin is the striking feature and verdict against the angular momentum and Nebular Theory.

Reading in our framework

The nearly circular path simply reflects little change in r, so v_{circ} changes little and v stays close to it. The retrograde spin is a **torque signature**—a result of pressure impulse with a lever arm acting in the opposite sense at birth. Gravity bends paths but cannot by itself create or flip spin.

Conventional note (for reference): Standard accounts appeal to early disk rotation and later tidal or collisional effects. We keep the observation but attribute the spin sense to **applied torque**, not to gravity.

One-minute check

Pick r = 0.723 AU. Compute v_{circ} and compare to 35.02 km/s (mean). The close match is the whole story for the path.

47.7.2 Earth–Moon — local control, tiny lunar pull, one face

Snapshot.

Earth orbits the Sun at v ≈ 29.78 km/s (near 30.03 at perihelion, 29.55 at aphelion). The Moon's orbital speed around Earth is about 1.018 km/s at the mean distance $r \approx$

3.84×10^8 m. Earth's inward pull on the Moon at that distance is about 2.70×10^{-3} m/s^2. (rising to 3.03×10^{-3} at perigee, falling to 2.42×10^{-3} at apogee). By contrast, the Moon's pull at Earth is about 3.3×10^{-5} m/s^2—tiny compared with Earth's own 9.8 m/s^2 at the surface.

Reading in our framework

The **path** of Earth around the Sun follows $v_{circ} = \sqrt{((GM_\odot)/r)}$; the small near–far speed change is exactly what the equality asks for. The **Moon** remains under Earth's control because Earth's inward pull at lunar distance is enough to demand about 1.0 km/s of tangential motion; that is what we observe. The **Moon shows one face** because, in our reading, it has **no independent spin** from torque; its motion is a **constrained straight-line curved by Earth's gravity**, not a separate axial rotation.

Tides

Inward pull at the surface is dominated by **Earth.** The oceans lag and lead the spinning solid planet; the Moon and Sun **modulate** the slosh but do not dominate it. The numbers above (Earth's 9.8 vs the Moon's 3.3×10^{-5} m/s^2 at Earth) make the scale clear.

Conventional note (for reference): Standard explanations describe the Moon–Earth system with tidal locking for the Moon and lunar-dominated differential tides. We keep the schedules and geometry but phrase them as **local control plus spin-led ocean response** under Earth's own gravity and the dispensable momentum.

One-minute check

At $r = 3.84 \times 10^8$ m, compute $v_{circ} = \sqrt{GM_\oplus/r}$ and recover ≈ 1.018 km/s. That single comparison reads the orbit.

Closing note for Section 7

Nothing new was needed: each case is the same equality in a different setting. The ellipse of Mercury, the nearly circular path of Venus with a torque-written spin, and the Earth–Moon bond all read from v versus $\sqrt{(GM/r)}$, with **spin** reserved for **torque** only.

47.8 Misreadings to Avoid

These are common traps and the short, plain fixes. Each uses the same ruler: compare the object's speed v with the local circular value $v_{circ} = \sqrt{(GM/r)}$; the escape value is $v_{esc} = \sqrt{2GM/r}$; inward pull is $a = GM/r^2$.

"Flat rotation curves prove extra matter."

Far out, v_{circ} falls as $1/\sqrt{r}$, but many stars still carry large tangential motion from earlier impulse. If v stays above the falling v_{circ}, curvature is weak and the plot looks flat. In our view that is slow escape, not proof of new substance.

"The Moon rotates once a month."

We always see one face. In our reading this is **constrained linear motion curved by Earth's gravity,** not independent axial spin. Gravity bends trajectories; **spin needs torque** (a pressure impulse with a lever arm).

"Tides show the Moon dominates Earth's oceans."

Earth's own inward pull near the surface (~9.8 m/s²) dwarfs the Moon's at Earth. Tides are oceans **lagging/leading** the spinning solid Earth under Earth's gravity; the Moon and Sun modulate the slosh and timing, and the dispensable momentum acquired by many small momenta in puts.

"Gravity can start spin."

A uniform inward pull produces no torque. It can only bend a path. True spin is a torque signature from pressure impulse (at birth or later).

"Capture is easy."

In vacuum there is no friction. Capture requires a brake that removes tangential motion—an opposite impulse, a collision, or a three-body trade. Otherwise, gravity only curves the flyby.

"Orbits need height (Newton's tower)."

Height is scenery, not cause. Direction and force matter. Give a tangential component plus inward pull and you get a curved path; purely normal projection gives rise–fall or escape.

"Nearby stars send us comets."

In our framework, comets are **local residents**. The Sun's practical reach (G-limit) ends near ~64 light-days; "nearby" stars at ~3–4 light-years are far outside that reach. Comet paths are very oblong because their projection is near the normal (radial) direction.

"Ellipses require curved spacetime."

You can read every ellipse with one equality: $v_{circ} = \sqrt{(GM/r)}$. Where v is below that value, the path tightens; where it is above (but below $\sqrt{2}v_{circ}$), the path stretches. No extra system is needed for the basic understanding.

"Day length changes because spin speeds up and slows down."

What mainly changes seasonally is orbital speed with distance; the spin state records past torque. The coin-toss picture helps: the spin can look different as the path geometry changes, though the spin itself is steady.

47.9 Case Notes: Outer Disk & Streams

These two mini-stories show how to "read" far-out stars and a short stream with the same one-snapshot test: compare the measured speed v to the local circular value $v_{circ} = \sqrt{GM/r}$. Escape at the same radius is $v_{esc} = \sqrt{2GM/r}$. The inward pull is $a = GM/r^2$. Use the core mass we adopted earlier for the Milky Way, $M_{core} = 9.3 \times 10^{10} M_{\odot}$.

47.9.1 Mini-story A — A far-out disk star that won't slow down

Picture a star at $r = 30$ kpc from the galactic core. For our M_{core}, the local circular value there is about vcirc ≈ 115.5 km/s. Suppose the measured star speed is v ≈ 200 km/s. Form the ratio $\chi = v/v_{circ}$. Here $\chi \approx 1.73$, which is above $\sqrt{2} \approx 1.414$. In our reading that star is already in slow escape at that radius: its tangential motion is larger than the circular need, and the core's curvature is too weak to turn it back tightly. On a speed–radius plot, this makes a flat segment—the speed stays near 200 km/s while v_{circ} keeps falling with distance. What the reader can check is simple: plug r into $v_{circ} = \sqrt{GM/r}$; if the real v stays above that ruler by a wide margin over many radii, the outer curve will look flat.

47.9.2 Mini-story B — A short stream peeling off a modest cluster

Take a cluster with $\mathrm{M_{cluster}} = 1 \times 10^5 \mathrm{M_\odot}$ orbiting the galaxy at $\mathrm{R} = 50$ kpc. The cluster's **control boundary** from our simple balance is $r \approx R\sqrt{(M_{cluster}/M_{gal})} \approx 52$ pc. Inside that radius, stars circle the cluster core; and beyond it, the **galaxy** starts to win.

Imagine a member star drifting out to $\mathrm{r} \sim 60 - 70$ pc from the cluster core. The cluster-only circular need there is a few km/s (about 3 k/s at the boundary; smaller a bit farther out). If that star carries ~$3 - 4$ km/s relative to the cluster and crosses the boundary, the galaxy's pull takes over and guides it along the **larger orbital path**. Now read the same star at the **galactic radius** $\mathrm{R} = 50$ kpc: for our core mass, $\mathrm{v_{circ}} \approx 89.4$ km/s. If the stream star is measured at $\mathrm{v} \approx 110$ km/s, then $\chi \approx 1.23$, which sits between 1 and $\sqrt{2}$: a **long ellipse** along the galaxy's path, gently opening—"slow escape in progress" if later measurements show χ creeping upward. The ribbon points along the cluster's motion; its width reflects how "tight" the cluster was. The two-plane picture holds: bound stars follow the cluster's own equatorial plane; the stream follows **the galaxy's plane** at R.

Takeaway. Far out, use the galaxy as the primary; near a cluster core, use the **cluster.** In both places, one ruler tells the story: compare v with $\sqrt{GM/r}$ at the relevant scale. The shape (tight circle, long ellipse, or slow escape) follows immediately.

47.10 For the Busy Reader — the whole book in one page

Everything we do reduces to a single, quick comparison. At a distance r from a primary of mass M, compute the local circular value $v_{circ} = \sqrt{GM/r}$. Compare the object's speed v. If $v < v_{circ}$, the path tightens inward. If $v = v_{circ}$, it is circular there. If v is between v_{circ} and $\sqrt{2}\,v_{circ}$, it is a long ellipse. If $v \geq \sqrt{2}\,v_{circ}$, it is in escape and, far from the core, keeps nearly the same speed (a flat segment on a speed–radius plot).

Gravity acts only inward (normal to the path). It bends straight-line motion but does not create spin. Spin is a torque signature—the result of a pressure impulse with a lever arm. Where there was no torque, there is no independent spin to adjust.

Long-lived tangential motion explains flat rotation curves and slow escape. Gravity has no sharp edge, but it has a practical reach set by mass and distance; beyond that efficient reach, curvature is weak and speeds look flat. No extra entities are needed in this reading.

Comets arc local to their star. In our framework the Sun's efficient reach ends near the G-limit (about ~64 light-days); "nearby" stars at ~3–4 light-years are far outside this reach. Solar comets are not controlled by other stars; their very oblong paths come from near-normal projection plus a smaller tangential component.

Capture is rare without a brake. Vacuum offers no friction. To capture a passerby, something must remove tangential motion: an opposite impulse, a collision, or a multi-body exchange. Otherwise, gravity only curves the path.

Clusters have two planes and a boundary. Member stars move in the cluster's own equatorial plane while the cluster is in control. The practical control boundary is where $\mathrm{GM_{cluster}/r^2 \approx GM_{gal}/R^2}$. Beyond it, stars keep their motion and line up as a stream along the galaxy's larger path.

If you remember one thing, remember this line: compare v to $\sqrt{GM/r}$. Everything else is vocabulary.

48. Epilogue: The Unity of a Mechanical Universe

The universe is a book that writes itself in motion. Every planet, star, and galaxy is a page turned by time—not the time of clocks, but the time of events. What began as a question about falling bodies has unfolded into an understanding of how all bodies, great and small, move under the same law.

This work has sought to restore a forgotten simplicity: that nothing moves without a cause, and that every cause must be real, observable, and repeatable. Through the twin forces of gravity and pressure impulse—the powers of aggregation and dispersion—we have traced the architecture of the cosmos from the swing of a pendulum to the flight of galaxies. The Massive Mass Ejection Theory is not an invention of imagination but a re-examination of nature's own language—the physics of locomotion written across every scale.

In the *Foundations*, we began with first principles. Matter was understood not as a by-product of space or time but as the axiomatic reality from which all else flows. Its inherent characteristics—mass, volume, gravity, pressure impulse, momentum, and thermal capacity—are the predicates of every physical phenomenon. Time and space, far from being agents of causation, were recognized as descriptive frameworks: the stage upon which matter acts, not actors themselves.

In the *Variables*, we explored how these characteristics interact. Momentum, divided into dispensable and indispensable forms, emerged as the true moving force of the universe—consumed and transferred in every motion yet inseparable from matter itself. Gravity was seen as the restraining influence acting only in the normal plane, never in the horizontal, while pressure impulse appeared as the initiator of motion, responsible for everything from the arc of a projectile to the ejection of stars from galactic cores. Temperature and energy gradients, too, were understood not as external conditions but as mechanical consequences of particle interactions.

The *Demonstrations* turned reasoning into experiment. Pendulums, projectiles, rebounds, and oscillations confirmed that nature speaks through measurable motion. The same relations that govern a falling stone govern the motion of celestial bodies. Every experiment, honestly observed, became a miniature universe in itself.

In the *Structure* of the solar system and galaxies, these principles showed their explanatory power. Planets and satellites were not assembled from a rotating nebula but from massive mass-ejection events in which the Sun launched matter outward with immense pressure impulses. Orbits were stabilized by the interplay of inherited momentum and gravitational restraint. Angular momentum and spin ceased to be mysterious inheritances and became mechanical results of initial impulses.

Extending outward to galaxies, the same mechanics held. Cores—masses of tens of billions of Suns—govern their systems through finite gravitational extents proportional to the square root of mass. Globular clusters appeared not as captured strays but as native offspring of early concentrated ejections: cores within cores. Flat rotation curves required no halos of invisible matter once core density was properly calculated, and galactic redshifts needed no expanding fabric of space but reflected the Doppler signatures of independent travelers propelled by their own accumulated momentum.

When turning to *Cosmology*, humility required us to stop at the axiomatic boundary of primordial particles. Their sudden presence, with immutable properties, set the stage for everything that followed. From their indivisibility, quantization, and fixed quantum speed limit arose the quantum domain; from their gravitational, thermal, and momentum capacities came the classical domain. The universe did not begin with the expansion of nothingness but with the appearance of something real: matter itself. And when we asked about the fate of that matter, the same principles provided continuity. Matter cannot vanish; it persists as the eternal inventory of the cosmos. Momentum, once imparted, is never lost but carried forward through the ages. Gravity bends it but does not erase it. The universe will not collapse into nothingness nor dissolve into emptiness. It will transform—stars will fade, galaxies will age, luminous processes will dwindle—yet matter and motion will remain, endlessly recombining, colliding, and dispersing.

In the final *Applications and Reflections*, understanding returns to use. The principles presented here invite verification, refinement, and extension. Prediction is not their limit but their test. Each motion observed, each orbit recalculated, will add precision to the same enduring truth: locomotion is the single thread uniting all scales of existence.

From first particles to galaxies in flight, from the spin of a pendulum to the drift of a cluster, the principle is one: the universe is a mechanical and material reality. Its truths are not hidden in abstractions but revealed in the phenomena themselves—simple, observable, and consistent. Mathematics here serves observation; philosophy reunites with experiment; reason bridges cause and consequence.

This book is not the end of discovery but the beginning of a renewed way of seeing. Future generations will refine, challenge, and expand these ideas, as they must. Truth does not fear correction—it thrives on it. What matters most is that inquiry continues, guided by observation, strengthened by logic, and tempered by humility before nature.

If this work has succeeded in one thing, it is to show that the universe is not an accident nor a mystery. It is a living demonstration of reason—visible to every honest observer. And though the author's words may fade, the motion they describe will continue eternally.

49. Appendices

49.1 Appendix A — Comparative Tables of Celestial Parameters

(All quantities are representative values expressed in SI units; roundings are given only to preserve scale. Light-time equivalents are included where useful.)

Table 49.1 Planetary Distances, Periods, and Velocities

BODY	MEAN DISTANCE FROM PRIMARY	ORBITAL PERIOD	ORBITAL VELOCITY	NOTES
Mercury	5.79×10^{10} m (193 s ≈ 3.2 min)	87.97 days	47.4 km s^{-1}	Innermost planet; high eccentricity
Venus	1.082×10^{11} m (360 s ≈ 6 min)	224.7 days	35.0 km s^{-1}	Dense atmosphere
Earth	1.496×10^{11} m (499 s ≈ 8.3 min)	365.25 days	29.8 km s^{-1}	Reference for 1 AU
Mars	2.279×10^{11} m (760 s ≈ 12.6 min)	686.98 days	24.1 km s^{-1}	Two small moons
Jupiter	7.785×10^{11} m (2 590 s ≈ 43 min)	11.86 y	13.1 km s^{-1}	Gas-giant; massive magnetosphere

Body	Mean Distance from Primary	Orbital Period	Orbital Velocity	Notes
Saturn	1.433×10^{12} m (4 780 s ≈ 79 min)	29.46 y	9.7 km s^{-1}	Rings from impulse fragments
Uranus	2.872×10^{12} m (9 580 s ≈ 2.66 h)	84.0 y	6.8 km s^{-1}	Axial tilt ≈ 98°
Neptune	4.495×10^{12} m (14 980 s ≈ 4.16 h)	164.8 y	5.4 km s^{-1}	Outermost major planet

Table 49.2 Masses and Radii of Planetary Bodies

Body	Mass (kg)	Radius (m)	Notes
Mercury	3.30×10^{23}	2.44×10^{6}	Small rocky planet
Venus	4.87×10^{24}	6.05×10^{6}	Similar size to Earth
Earth	5.97×10^{24}	6.37×10^{6}	Reference standard
Mars	6.42×10^{23}	3.39×10^{6}	Thin atmosphere
Jupiter	1.90×10^{27}	7.15×10^{7}	Dominant mass of system
Saturn	5.68×10^{26}	6.03×10^{7}	Low density

BODY	MASS (KG)	RADIUS (M)	NOTES
Uranus	8.68×10^{25}	2.56×10^{7}	Ice-giant
Neptune	1.02×10^{26}	2.48×10^{7}	Ice-giant
Moon (Earth)	7.35×10^{22}	1.74×10^{6}	Bound satellite
Sun	1.989×10^{30}	6.96×10^{8}	Central primary of system

Table 49.3Galactic Parameters

GALACTIC PARAMETER	SYMBOL	TYPICAL VALUE	COMMENT
Solar galactocentric distance	$r_{\odot}$	2.47×10^{20} m $\approx 26\,000$ ly	Radius from Milky-Way core
Solar orbital speed	$v_{\odot}$	2.2×10^{5} m $s^{-1} \approx 220$ km s^{-1}	Mean circular velocity
Effective core mass (Milky Way)	M_{core}	$\approx 9 \times 10^{10}$ M⊙	As derived in text
Gravitational extent (r_{EGE})	—	$\approx 6 \times 10^{20}$ m $\approx 65\,000$ ly	Outer boundary of control

49.2 Appendix B — Mathematical and Physical Constants

QUANTITY	SYMBOL	VALUE (SI UNITS)	NOTES
Gravitational constant	(G)	6.674×10^{-11} m³ kg⁻¹ s⁻²	Universal constant of gravitation
Speed of light	(c)	$2.997\,924\,58 \times 10^{8}$ m s⁻¹	Quantum speed limit; intrinsic to EM origin
Astronomical unit	AU	$1.495\,978\,7 \times 10^{11}$ m	Mean Earth–Sun distance
1 kiloparsec (kpc)		$3.085677581 \times 10^{19}$ m	
Light-second	—	2.9979×10^{8} m	Used for intuitive distance comparison
Light-minute	—	1.7987×10^{10} m	60 × light-second
Solar mass	($M_{\odot}$)	$1.988\,47 \times 10^{30}$ kg	Standard gravitational reference
Solar Gravitational Parameter	$GM_{\odot}$	$1.32712440018 \times 10^{20}$ m³/s²	
Solar radius	($R_{\odot}$)	6.957×10^{8} m	—
Earth mass	$M_{\oplus}$	$5.972\,2 \times 10^{24}$ kg	—

QUANTITY	SYMBOL	VALUE (SI UNITS)	NOTES
Earth Gravitational Parameter	GM	$3.986004418 \times 10^{14}\ m^3/s^2$	
Earth radius	$(R_\oplus)$	6.371×10^6 m	Mean radius
Standard gravitational acceleration	(g)	9.80665 m s^{-2}	At Earth's surface
π (pi)	π	3.141 592 653 5	Geometrical constant
Year	—	$3.155\ 76 \times 10^7$ s	Mean solar year

Mathematical Relations Derived from Observed Phenomena

Nature moves first; numbers follow. These relations are not causes of motion but mirrors of how motion already occurs in the universe.

Pendulum & Orbital Balance

$$v = \sqrt{ar}\,, \quad a = \frac{v^2}{r}, \quad a = \frac{GM}{r^2},$$

$$r = \sqrt{\frac{GM}{a}}, \; GM = ar^2\,.$$

Momentum, Force, Impulse

$$P = mv, \quad p_{disp} = m\, v_{initial}\,, \;,$$

$$F = m\,a\,, Impulse = F\Delta t = \Delta P\,.$$

Gravitational Force

$$F = \frac{GMm}{r^2}\,, a = \frac{F}{m} = \frac{GM}{r^2}\,,$$

$$M = \frac{ar^2}{G}\,, G = \frac{ar^2}{M}\,.$$

Orbital Mechanics (Kepler form)

$$T = 2\pi\sqrt{\frac{r}{a}}\,; T = \; 2\pi\sqrt{\frac{r^3}{GM}}.$$

Equation & Value Index

- $v = \sqrt{GM/r}$ — circular-path speed at radius r.
- $v_{esc} = \sqrt{2GM/r}$ — escape speed at radius r.
- $v = \sqrt{ar}$ — pendulum/centripetal equality.
- $\mathrm{a} = \mathrm{GM}/\mathrm{r}^2$— gravitational acceleration at radius r.

Author's Note on Method and Sources

This work was not written by following any single textbook or modern research paper. It grew instead from long contemplation of the ideas that have shaped natural philosophy from antiquity to the present. The thoughts of Aristotle, Galileo, and Newton have been my constant companions—not as authorities to be quoted, but as fellow travelers in the search for truth. Their questions, rather than their formulas, guided the course of these pages.

In the study of cosmology, the boundary between ancient insight and modern observation is thin. The principles that explain a falling stone still govern the galaxies. I have drawn upon the heritage of classical philosophy, the experiments of early physics, and the collective results of contemporary astronomy, yet the conclusions reached here are my own. They arise from reasoning upon phenomena, not from reliance on external citations.

For this reason, the Bibliography that follows is selective rather than exhaustive. It acknowledges the enduring sources of understanding that have nourished this inquiry, and it honors the spirit of all who sought to see the universe as it truly is.

50. Bibliography and References

(All titles are cited in the edition most commonly available in English translation. Ancient and classical works are listed by author and era; modern references and technical constants follow. This list represents intellectual influences rather than direct textual citations.)

Classical and Philosophical Sources

Aristotle. *Physics*, *Metaphysics*, *On the Heavens*, and *Posterior Analytics.* Translated editions consulted in various sources.

Plato. *Timaeus*, *Republic*, and *Phaedo.* Dialogues forming the early foundation for cosmological thought.

Empedocles of Akragas. Fragments on the four roots and the forces of Love and Strife.

Strato of Lampsacus. Fragments on natural motion and vacuum.

Galileo Galilei. *Dialogues Concerning Two New Sciences.* 1638. Primary foundation for the present method of observation, reasoning, and experiment.

Isaac Newton. *Philosophiae Naturalis Principia Mathematica.* 1687. Classical mechanics and gravitation.

Johannes Kepler. *Astronomia Nova* (1609); *Harmonices Mundi* (1619).

Giovanni Battista Riccioli. *Almagestum Novum.* 1651. Important for early comparative reasoning in astronomy.

Laplace P.S *Celestial mechanics.* 1799

Schneider. and Michael *S* *A Beginner's Guide to Constructing the Universe: The Mathematical Archetypes of Nature, Art, and Science.* 1994

George Grote. *Plato and the Other Companions of Sokrates: Vol. 1 of 4*

Historical and Conceptual Influences

Albert Einstein. *Relativity: The Special and the General Theory.* 1916 (English translation).

Roger Penrose. *Cycles of Time.* 2010 — modern cosmological reflection.

Reference Texts and Data Sources

NASA Planetary Fact Sheets (online compilation, various revisions).

European Space Agency – Gaia Mission Data Release Summaries.

IAU Astronomical Constants, 2015 Revision.

CODATA Recommended Values of the Fundamental Physical Constants (2022 update).

Philosophical and Contemporary Commentaries

The Cambridge Companion to Aristotle, ed. J. Barnes. Cambridge University Press, 1995.

The Discoveries and Opinions of Galileo, trans. Stillman Drake. Anchor Books, 1957.

The Life of Isaac Newton, Richard Westfall. Cambridge University Press, 1980.

51. About the Author

Dr. Sayyad Masthan Vali is an independent researcher whose life-long pursuit has been to understand the real motion of the universe through observation, reasoning, and classical mechanics. Trained in medicine yet drawn irresistibly to natural philosophy, he has spent more than two decades studying the physical foundations of loco-motion—how matter truly moves and why every structure in the cosmos endures.

In *The Universe*, Dr. Sayyad introduces the **Massive Mass Ejection Theory**, a comprehensive model that explains the formation and motion of stars, solar systems, and galaxies through observable physical causes rather than speculative assumptions. His work is built on three essential insights: **gravity acts only in the normal plane, pressure impulse operates in all directions as the creative force**, and **dispensable momentum—momentum acquired and contained within bodies—is the active engine of universal motion**.

Writing in the tradition of Galileo and Newton, Dr. Sayyad combines observation, experiment, and logic to restore physics to its classical clarity. *The Universe* stands as the culmination of a life-long effort to reconcile the behavior of the smallest particle with the movement of galaxies, guided by one conviction: that truth in science must always begin with phenomena and end in understanding.

www.ingramcontent.com/pod-product-compliance
Lightning Source LLC
LaVergne TN
LVHW091313100726
842905LV00029BA/281